# EFFECTIVE
# SPEAKING AND
# PRESENTATION
### for the
### company executive

# EFFECTIVE SPEAKING AND PRESENTATION
## for the
## company executive

*Clive T. Goodworth*

**BUSINESS BOOKS**
*London — Melbourne — Sydney — Auckland — Johannesburg*

Business Books Ltd
*an imprint of the Hutchinson Publishing Group*
24 Highbury Crescent, London N5

Hutchinson Group (Australia) Pty Ltd
30-32 Cremorne Street, Richmond South, Victoria 3121
PO Box 151, Broadway, New South Wales 2007

Hutchinson Group (NZ) Ltd
32-34 View Road, PO Box 40-086, Glenfield, Auckland 10

Hutchinson Group (SA) (Pty) Ltd
PO Box 337, Bergvlei 2012, South Africa

*First published 1980*
*Reprinted 1981*

*Photoset in 10 on 12 point Baskerville*

Printed in England by The Anchor Press
and bound by Wm Brendon & Son Ltd,
both of Tiptree, Essex.

**British Library Cataloguing in Publication Data**

Goodworth, Clive T
  Effective speaking and presentation for the
  company executive.
  1. Public speaking
  2. Executives
  I. Title
  808.5'1    PN4121

ISBN  0 220 67028 5 (Cased)
       0 220 67031 5 (Limp)

*Dedicated to the*
*Chief Executive who showed me the way —*
*and then booted me on it.*

# Contents

**Part One**   **BY WAY OF STARTERS**

*Chapter 1*   **Relax — this will only hurt a little**     *3*

Introductory tales of woe and setting the scene

*Chapter 2*   **. . . but this may hurt a bit more**     *9*

A word on the language — Accent and dialect —
The 'speaking personality' — Sincerity —
Rhythm, phrasing and tone — Vocabulary —
Logicality of approach — Mobility — Attitudes
— Bloomers — Humour — Self-tutorial

**Part Two**   **DOING ONE'S THING IN THE DAILY ROUND**

*Chapter 3*   **Orders is orders. . . .**     *23*

Some opinions on giving orders — The parts of
an order and the factors involved — Types of
order — Advice from an old sage — Passing the
buck — The retiring violet — Self-tutorial

*Chapter 4*   **Rockets — and how best to launch 'em**   *31*

Golden rules for the launch-pad — Types of
rocket — Thoughts on rockets in general —
Self-tutorial

*Chapter 5*   **Defusing the grievance bomb**   *39*

Some views on handling grievances — A
grievance checklist — Following the grievance
up — Ducking the issue — Self-tutorial

*Chapter 6*   **Let's have a discussion**   *44*

Some discussion 'nasties' — Conduct of the
discussion — A catalogue of discussion sins —
Self-tutorial

*Chapter 7*   **A dollop of praise**   *52*

Some instances of praise misused — Choosing
the right words — Individual or corporate
praise? — Coping with the retirement presentation — Self-tutorial

*Chapter 8*   **Appraising the hell out of people**   *60*

Appraisal and subjectivity — An appraisal
horror story — Open or closed appraisal? —
Playing the appraisal game — Weaknesses and
pitfalls — It's the form that counts — A checklist for the appraisal discussion — A possible
approach to appraisal — Self-tutorial

**Part Three**   **DOING ONE'S THING BEFORE AN AUDIENCE**

*Chapter 9*   **Composing the beast**   *81*

Opinions and difficulties — Getting the address
into perspective — The component parts of an
address — Self-tutorial

*Chapter 10*   **Be prepared, boys — be prepared!**   *89*

A tiny tale of disaster — The 'get it all down'
syndrome — All about speaking notes — Preparing the committee-type report — The
infernal business of rehearsal — Self-tutorial

*Chapter 11*  **The dreaded heebie-jeebies**  *101*

Another tale of disaster — More on subject
knowledge — How to live with nerves — Some
palliatives, good and bad — Self-tutorial

*Chapter 12*  **Surveying a sea of faces — and winning**  *109*

The planned event — Essential reconnaissance
— Some useful preliminaries — Dress —
Apologies — Volume — Dealing with questions
— Tackling the impromptu event — The grand
art of toasting — Self-tutorial

*Chapter 13*  **Speak to the press — not on your life!**  *118*

Attitudes to the press — Acting as the company
spokesman — The impromptu occasion — The
press conference — Self-tutorial

*Chapter 14*  **Meetings — and how to keep one's end up**  *124*

On meetings generally — Rules of order —
Speaking the language — Informal meetings —
Personal performance at meetings — Self-
tutorial

*Chapter 15*  **It's not all chalk and talk**  *136*

A letter to a training manager — Know your
onions — So you know it, but can you show it?
— Know your people — Methods of imparting
knowledge — Visual aids — A tale about a guest
speaker — Self-tutorial

*Chapter 16*  **On being a good candidate**  *147*

An introductory homily — Know thine adversary
— Interview tactics and gamesmanship —
Starting off on the right foot — Answering
questions in the right way — 64,000 dollar
questions — A bag of dirty tricks — Self-tutorial

*Chapter 17*  **Happy days with shop stewards**  *159*

Firstly, some opinions — The developing scene
— The TUC programme for shop stewards —
Matching skill for skill

**Part Four   BACK TO SCHOOL**

*Chapter 18*   **H'articulating and uvver 'orrors**                    *165*

The factors that affect articulation — Sugaring
the pronunciation pill — Acronyms and slang —
Self-tutorial

*Chapter 19*   **A postscript on burning the communication**          *173*
**candle at both ends**

Formal communication — Consultation — Informal communication — A speaking checklist
for the company

*Chapter 20*   **Strictly for the keen type**                          *177*

A comprehensive test on what has gone before,
and a lot more besides — Answers-cum-crib-
bank

*Appendix*   **Tribunal tribulations**                                  *193*

The industrial tribunal environment — Tribunal
proceedings — The business of cross-examination — Demeanour — Forms of address — A drill
for the tribunal witness

*Recommended reading*                                                  *199*

*Index*                                                                *201*

# Part One
# BY WAY OF STARTERS

They never taste who always drink;
They always talk, who never think.

**Matthew Prior (1644-1721)**
*Upon this passage in the Scaligeriana*

# 1
# Relax — this will only hurt a little

Reader, relax — before we plunge merrily off the deep end into the somewhat murky waters of effective speaking and presentation, I would like to set the scene with a few anecdotes. The name of the game is recognition, and whilst I have invented a few pseudonyms in a sporting attempt to protect the guilty, if a clammy finger does touch upon the odd raw spot — why, all well and good, the sticking-plaster will come later.

## A memorandum to a training manager

*CONFIDENTIAL*

> *To:*    Geoffrey White
> *From:*  Managing Director
> *Date:*  10 Jan 79

Thank you for your efforts in connection with last Friday's management seminar on Unfair Dismissal which, in general, seemed to be a great success and highly relevant to the needs of the participants.

However, having said this, I feel bound to comment that the single presentation on 'ACAS' by your training officer, Roger Eastwood, marred an otherwise pleasant and instructive day. This man's ability as a speaker is little short of deplorable, and whilst I do not doubt the extent of his specialist knowledge, I am alarmed at his attempts to communicate this knowledge to others. Plainly, this is a serious failing in a training officer, and I would like to see you in my office at 3 p.m. on Thursday next in order to discuss the matter further.

Brian Willis
*Managing Director*

## Sowing the seed of doubt

James Longton, Managing Director of Porson Industries, leaned his elbows comfortably on the rosewood desk and, puffing steadily at his pipe, re-read the narrative section of the performance report which had been passed to him earlier that morning by the director of personnel.

In sum, Brown has performed well since his promotion to group personnel manager some eight months ago. A number of serious industrial problems have occurred during the period and I have been impressed by his personal effectiveness as a negotiator, and by the manner in which he has secured union agreement on several difficult issues. Bearing in mind that Brown was formerly a company personnel manager within the group for which he now has overall responsibility, he has achieved a notably successful working relationship with the eight personnel managers who were previously his peers. Similarly, he has recognised the vital need for diplomacy and tact where the company general managers are concerned, and appears to have scored well in this respect. There has been considerable praise for his work and, to my knowledge, a total lack of criticism. He has been heavily involved with the implementation of the new employee benefits package, and it is largely due to his personal efforts that the scheme has enjoyed such an initial success.

As a senior executive, Brown is a member of the group management committee, and it is in this context that I must admit to some reservations in terms of his performance and adaptability. There have been several occasions when, despite his achievement in creating a commendable rapport with subsidiary company management, he has not displayed a similar acumen at the group management meetings. Whilst I make due allowance for the fact that Brown is very much a 'new boy' at group level, I have not been impressed by the way in which he has reported various topics to the committee or, for that matter, by the manner in which he has participated in certain discussions. There is little doubt that he has annoyed some of the more senior members of the committee by resorting to a degree of impetuous and ill-advised comment, and there have been times when his presentations have suffered from the use of injudicious, off-the-cuff statements. A further consequence of this weakness is that his new colleagues are not presented with a clear picture of his undoubted ability,

4

which is a matter for some concern. I have had a long discussion with Brown on this question, and he has expressed some surprise and disagreement with my views.

Peter J. Howells
*Director of Personnel*

*Comments by manager being appraised*

Whilst very gratified with the numerical assessments and narrative report on my performance at company level, I cannot agree with the references to my apparent failings at group management meetings. I always devote a great deal of time and care to the preparation of reports for the committee, and I cannot accept that I display such untoward attitudes in my dealings with the members.

Be that as it may, mused the managing director, it will be necessary to keep an eye on this young man. Picking up the telephone, he dialled the personnel director's number. 'Peter, Jim Longton here — look, I've read your report on Brown and, frankly, I'm rather concerned that you haven't mentioned this matter earlier. . . . What's that?. . . . Well, in my book, misguided comments point to misguided attitudes — and if Brown is upsetting the apple-cart at group, it's quite likely that he's doing the same thing at company level. . . . Yes, I know that you are happy with the situation in that quarter, and I agree that Brown has done some good work — but I'm beginning to have some serious doubts. . . .'

## Speech is the small change of silence. . . .

General Sir Arthur Peregrine Emmett, Bt, director of thirteen different companies and chairman of Pan-Oceanic Development Ltd, was happy in the knowledge that the annual general meeting was proceeding at the accustomed, equable pace. Hopelessly in love with the sound of his own voice and inordinately fond of addressing captive audiences, the elderly baronet rose to his feet and, clearing his throat, launched into the first of many planned, and quite superfluous, supplementary remarks. 'Er — ladies and gentlemen — I am sure you would wish me to comment in greater detail on the outstanding success enjoyed by your commercial division. . . .'

'Mr Chairman. . . .' A quiet yet penetrating voice, emanating from the shadows at the rear of the hall, brought Sir Arthur's soporific monologue to an abrupt and premature halt. Irritated at the sudden interruption and experiencing a vague sense of unease, the chairman surveyed the gathering in a vain attempt to locate the source of the unwanted interjection.

'Mr Chairman. . . .'

Dammit, there it was again. Sir Arthur, who was not accustomed to being interrupted, particularly during the sanctity of a public address, made a swift and, as it turned out, unwise decision to ignore the unknown challenger. 'Ahem, yes — well, ladies and gentlemen, as I was about to say — the group's commercial division has exceeded all our hopes. . . .'

'*Mr Chairman, I will be heard.*' The sheer emphasis of the statement, uttered with mellifluous assurance, severed Sir Arthur's stumbling words with surgical precision. Irresolute and anxious, now completely jerked from the rails of his much-rehearsed speech, he swallowed nervously and — looking forlornly for help from his fellow-directors, who were all intent on staring steadily into the middle distance — gave a slight nod of surrender. Two hundred and fifty-three shareholders, pleasantly aware that the afternoon was about to produce some unexpected entertainment, stirred in their seats and, with craning necks, sought a better view of their intrepid colleague.

'Thank you, Mr Chairman.' The speaker rose to his feet and a murmur of surprise rippled through the assembly. Standing at the back of the hall was a scrawny, sad figure of a man who, clutching a worn briefcase to his chest, gazed diffidently at the chairman.

Sir Arthur, who had expected a more imposing adversary, could hardly believe his eyes — was this the creature who had dared so rudely to interrupt the proceedings? Vastly encouraged by the physical insignificance of the man who faced him across the serried rows of shareholders, the baronet made his second mistake. He spoke in a deliberately supercilious tone, 'You will be aware, sir, that there will be an opportunity for questions later. . . .'

'The time to speak, Sir Arthur, is *here and now*. . . .' The man's voice carried such modulated intensity that the hapless chairman, realising the futility of further resistance, gave up and stood miserably as the speaker continued. '. . . for I fear that we have all listened to too much for far too long. Whilst it may be politically expedient for you, Mr Chairman, to sing the praises of the commercial division — and, sir, how you have sung! — I venture to suggest that the interests of the shareholders would be more adequately served if you were to make accurate and detailed comment on the abject failure of the *exploration* division. I refer, of course, to the reckless, monstrously expensive and wholly abortive drilling activities in Trinidad which, despite the best expert advice, your board appears hell-bent on continuing to support, whatever the cost. . . .'

Pan-Oceanic's exploration director, who had been eyeing the speaker closely, nudged the company secretary with his elbow. 'I've just realised who that is', he whispered urgently. 'It's Professor Middleton — and, believe me, we're in trouble. That chap knows more about Trinidad operations than the rest of us put together. For goodness sake, catch old Emmet's eye and make him pass the buck to one of us — he won't stand a chance once Middleton gets going, the man's out for blood!'

The company secretary nodded and swiftly pencilled a brief note which, with studied nonchalance, he placed on the table in front of the chairman's erect figure. But it was to no avail. Sir Arthur, despite his initial fears, came from several centuries of soldiering stock and he was not a coward. The shareholder's indictment had kindled a burning resentment — the dratted fellow just had to

6

be put down. Thus, the note went unheeded and the die for corporate disaster was cast.

'*No, sir,*' the baronet thundered, his face red with indignation, 'I will not accept such unwarranted remarks! If you read the annual report, you will see that. . . .'

'It so happens, Mr Chairman, that I have studied the document at length.' Once again, the shareholder's voice had interrupted Emmett with consummate ease. 'However, I am grateful to you for reminding me that the annual report is, in fact, the primary cause of my concern. Perhaps, Sir Arthur, you would kindly explain to the meeting why, when reporting on the group's Trinidad activities, your board chose to suppress certain vital information — including, for instance, the fact that Pan-Oceanic, under your direction, persisted in drilling no less than seventeen wells in an area of almost textbook sterility, with the result that all seventeen were dry and abandoned.'

The revelation — for revelation it was — stunned the assembly into momentary silence. Then, as the shareholders recalled the honeyed tones of the report on the Trinidad enterprise and realised that, in all probability, they had been duped, the hall echoed with cries of protest. The exploration director, painfully aware of the crisis and the chairman's inability to match the questioner's expertise, rose hurriedly to his feet.

'Mr Chairman — perhaps I can deal with Professor Middleton's observations', he said, desperately trying to warn Emmett that he was on dangerous ground and facing a powerful opponent. As it turned out, it was a forlorn attempt and doomed to failure.

When, some years previously, the baronet had accepted the chairmanship of Pan-Oceanic, the directors had been highly pleased with what they regarded as a significant business acquisition. The dictates of organisation vanity had been satisfied, and the group had obtained a real-life peer of the realm as an eminently respectable and imposing figurehead for the company — and that was all that really mattered. The fact that the ageing chairman knew next to nothing about the group's activities presented no difficulty to the board and was of little personal concern to Sir Arthur — for, after all, in his view he was a gentleman dealing with gentlemen, and trust was everything. He performed the duties of chairman with Harrovian loyalty and applied his slightly Victorian rubber stamp to all and sundry without doubt or demur — and much enjoyed the dignity of the process.

Thus it was that, faced with Professor Middleton's condemnation of the annual report, Sir Arthur gave no thought to the possibility that the shareholder's assertions were correct — no, this was a clear attack on his personal integrity, the damned fellow was accusing him of some vile form of skulduggery. Beside himself with anger, he spurned the exploration director's anxious attempt to save the situation.

'No, David!' he spluttered. 'I will deal with this — this man.' He turned to the restive audience and glared at Middleton. 'How dare you, sir — how dare you accuse me of presenting less than the truth! Your words are clearly actionable, sir, and I demand — I insist — that you withdraw them. . . .'

'Mr Chairman, you are in no position to make demands and I propose to tell you, your directors and my fellow shareholders exactly why. . . .' With these words, Professor Middleton launched into a precise and merciless exposition of the group's shortcomings and, in so doing, inflicted upon the unfortunate and vainly expostulating chairman the death of a thousand verbal cuts. The oil expert gave no quarter, and Emmett, a brave fool at heart, blustered on until at the end he was revealed for what he was — an ineffective, pompous man who had allowed himself to be manipulated, a self-important sheep in baronet's clothing. He never spoke in public again.

* * *

Enough then of anecdotes and setting the scene. We are about to set off on a lengthy toddle through the speaking jungle — but first a word of explanation. This book is all about speaking or, in case you have an appetite for textbook terminology (which I hope you don't), verbal communication — and I do not just mean a book on the nuts and bolts of giving a public address. Although the techniques of delivering a speech form an important weapon in the speaker's armoury, the average company man — if there is such a beast — spends most of his time coping with other aspects of the game. We are going to examine and dissect as many speaking activities as possible and, with fingers and toes firmly crossed, come up with a fair selection of tips and remedies — a kind of Bertie Bloggs's *vade mecum* for speaking in general. If the company chap cares to examine his scars, he will find that a goodly number can be attributed to wounds sustained during his day-to-day dealings with subordinates, colleagues and, evil thought, his seniors. We will therefore be taking a close look at the nitty-gritty of such daily engagements — and, with bags of optimism, seek to disarm some of the booby-traps that bestrew the no-man's-land of issuing instructions, giving rockets, coping at meetings, supporting, opposing and — because we know it happens — creeping and crawling. The bill of fare will also offer a selection of do-it-yourself homilies on such vexed topics as speaking to the press, surviving at tribunals, saving one's soul at seminars and so on. Ah, yes, and somewhere in the honey-pot, a hefty dose of tips on public speaking. All set, then? Good, let's get cracking.

## The aims and objectives of effective speaking

I have a hearty dislike for erudite, turgid textbooks, and the reader who expects a lofty, chalk-and-talk discourse on the aims of effective speaking will be mightily disappointed with that which follows. To the company man, galloping for his life in the Rat-Race Handicap, speaking ability is a prime ingredient in the vital mix — the recipe which, cooked and served by Nemesis, will determine whether he survives the course. In short, the aims and objectives of effective speaking are, quite simply, to know what to say, when to say it and how to say it — and *that* is what this book is all about.

> A thing well said will be wit in all languages.
> **William Drummond (1585-1649)**
> *Essay on Dramatic Poesy*

# 2
# . . . but this may hurt a bit more

## Before looking at the potter, a peep at the clay

At the last count of words in the English language (the mind boggles — 'Jim, I have a little job for you. . . .') the sobering fact emerged that, provided we know them all, we can wrap our tongues round no less than 750,000 words without repeating ourselves. Thanks to our oft-maligned forbears and their habit of popping off to foreign parts with the sterling cry, 'Good morning, natives — you may not know it, but you're British now,' well over 300 million people spread across this crowded globe speak English as their mother tongue, and a further 200 million-odd bounce it around with varying degrees of skill as a second language. Our ancestors' acquisitive nature went a little beyond the yen to plonk British flags in other people's gardens; they also pinched words — with the result, for instance, that nearly half the English vocabulary should either bear the stamp, 'Made in France', or the declaration, 'Contains pure essence of Latin'. However, this matters little — the fact is that English has become the language of the international businessman, the scientist, the pilot and a whole host of other folk. It is the most widely spoken language in the world, a true *lingua franca*, a common language. So, reader, that is the clay — we must now concern ourselves with the potter.

## Wot abaht me accent, then?

The purpose of this chapter is to have a quiet nibble at a miscellany of factors that tend to influence the inexperienced speaker in his approach to the game, and in my view the worrying question of accent must take pride of place on the menu. One of the curses of this modern age is the fact that many of us have had the doubtful pleasure of listening to our own voice on a tape recorder; do you remember your initial reaction? Let me tell you mine — I could not believe my ears, I was quite horrified. What I had fondly imagined to be a fairly pleasant, 'better-than-average', London-type voice emerged from that electronic box of tricks as a ghastly, adenoidal, suburban twang — and it worried me stiff. Then, as time wore on and a combination of circumstances literally pitchforked me into a number of speaking roles, the worry subsided and, would you believe, I actually began to enjoy addressing an audience, twang or no twang. I like to think that I came to terms with this business of accent and, just maybe, I can help you to do the same.

Strictly speaking, there are two aspects to be considered: dialect (a style of speech which is peculiar to a certain area) and then accent (variants, if you like, on a given dialect theme). Taking a rather simplistic view, the increased mobility of our population is bringing about the swift death of dialect whilst, for the same reason, a hotchpotch of accents is on the increase. Acknowledging that there will always be a certain amount of prejudice against any dialect, the owner of a 'pure' example would do well to appreciate that, whatever his feelings may say to the contrary, he is richly endowed. The owner of an 'impure' dialect — my 'London accent', for example, with a touch of Cockney, a sprinkling of this and that, and not much of anything — is not quite so fortunate, but is still far from being doomed as a speaker. Remember, we are amateur speakers, people who seek a modicum of prowess and self-confidence in order that we may acquit ourselves with fair success when the occasion arises — let the would-be professional speaker who seeks the Queen's English, whatever that may be, worry about lessons in elocution. *We have a far more urgent aim, an objective which transcends any need to modify accent or dialect - and that, quite simply, is to persuade and convince those to whom we speak that we are worthy of their attention.*

So — wot abaht yer accent, then — enjoy it — and forget it!

## It's personality that counts

Too right, of course, personality counts. However, this does not mean that, to succeed in his ambitions, Ernie Ramsbottom, deputy-assistant-undermanager at Curdles Dairies, has to become the Laurence Olivier of the speaking world. Nor does it mean that, having eyed this paragraph, dear old Ernie — or *you* — can lightly afford to give a faintly patronising smile and pop off for a cup of coffee. To the company man who wishes to persuade and convince, it means accepting that there is such a thing as a 'speaking personality'. It means swotting up the recipe and engaging in a very frank self-appraisal, pinpointing and admitting one's weaknesses, taking a hearty pinch of the necessary ingredients, and putting them to effective use.

The 'speaking personality' is a little more than a collection of desirable characters and attributes, for, whilst these are all-important, it is necessary for the persuasive speaker to project his personality and, as will be seen, this entails the use of some 'physical' abilities — a vital mix of the following:

*Sincerity* To convince listeners that he is sincere, a speaker must demonstrate that he is something more than a mouthpiece, a mere *simulator*, and he achieves this by utilising a careful choice of words and by employing an adequate warmth and depth of expression, both oral and facial. Think of it from this viewpoint — do the following strike you as sincere speakers?

a    With his eyes fixed steadfastly on his notes, Michael addressed the audience in a monotonous, I-am-forced-to-read-this-bilge voice. . . .

b    John listened to the foreman's well-justified complaint and, uncomfortably aware that the matter had reached a critical stage, replied to the indictment. 'Er, yes — all right, Jack, I'll see — er — what can be done. . . .'

c    The manager fidgeted with the papers on his desk, frantically trying to think of something to say. Then, looking his subordinate briefly in the eye, he replied, 'Well, Derek, the trouble is — it's the directors, they're chasing me for these figures. . . .'

d    The master strolled to the window and stood with his back to the class. 'Right, all of you,' he intoned. 'Take down some notes — oil is a viscous liquid of either animal, vegetable or mineral origin. . . . the mineral oils. . . .' His voice tailed into silence as, basking in the warmth of the bright sunlight, his mind turned to the attractive prospect of the approaching holiday. . . .

Sincerity in speech, then, is conveyed by:

1    Choosing the right words and uttering them with a shade of meaning, an inflection, an emphasis — a whole range of nuances which are denied to the writer, but fully available as a vital aid to the speaker.

2    The use of carefully selected and modulated gesture and facial expression — remembering that the eyes can say many things. . . .

Yes, sincerity counts — if, that is, you wish to be respected, believed and, on the odd, sublime occasion, applauded.


*Rhythm and phrasing* These ingredients are concerned with the manner in which the effective speaker will stimulate the listener's emotions — provoke him to listen, to take an interest in that which he hears. An unchanging rhythm in speech may be an ideal tool of the trade for an aspiring hypnotist, but the speaker will find little joy in lulling his audience off to sleep. Unluckily, in very many cases a sense of rhythm is largely an instinctive ability, but much can be gained from practice — and the best forms of practice are to read aloud in private and to engage in as many conversations as possible, *but carrying out both activities with the following aims in mind:*

1    To introduce *variation* in rhythm, but not to the extent that rhythm 'takes over' and the significance of the words is lost in a welter of symphonic composition. A theatrical style of rhythm, for instance, may be wonderful

stuff when declaiming lines from Shakespeare, but a trifle incongruous when giving young Willie, the office junior, instructions for the day.

2　　To achieve the correct arrangement of stressed and unstressed words, and to recognise that the sense or import of a sentence can be drastically changed by the use of varying rhythms.

Remember also that an unwise choice of rhythmic composition can result in the speaker sounding rather akin to a story-teller on Children's Hour — which is marvellous if he happens to be addressing five-year-olds, but a trifle odd if the audience is composed of hairy foremen.

Phrasing is concerned with delivering whatever one has to say in *manageable chunks*. The John Gilpin of a speaker who gallops at full tilt through his piece, without regard for punctuation or drawing breath, will swiftly come to be regarded as a panting nonentity. Conversely, the human sloth, the speaker who unknowingly employs a kind of verbal Chinese water-torture, can make life well nigh intolerable for those who are forced to listen:

'Er — I am — er — glad to — um — have this — er — chance to — er — speak — ahem — to all of you — um — this evening. . . . (*Pregnant silence*) — I — er — would like to — um — thank. . . .'

*Tone*　With 'tone' we threaten to come full circle and verge on 'sincerity', but there are some aspects to be considered. Think on't:

a　　*Disciplinary matters:*
　　　The employment of a '*cold, forceful*' voice?
　　　'*Cold*' — the *tone* which is sincerely expressed.
　　　'*Forceful*' — the *tone* of the sincerity — the measure of it.
b　　*Laudatory matters:*
　　　The employment of a '*warm, congratulatory*' voice?
　　　'*Warm*' — the *tone* which, again, is sincerely expressed.
　　　'*Congratulatory*' — another measure, an evident yardstick, of sincerity.

There is an ideal tone to suit every statement — and every meaning behind that statement. Identify and use them.

*Vocabulary*　Clearly, the possession and use of an adequate vocabulary has much to do with the projection of a 'speaking personality'. Note, if you will, that I use the word 'adequate', for whilst it is obviously a great advantage to have an *extensive* vocabulary at one's fingertips, many inexperienced speakers worry overmuch on this score. *Reading* and *listening to others* will increase one's 'word battery', but beware of the mighty pitfalls which lurk in the area of specialised language. Our modern community contains and is founded upon a positive army of technologists, computer people, scientific wizards, administrators and the like, who are all busily engaged in building their own jargon mountains — and they are finding it increasingly difficult to open their mouths without befuddling us with hocus-pocus. Increasing one's vocabulary or using one's existing word battery does *not* mean striving to communicate by means of jargon — except of course when addressing fellow-members of the coven!

*Logicality of approach* In one sense, speaking is much easier than writing, for most of us tend to make use of words and phrases in speech which we would not dream of using when committing pen to paper. However and unluckily, this does not mean that it is easier to be a good speaker than a good writer — the spoken words, easily chosen, are often 'easily wrong'. The effective speaker must employ a logical approach to his subject and not fall headlong into the trap of an 'easy come, easy go' selection of words and phrases.

*Mobility* Mobility does not mean dashing up and down the platform or round the office like a blue-arsed fly — it simply means ensuring a mobility of stance and expression. The speaker who remains transfixed in stance and expression, resembling a Red Admiral in a butterfly collection, will look rather akin to a human totem pole — but few will respect him, let alone worship the creature.

That, then, is the general recipe for the attainment of a 'speaking personality', but — remembering that this chapter is a kind of nitty-gritty doormat for the more specialised chapters which follow — there are a number of other grisly things to be taken into account, so here goes.

## Attitudes

A speaker's attitude, whether he be addressing a vast public audience or simply talking to young Jones in the office, can make or mar the occasion. A revealed attitude may stem from a particular bias or prejudice or, more unfortunate, be the hallmark of an individual's very mode of existence. It is usually possible for the frank person to identify the former cause and, if he so wishes, do something about it — but an attitude which is part-and-parcel of the very fibre of a guy's outlook is something else. It may be possible for a leopard to change his spots — but, being realistic, *not* as a result of a few paragraphs in a book — but I must still try to work the oracle!

*Aggression* The barrister cross-examining a recalcitrant witness, the propagandist in wartime, the radical politician — such worthies possess, whether we like it or not, an in-built licence for aggression and, more to the point, it is generally expected that such people will use it to the full in the exploitation of their aims. But, and it is a big but, a licence for aggression does *not* extend to the everyday, run-of-the-mill speaker. The manager who reprimands an employee, investigates an incident, interviews a candidate for employment, the teacher taking a class of unwilling pupils, the speaker addressing a disinterested audience — these and countless other examples *represent occasions when a display of aggression is tactically bad, reprehensible and totally unforgivable*. The imposition of a firm and friendly authority — or a firm and *cold* authority — is a tool of the everyday speaker's trade. Aggression is simply the resort of the bully or, funnily enough, the coward who, being afraid of revealing shortcomings in his personality, takes refuge in the adage that attack is the best form of defence. Aggression is *out*.

*Argument* I am not referring to argument in the legal or reasoned sense, which is clearly necessary and entirely permissible on a vast number of occasions — no, I have in mind those miserable, niggling individuals who cannot open their mouths without engaging in argument or continued dissent. There are a few thousand miles between perfectly valid discussion and this form of insensate argument. Do *you* offend in this manner — or are you going to argue the point?

*Domination* The professional public speaker knows exactly when and how to dominate his audience but, let me repeat, we are amateurs who seek to convince and persuade whenever we open our mouths — and domination is not the method by which we should try to achieve these laudable aims. Some of us are born with that brand of extroversion that compels us to exude floods of personality — hearty, back-slapping, everything-in-life-needs-a-push types. Others among us tackle the job of communication by emulating the extrovert and assuming a form of *ersatz* domination which, if anything, is a jolly sight worse than the genuine article. Projected ebullience — natural or assumed — will inevitably result in the true import and purpose of what is said being unduly 'overlaid' with the attitude, to the detriment of the occasion.

*Insistence on showing authority* A very common complaint of the working man or woman with responsibility is the propensity to constantly remind others of their authority and, of course, of the magnificent saga of achievement which has propelled them to their exalted perches. Insistence on showing authority is usually a symptom of the insecure — and in these days of rat-race, redundancy and rationalisation, there is more than enough genuine insecurity dogging our lives — but this is no excuse for allowing that which we say to be polluted with the words of the braggart. Reader, if you are a 'self-made man' or you have clawed your way up the ladder the 'hard way', be proud of your achievement — but do put a sock in it, modesty is a divine virtue. . . .

*Fear and dislike* If a speaker — or, for that matter, his audience — is governed or motivated by fear or dislike, effective communication will fly straight out of the window. I know (and, boy, how do I know) that many top dogs in industry and commerce attain and hold their positions by the simple expedient of treading on the necks of others — a case of size eleven boots descending on size seven necks — but the imposition of fear and the manifestation of dislike are works of the Devil; do not enlist as his disciple. Incidentally, the advent of all that employment legislation heaped around our ears has had the effect of plonking salt on the tails of many petty tyrants — but, law or no law, speak fairly and be regarded as fair.

As for the speaker who *feels* fear, there is little use in offering honeyed, palliative words. The nervous individual will not need reminding that fear is a very cogent and destructive emotion — but he may need reminding that there are ways and means of living with the affliction, and Chapter 10 sets out to probe and dissect this unwelcome bedmate. For the moment, suffice it to say that the hairy old advice about preventing an attacking dog from sensing one's fear is extremely relevant when it comes to addressing people. The human animal has an inherently vicious streak in his make-up (there's an original gem for you) and often takes pleasurable advantage of someone in the herd who is afraid of him. So, one moral must be to refrain from *showing* fear, however much one is quaking inside. Similarly, the wise speaker will conceal any feelings of dislike, however justified, that he may have for his audience, for it will only provoke a like response.

## Some further nasties

*Bloomers*   Mis-statements, gaffes, clangers, inaccuracies — call them what you will — the hard fact is that we all commit them, particularly during times of stress or crisis. The company flapper, the every-minute-a-disaster panic-merchant, is a professional at the art of dropping one-ton clangers, but there are also well-meaning folk (you, kind reader, excepted — or are you?) who, quite calmly and at the drop of a hat, commit the most awful verbal boners. They range in extent from malapropisms (named after Mrs Malaprop, a richly wonderful character in Sheridan's *The Rivals*, who does such terrific things as describing another character as *'the very pineapple of politeness'*, and expresses the pious hope that her daughter, who has just been recommended to *'illiterate'* a certain gentleman from her memory, will never become a *'progeny of learning'*) to positively horrendous spoken errors, of which the history books and dismissal registers are full. With Mrs Malaprop in mind, the rule must be, 'Think before you open your mouth and, when you do open it, don't put your foot in it', or something like that. . . .

Unfortunately, our skill at committing bloomers is seldom matched by our candour in admitting and correcting them, particularly when the good old spoken word is concerned:

*Manager*   *(Testily)*   'Mrs Jones, I've asked you twice to get me the sales figures for March — where are they?'
*Mrs Jones*   *(Slightly affronted)*   'But — I put them on your desk this morning, Mr Williams. . . .'
*Manager*   'Er — yes, so they are — but why it is that I have to keep chasing these things?'

*Lecturer*   '. . . the war was only weeks old when, on the 14th of October 1939, the Royal Navy suffered a major disaster — the sinking of the *Ark Royal* at her anchorage in Scapa Flow. . . .'
*Student*   'Excuse me, Mr Booth — but surely you mean the battleship *Royal Oak?*'

*Lecturer*    *(Who dislikes being interrupted, let alone corrected)*    'No, no — I mean what I say, the aircraft carrier *Ark Royal*. . . .'

*Student*    *(Who plainly knows his facts and is not to be put off)*    'But the *Ark Royal* was sunk by U-boats in the Mediterranean. . . .'

*Lecturer*    'Look, old son, I *remember* World War 2 — I was *in* it — you weren't even a glint in your dad's eye! Take it from me, it was the *Ark Royal*. Now, for goodness sake, let's get on. . . .'    *(Student immediately loses faith in every word uttered by our impatient and totally incorrect hero.)*

*Manager*    *(Addressing staff)*    'I want you to know that I've had a copy of a circular memo from the managing director on the subject of staff lateness. . . . I take a very serious view of this, and so far as this department is concerned, I am going to insist on punctuality — is that clear?'

*Supervisor*    *(Acting as spokesman for the muttering group)*    'Mr Fox, there hasn't been a single instance of lateness in this department for months.'

*Manager*    'Well, then — let's keep it that way. . . .'    *(Exit staff, thinking and planning mayhem.)*

A frank admission of an error is a fine attribute and is much admired by subordinates and audiences alike. The vintage comment, 'What I like about the man is that he always admits when he is in the wrong', can be a valuable accolade.

*Humour*    A speaker-acquaintance of mine is a born comic. Possessing a very retentive memory — for gags, that is, but precious little else — he can render any company into stitches of laughter and nearly always does. That is the trouble, of course; he can hardly open his mouth without making a funny, with the inevitable result that his audience is completely distracted from the subject in hand. Such a speaker is a poor communicator of everything but jokes, and very swiftly loses the respect of his audience, however much they may laugh. I know of another speaker who often lands in similar trouble, but by travelling a different route — for he is not a born comic and has a rotten memory for jokes. This guy's lethal frailty is simply that he puts everything he has got into the telling of what he regards as a magnificently funny story, only to find that he has recounted the oldest chestnut in the bag. On such awkward occasions, and I am afraid they are legion, he realises halfway through the story that he 'has done it again' by the manner in which the glazed-eye ratio zooms up to critical level — but by then it is too late. No, humour in overkill doses or humour from all too dusty bottles can be the speaker's downfall.

The professional raconteur and the experienced comedian know that humour, like women's fashions, enjoys a multiplicity of popular and often slightly incomprehensible 'in' seasons. The blunt austerity of Second World War 2 'Adolf and Hermann' jokes — supreme morale-boosters of their age — ushered in the golden era of the long hemline, highly-padded 'Englishman, Irishman and Scotsman' mode, which proliferated within the ranks of jokers

16

who yearned for the fripperies of peace. Then as a cynical world discovered the fallibilities and price of enduring peace, the *haute couturier* of humour sprang the 'hard line' on an unsuspecting world — and a welter of sharply-critical, dig-thy-neighbour gags hit the fashion market. The English, for example, swiftly developed a predilection for 'Irish' gags:

*Pilot, calling London Airport* 'Heathrow, may I have a time-check, please?'
*Heathrow Tower* 'Yes, certainly. If that is a Lufthansa flight, the time is 13.50 hours, precisely. If it is British Airways, the time is ten-to-two. If it is Aer Lingus calling, Noddy is on the ten and Big-Ears is on the two. . . .'

Poor, undeserving Aer Lingus — the splendid airline came in for more than its fair share of English digs:

'Oi — how do you recognise an Aer Lingus captain?'
'I don't know — how *do* you recognise an Aer Lingus captain?'
'He's the one with gold rings round his wellies. . . .'

Canadians relished 'Newfie' jokes (to the uninitiated, the much-maligned folk of Newfoundland), the Irish — who were obviously sick of being a target — entered the field with innumerable digs at the Kerrymen, Americans gained a somewhat unhealthy appetite for Polack gags (one wonders how the Polish immigrants got *their* revenge), and even the Arabs entered into the spirit of things by choosing the Bedou desert-dweller as a butt for their humour. All of which means very little except, perhaps, to make the point that an intending humourist should ensure that his funnies are in-season — for jokes, unlike wine, do not improve with keeping.

Another thing for the speaker to watch is the question of propriety. One man's meat is another man's poison, and it may well be that the august members of the East Cringe Mothers' Guild will not take very kindly to that carefully nurtured yarn about the pretty girl, the elephant and the toothpick. To regale a predominantly Irish audience with gags about the Irish might be a resounding success on some occasions — and an invitation for a shillelagh round the ears on others. Consider the joke with care but, above all, consider the audience.

A good tip for the intending humourist is to keep on the lookout for real-life anecdotes and stories — for, humans being what they are, the funniest things are those that actually *happen*. Take, for example — and forgive me, for I cannot get away from the Emerald Isle — the true story of the Irish community who were very proud of the historic, ruined church that lay just beyond their village. Aware that the ruins were in danger of further damage by vandals, they engaged in intensive fund-raising activities until, at long last, there was sufficient money to have a decent stone wall built round the hallowed site. When the wall was completed, a string of church and other dignitaries went to the site to carry out a dedication ceremony — only to find that the ruined church had disappeared. . . . Begorrah, t'is true.

Remember, humour should be fun — especially to those who listen.

## Self-tutorial (Part One)

## A GENERAL QUIZ ON THE PRECEDING CHAPTER

Reader, play the game and attempt this type of quiz by covering all but Question 1 with a piece of paper — and then move the paper down as you proceed from question to question. Remember, no peeping, it does no harm to exercise your memory.

**Answers**

**Questions**

1 How does a speaker convey sincerity?

1 By choosing the right words — by uttering them with a convincing inflection and emphasis — and by the use of carefully controlled and effective facial expression and gestures.

2 What is meant by the use of 'phrasing' in speech?

2 The delivery of what one has to say in a well-punctuated and easily understood fashion, i.e. in manageable chunks.

3 Should a speaker set out to dominate his listener?

3 Never! There is a world of difference between dominating a conversation or discussion and *controlling* it.

4 If a speaker fails to convey sincerity, what will be the overall effect?

4 It will be felt by the listener that the speaker is merely *simulating* interest and concern; he will not be believed.

5 The chapter condemns 'argument' as a weapon in the speaker's bag of tricks — does this mean argument should *never* be used?

5 Of course not — *reasoned* argument has an important place in the work scenario. Argument for the sake of argument — an inherent attitude in many — is the forbidden fruit; bite it not!

6 An employee requires to be verbally reprimanded following a minor offence. He attempts to argue further his point of view during delivery of the reprimand — is there valid cause for the use of aggression on such an occasion?

6 No, there isn't. Aggression is a cardinal weakness of the manager who is poor at his profession, and there is no excuse for the attitude — particularly during any form of judicial proceeding. (Many

7 To recap, what are the essential ingredients of a 'speaking personality'?

18

managers tend to overlook the
vital fact that a verbal reprimand,
however trivial, is the outcome of
a judicial procedure — and should
be treated as such.)

7   Sincerity — correct rhythm and
    phrasing of speech — correct tone
    of speech — adequate vocabulary
    — a logical approach to the subject
    — mobility.

8   The 'temperature' of what is said
    — a warm, cold, icy, friendly, etc.,
    tone.

9   The ability to enhance what is said
    by movement and expression —
    the good opposite of a 'dead-pan'
    speaker.

8   What is meant by 'tone'?

9   What about 'mobility'?

## Self-tutorial (Part Two)

Bearing in mind that effective phrasing for verbal delivery does *not* just mean
sticking religiously to punctuation marks, read the following passage out loud:
1   'As it comes' (your normal reading voice).
2   With effective phrasing.

Today's methods of communication with the public at large — the mass
media of press, radio and television — ensure that the man in the street is
made well aware of what is going on in the world and, very often, is in the
position of witnessing events as they actually take place. The advent of the
'instant report', the television camerman filming an industrial
confrontation on the picket line, with instantaneous transmission to the
homes of several million viewers, means that communication is achieved
with a degree of impact hitherto unknown. In short, the public is fed —
almost, it might be said, force-fed — with an almost continuous stream of
information and opinion on all types and varieties of events which, in the
view of the transmitting authority, are deemed to be newsworthy and 'in
the public interest'. Whilst there can be little doubt that the mass media
perform a valuable service — in a free society, man is entitled to be
informed — there is equally little doubt that much information is presented
in a heavily edited and 'slanted' form. To the media, bad news is always
'good news', for it is the disaster or emotive issue that sells newspapers
and glues people to the radio or telly. When the television camerman
zooms in on an ugly picketing scene, with the news reporter conducting
off-the-cuff interviews with a haphazard selection of aggrieved

participants, it is extremely easy for a relatively uninformed viewer to be emotively and inaccurately influenced by that which he sees and hears.

Now — imagine that you are facing an audience, and read it again!

## Self-tutorial (Part Three)

Here is a second exercise which involves reading aloud — stick with it, and never mind what the missus has to say. This time we are concerned with effective phrasing *and* tone. Same drill — read the passage several times until you achieve the desired effect:

> Speak the speech, I pray you, as I pronounced it to you, trippingly on the tongue: but if you mouth it, as many of your players do, I had as lief the town-crier spoke my lines. Nor do not saw the air too much with your hand, thus; but use all gently: for in the very torrent, tempest, and, as I may say, the whirlwind of passion, you must acquire and beget a temperance that may give it smoothness. Oh, it offends me to the soul, to hear a robustious periwig-pated fellow tear a passion to tatters, to very rags, to split the ears of the groundlings, who, for the most part, are capable of nothing but inexplicable dumb shows and noise: I could have such a fellow whipped for o'erdoing Termagant; it out-herods Herod: pray you, avoid it.

Familiar stuff — yes, but very good advice. But the second part of Hamlet's stirring lesson to the players constitutes an even bigger challenge when it comes to implanting effective phrasing and tone. So if you are feeling brave, have a shot at this:

> Be not too tame neither, but let your own discretion be your tutor: suit the action to the word, the word to the action; with this special observance, that you o'erstep not the modesty of nature: for anything so overdone is from the purpose of playing, whose end, both at the first and now, was and is, to hold, as 'twere, the mirror up to nature; to show virtue her own feature, scorn her own image, and the very age and body of the time his form and pressure. Now, this overdone or come tardy off, though it make the unskilful laugh, cannot but make the judicious grieve; the censure of the which one must, in your allowance, o'erweigh a whole theatre of others. Oh, there be players that I have seen play — and heard others praise, and that highly, not to speak it profanely, that neither having the accent of Christians, nor the gate of Christian, pagan, nor man, have so strutted and bellowed that I have thought some of nature's journeymen had made men, and not made them well, they imitated humanity so abominably.

Now, it is time for some soul-searching. Was your reading slightly flat and, as a result, uninteresting — or, on the other hand, did you fall into the traditional amateur's trap of reading Shakespeare 'larger than life'? Lastly, have you taken the Bard's advice to heart?

# Part Two
# DOING ONE'S THING IN THE DAILY ROUND

Yet seemed that tone, and gesture bland,
Less used to sue than to command.

**Sir Walter Scott (1771-1832)**
*The Lady of the Lake*

# 3
# Orders is orders

The vexed business of issuing orders and instructions looms large on the horizon of almost any manager, yet relatively few of us are prompted to give much thought to the manner in which we implement the process. With the notable exception of the armed services and a handful of other worthy bodies, the powers-that-be who promote us to positions of authority seem to assume that the very act of promotion bestows a heaven-sent ability to stir people into action — 'You're a manager now — get out there and manage. . . .' Little wonder then that one finds a wide spectrum of individual views on the subject:

'Orders is orders, m'lad, and if yer knows wot's good f'yer, yer'll bloody well obey 'em. . . .'
*(Ever-to-be-remembered comment made to the author by a fatherly Flight Sergeant of the 'old school')*

'No, I don't have any difficulty giving instructions to my staff — why should I? It's simple really — go by the book and you can't go wrong. What d'you mean by *how* do I give orders? Attitudes — style— Oh, I leave that kind of thing to the trick-cyclists — after all, I'm a manager, not a social worker. If there's something to be done, tell 'em to do it — and that's the end of the matter.'
*(Comment at a seminar by a production manager)*

'I suppose my difficulty is that I work right alongside my staff, and because of the nature of the work, things are very informal. I like the nice, easy atmosphere — except, that is, when I have to issue instructions. Sometimes, I get a kind of back-chat, and while it's never anything serious, I often feel that my authority is being questioned — but don't all managers get this at some time or other?'
*(Excerpt from a taped discussion with a young accountant)*

'Let's be honest — who gives orders or instructions these days? Polite requests, maybe. . . .'
*(Comment at a seminar by an office supervisor)*

And so on, *ad infinitum.*

There is a little more to giving orders than merely stirring people into action — after all, a hand-grenade would have that effect. A properly constructed order has several component parts:
1   *First vital element*   The 'stirring' bit — but, wait for it, there is more — the order must stir people into action *to achieve an aim.* No objective — no order.
2   *Second vital element*   The 'allocation' bit — the notification that Mr So-and-So is going to be held responsible for the achievement of the objective.
3   *Third vital element*   The 'motivation' bit — if Bertie Bloggs is to give of his best in achieving the objective, he must be 'put in the picture'. Many managers choose to condemn this element as a form of toadying to the subordinate — pure regression to the 'orders is orders' syndrome — and then wonder why the particular task is performed unwillingly. *Motivation is essential.*
4   *Fourth vital element*   The 'consultation' bit — the provision of an opportunity for dear old Bertie to consult and participate in the given situation. It must be remembered that subordinates who are denied such opportunities are, in fact, denied the essential right to display capabilities and potential for promotion. Let me rub the salt in — the manager who refuses the right of consultation is often an insecure manager, and he had better watch out. . . .
   Having looked at the component parts of an order, it is now necessary to note the obvious fact that the manner in which an order is given is of supreme importance. The office manager who strides into his little empire and suddenly bawls out, *'Right, you lot - stand by your desks!'* has not only forgotten all about the component parts of an order, but is also inviting, at the very least, a silent barrage of raspberries from his staff. Plainly, the *type* of order to be given will be dictated by a number of factors:
1   *The status level, personalities - call it what you will - of the people involved*   I venture to say that an order given to a group of university dons would be expressed in quite different terms to the same order when given to a gang of road-workers — for example, the order to the road-workers would have to be much more polite. . . .

2    *The job involved*   Many factors come to mind — the complexity of the job, the general conditions under which it is to be performed, the degree of urgency involved, whether the task will have any effect on future relationships and so on.

3    *The general environment*   The quality of relationship between the person giving the order and those who are required to obey — in other words, the 'climate'. There may also be external influences to be taken into account — union attitudes, legal restrictions, etc.

And, last but not least, the indigestible factor —

4    *The personality of the guy or girl giving the order*   And, as you will guess, this prime factor cannot be dismissed in a few words — bide a wee while and we will look at this 'nasty' in some depth.

That, then, is the list of ingredients — let us examine the type of order which can emerge:

*(a)   The command*   In the bad old days of dark, Satanic mills and all that jazz, most orders were issued in the form of commands, but, as we are constantly reminded, we now live and work in a more enlightened age — and commands are considered the height of naughtiness. Suffice it to say, then, that this type of unilateral communication has somewhat limited uses, except — as one authority rather charmingly puts it — when more diplomatic methods fail or, of course, when a state of emergency prevails.

*(b)   The instruction*   What's in a name, do I hear you ask? Well, it is true that the only difference between a command and an instruction may be based in semantics — but I like to think that the latter version has a less emotive ring about it. Certainly it is possible to phrase an instruction without it sounding too much like a command:

> *Instruction*   'Mr Jones, I'll see the other candidate now — bring him in, please.'
> *Command*   'Mr Jones, bring the other candidate in.'

*(c)   The request*   In certain circumstances, there is a great deal to be said for shrouding an order within the tactful mask of a request:

> 'Brian, I wonder if you would mind getting out the Hackett file for me?'

> 'John, could you look into this business of the tribunal order and find out who is at fault?'

There is little doubt that the request — delivered by the right personality and in the right way, more of which anon — goes a long way towards establishing a rapport between the manager and his subordinates.

*(d)   The suggestion*   Note how we are sliding headlong down the 'scale of emphasis' but, for all that, it is possible on many occasions to utilise a suggestion and achieve the effect of an order:

'Peter, I'm not very happy about the state of the lubrication bay. . . .'

Such a suggestion may be entirely sufficient to prompt Peter to crack the whip with the grease-monkeys; the hint has been made and he is smart enough to appreciate the true import of the comment. The manager who enjoys a good rapport with his subordinates will find the occasional use of the suggestion a handy and tactful tool of management.

*(e) The plea* Now, of course, we have reached rock-bottom, the nadir of the manager's 'order spectrum' and last resort of the chap who has failed. The tragic and utterly frustrating fact is that there are many folk who, promoted beyond their levels of competence, cling desperately to the reins of authority, pleading and even bribing their way through management life:

> 'Mick, I know you don't agree, but I'm getting hammered by the directors about this — do it for me, there's a good lad. Tell you what — get the job done, and I'll see if I can arrange for you to have some time off. . . .'

> '. . . but, Howard, please — you've got to do it, or there'll be holy hell to pay from the boss. . . .'

And that seems a good point at which to return to the thorny business of personality. . . .

## Anyway, who the heck does he think he is?

The war-cry of the indignant subordinate — and very often it pays the manager to give serious thought to the question. Be a devil, engage in some frank heart-searching and, remembering that we are concerned with the art of giving orders, see if any of the following accounts strike a responsive chord — and if so, do something about it!

*All pals together* Recall, if you will, the excerpt from the discussion with a young accountant: '. . . I like the nice, easy atmosphere — except, that is, when I have to issue instructions. . . .' The one big snag with maintaining an informal relationship with one's subordinates is that if things go too far, it is extremely hard to revert to a formal situation whenever necessary without upsetting the proverbial apple-cart. Many moons ago, when posted to my first appointment as a newly commissioned, sprog pilot officer, the station adjutant did the traditional thing and clobbered me with a 'secondary duty' — officer-in-charge of the Corporals' Club. T'was Christmas time and the corporals, who, on this station, ran a most excellent club, decided to hold a party, and yours truly received an official invitation. Despite the fact that I had been well drilled on such matters ('. . . as an officer, you will be required to attend NCO's functions — maintain a pleasant dignity, stay sober and depart early', and so on), I was a wee bit timorous about the whole thing. My flight sergeant, a grizzled and expert veteran of many years' service, heard that I was going to the shindig, and weighing me up with that marvellous expertise which is peculiar to servicemen of his stature, chose to give me some advice.

'Excuse me, sir, for being so bold, but seeing as it's your first official visit, like, to the corporals' club. . . .' There was a tactful pause and then, sensing correctly that his words would not be unwelcome, he continued. 'Well, it's like this, sir — they're a good bunch of lads on the whole an' I don't expect they'll take any liberties, 'specially if they see that you're enjoying yourself and, if you'll pardon the expression, sir, not being kind of stand-offish. As I see it, the big secret is to be your natural self, like, but not so natural that they forget you're the boss. . . . Show 'em you're man enough to like 'em and that you appreciate their company — and, well, man enough to change hats when it's necessary and be a — er, bastard, sir — but *only for as long as it's necessary. . . .*'

The company man would be well advised to follow the flight sergeant's advice and seek to achieve the elusive 'happy medium' of informality with his subordinates. Then, and only then, will he find that the transition to a formal situation can be a relatively smooth and painless process, and the issue of instructions an effective, but commonplace, occurrence.

*I'm the Lord High Executioner. . . .* There are managers who should be forced to spend their lives staked to the nearest barrack square. I refer of course to that unfortunate breed of tragicomic characters who, knowing next to nothing about sergeant-majors, try to emulate them in the management and control of their juniors. Perhaps you will forgive a parody of the serviceman's old, old lament:

They stand at their desks
And they bawl and they shout
They shout about things
They know fuck-all about!

We have all encountered them, and many of us have had the misfortune to serve under their abysmal ministrations. Always on the move, usually at the gallop, these worthies rarely draw breath for fear of interrupting the constant spate of useless, superfluous and intimidating orders which they spew forth, all capped with reminders of the dire penalties for disobedience. Some enlightened day, there will be a corporate garrotte for these management loud-mouths — so, reader-in-a-hundred, if the cap fits, keep looking over your shoulder.

*It's not me, chaps, it's the people upstairs* If we are truthful, every man-jack of us has passed the buck at some time or other when issuing instructions — a number of us are professionally qualified at the art. If there is a difficult or unpleasant task to be done, it is all too easy to cap the instructions with the buck-passing classic, 'Sorry, but it's the boss — he wants it done'. I am reminded of a certain 'manager' in further education who has become so adept at passing the buck

27

that whenever he originates an instruction, he commences it with the words, 'Mr So-and-so (*the man's boss*) requires you to. . . .' The poor old boss has no idea that his name is so constantly taken in vain, and would probably be very annoyed if he found out. Subordinates are not fools — in fact, the keenest appraisals of managers are those carried out by their juniors — so, beware, if your buck-passing slip is showing; they will spot it.

*The shy and retiring type*   I have nothing but genuine sympathy for the manager who finds it difficult to issue instructions because he feels shy or ill-at-ease. In the good old USA, one can combine the Saturday shopping with a quick nip-in and tune-up with Your Friendly Headshrinker, but on this side of the pond, we are a bit more inhibited about such things — and the shy manager usually goes through a quiet hell all on his own. There are many manifestations of the ill-at-ease syndrome, ranging from a total dread of confronting people to, for instance, the immobilising inability to look a person in the eye without twitching, blushing, or feeling and looking awkward. Many books have been written on the subject of building self-confidence, and there are a number of management courses which claim to help the shy executive — perhaps he should give them a try. It is not my intention to pour out honeyed words of encouragement for, as I have said, I have nothing but genuine sympathy to offer.

## Orders in a nutshell

You can win half the battle of giving orders by simply thinking before opening your mouth — and think along these lines:
1    What *type* of order does the situation require?
2    Has the order been *planned* to include:
    *a*    Adequate information on the situation?
    *b*    Effective allocation of responsibility?
    *c*    A means to inspire enthusiasm and motivate for success?
    *d*    An opportunity for consultation/discussion?
3    Last but not least, is the way clear for efficient feedback/follow-up of the results?
Right, then, get to it! And that's an order. . . .

## Self-tutorial (Part One)

In the preceding chapter, I offered that orders can be categorised on a five-point 'scale of emphasis':

Commands
Instructions
Requests
Suggestions
Pleas

You will have noticed that the choice of words determined the type of order that emerged in the examples. But is this the end of the story? Look at the following example, which, so far as the words are concerned, appears to constitute a request:

'Mr Brown, would you bring me the other schedule, please?'

Now repeat the request to yourself, but this time lay stress on the word which is italicised as follows:

a  'Mr *Brown*, would you bring me the other schedule, please?' Has Brown been caught daydreaming. . . ?

b  'Mr Brown, *would* you bring me the other schedule, please?' Is a favour being asked — or is this the second time of asking?

c  'Mr Brown, would *you* bring me the other schedule, please?' Brown, and no one else, is to bring the schedule. . . .

d  'Mr Brown, would you *bring* me the other schedule, please?' Don't talk about it, Brown, *bring* it. . . .

e  'Mr Brown, would you bring *me* the other schedule, please?' Don't take it to *him* — bring it to *me*. . . .

f  'Mr Brown, would you bring me the *other* schedule, please?' Not *this* schedule, you idiot, the *other* one. . . .

g  'Mr Brown, would you bring me the other *schedule*, please?' I don't want the *catalogue* — I want the *schedule*. . . .

h  'Mr Brown, would you bring me the other schedule, *please*?' For the tenth time of asking, Brown — bring me the schedule. . . .

Plainly, the act of laying stress on particular words can drastically affect the meaning and import of any statement, but where orders are concerned, it is very important to get it right first time. The employee who greets a wrongly stressed instruction with raised eyebrows has made an effective point — the damage has been done. Laying stress is a fairly automatic function with most individuals, and if a person happens to be a naturally sarcastic character, his orders will reflect this weakness — to the detriment of good working relationships.

Note, also, that *inflexion* plays a similar part in the process of giving orders. Repeat to yourself the request to Mr Brown, using rising and falling inflexions — and see the difference that it makes.

## A GENERAL QUIZ ON THE PRECEDING CHAPTER

**Answers**

**Questions**

1 What should first be considered before issuing an order?

1 What *type* of order the situation requires

2 And, for convenience, how may orders be categorised?

2 Commands, instructions, requests, suggestions and — pathetic last — pleas

3 What is meant by the 'motivation content' of an order?

3 The encouragement — *not* bribery — element of an order, to provoke the recipient to give of his best

4 What factors will influence the *type* of order to be given?

4 The status and personalities of the people concerned, the type of job involved, the relationship between the person issuing the order and the recipients

5 Anything else?

5 The personality of the person who issues the order — *you*

6 When, in general, may commands be freely issued in the normal business environment?

6 In times of emergency or crisis

7 Should the reason for a given task be explained when the order is issued?

7 Yes — for this is an important element in the motivational content of an order

8 What is meant by the 'allocation content' of an order?

8 The clear allocation of responsibility for the task

Severity breedeth fear, but roughness breedeth
hate. Even reproofs from authority ought to be
grave and not taunting.

**Francis Bacon (1561-1626)**
*Of Great Place*

# 4

# Rockets — and how best to launch 'em

The average manager — there I go again, but you know what I mean — never really enjoys giving reprimands, but in today's democratic world with the storm-clouds of a chilling array of employment law poised to descend on him from a great height, he positively hates the idea. The fine old honest-to-goodness rocket, the verbal raspberry with no holds barred and words chosen with gay abandon, is very much a thing of the past. Whilst the onerous clauses of the Industrial Relations Code of Practice legitimise the existence of the informal warning, many of us know — and some to our cost — that the word 'informal' has a very hollow ring about it. When events demand the issue of a verbal warning, the preparation and delivery of the wretched thing involves a great deal of formality — if, that is, the manager seeks to avoid the dripping fangs of union or legal carnivores. T'is a vexed business, and it is the purpose of this chapter to offer some help.

## The golden rules for launching rockets

1   *Get the facts right*   The boss who sails into battle and delivers a reprimand which is based on faulty information will reap, and certainly deserve, the accolade of MMM — Management Mug of the Month.
2   *Manager – unconscious contender for the MMM*   'Smith, I'm given to under-stand that yesterday, at cease-work — despite standing instructions on the

subject — you saw fit to go home without ensuring that the confidential file on Jefferson was locked away. Fortunately, Mr Fox happened to go into your office and found the folder on your desk, open for all to see — otherwise, there would have been an even worse breach of security. Be that as it may, I take a most serious view of your laxity — what have you to say for yourself?'

3  *Smith – hell-bent on awarding the MMM*  'Well, there is one thing, sir — if you recall, I've just returned from three days' leave, I wasn't in my office yesterday. . . .'

The facts and background information on a situation which may entail the issue of a reprimand should always be checked with care, and particularly when one is 'acting on information received'. Then, and only then, should the offender be placed on the inquisitorial mat, and a *second* check-cum-investigation commenced. Every alleged sinner is entitled to be regarded as innocent until proved guilty, and his version of the affair should be allowed to emerge before the manager succumbs to pontification or pronouncement of sentence.

*Be human, not a parody of the Lord Chief Justice*  Give some managers the task of delivering a reprimand, and, lo and behold, out of the desk drawer comes a special po-face which is reserved exclusively for such occasions — and mighty false it looks too. There is no such thing as a judicial expression; it is the wig and gown that makes His Lordship look that way — so, manager-mimic, beware. Another favourite trick employed by this quaint breed of manager is the adoption, again specially for the occasion, of a 'judicial stance'. Before the hapless miscreant enters the inner sanctum, everything on the desk is positioned and squared-off to the nearest millimetre and the manager struggles from his accustomed slouch to a bolt-upright position of rectitude — with, if he is nervous, his arms folded and trying for all the world to look like a lounge-suited Buddha. Employees notice these things. . . .

*Be fair*  Extend a helping hand to the employee. In addition to establishing the facts, win the offender's confidence — it is possible to do this without being unduly friendly — and ascertain if, just perhaps, there was an important, underlying reason for what he did:

1  *A gambit for, say, the 'thinking' employee*  'From what you have told me, Brian, there is no doubt that you were fully aware that you were breaking company regulations, but I've always regarded you as a pretty level-headed individual — you must have felt there was a good reason for doing so-and-so. Care to tell me about it?'

2  *A more direct approach, with a hint that justice will prevail*  'Right — so we've established that you disobeyed my instructions — but I'd be a poor manager if I left it at that — in fairness to you, I want to hear *why* you did so-and-so. . . .'

3  *A possible approach for the employee who appreciates being dealt with in a man-to-*

*man style* 'John, you've been very frank with me and that's a quality I admire. Now — be equally frank and tell me *why* you did. . . .'

*Be a good listener* There is precious little use in encouraging an offender to give his version of the affair if his cry from the heart or pack of lies is constantly interrupted by a space of how, why, when and buts from a Doubting Thomas of a manager. Certainly the arrant knave or the employee with verbal diarrhoea will require to be silenced, but in most cases an attentive expression and occasional nod will convince the individual that he is receiving a fair hearing.

*Don't be a sarcastic brute* Some 'managers' are naturally sarcastic and, horrible breed that they are, regard any form of disciplinary hearing as a heaven-sent opportunity to expand and develop their scurrilous art. The use of sarcasm when dealing with subordinates is a reprehensible practice at the best of times, but the manager who allows his vituperations to taint a disciplinary hearing deserves to be hanged, drawn and quartered.

*Hold on to your temper* There will be times when a rascal of an offender will have you clinging desperately to the last threads of self-control — and cling you must! Remember that the disciplinary hearing is a stressful occasion for all but the worst of employees, and that some will allow their tongues to run away with them. Obviously, outrageous comments and attitudes demand a firm response, but never, ever lose your temper.

*The rocket itself* Many of us experience difficulty with the actual wording of a verbal warning or reprimand, and some make the total mistake of believing that such an occasion merits a lecture. In short, it does not — the aim is to censure, not harangue. The key to an effective and telling reprimand is to ensure that it is brief and succinct. If the offender has been given a fair crack of the whip — acquainted with the facts and permitted his say — then, when it comes to the reprimand itself, there is little sense in prolonging the issue with any kind of homily, for the employee will be well aware of his guilt and the extent of his transgression.

Consider, then, the wording of the rocket, remembering that although the procedure bears the official tag of informality, this is merely intended as a means of distinguishing between the verbal and the written process — the *words* which are used should convey a high degree of formality. But, what words? The existence of an all-embracing disciplinary procedure may inhibit one's choice, but otherwise the field is wide open. Here are a few examples which may serve as useful 'triggers' for the chap in need:

'. . . and, as a consequence, it has been established that you disobeyed a clear instruction from Mr Champion, your supervisor. You are therefore reprimanded and warned that any further instances of misconduct may result in more formal proceedings being taken against you. That is all. . . .'

33

'. . . on this occasion I have decided to award you a verbal reprimand. You should note that this is the first stage in the company's disciplinary procedure, and that further misconduct on your part may result in more formal action being taken. That is all. . . .'

'I take a very serious view of this matter, Simon, and I wish to make it quite plain that I will not tolerate such behaviour in the office. Make no mistake about it, any further instance of this nature and you will find yourself in very deep trouble. You are a sensible chap at heart — heed my warning and don't place your future in jeopardy. . . .'

'I am satisfied that you have committed a clear breach of company regulations and, as a consequence, I am now awarding you a verbal reprimand. This fact will be duly noted in your personal file, and you are warned that any further act of misconduct may lead to more formal action being taken by the company. . . .'

'Brian, I find this a sad and painful business — I have no option but to award you a reprimand, and this, of course, will be noted in your personal file. I'm sure that I do not have to remind an employee of your calibre that any further instances of this nature can only result in very serious consequences. . . .'

'. . . and, as a result, White, I am now giving you an informal reprimand. This means that you have incurred the first stage of the company disciplinary procedure and that if you commit any further acts of misconduct, more formal action may then have to be taken. . . .'

'I find that the complaint against you has been proved, and since this involved a clear breach of company rules, I am verbally reprimanding you. I must warn you that. . . .'

*Remember the rules*   If your company has an established disciplinary procedure, you will not need reminding that it would be fatal to step outside it. Remember such points as the possible rights of the offender to have a union or other representative present at the hearing, and if the procedure includes a right of appeal against sentence, remember to explain this to the employee.

## Some thoughts on rockets in general

It has been said many times that imposed discipline is, in fact, a *negative* form of discipline, and that the thinking manager will strive for a better work climate where *positive* discipline — the motivation of employees to conform — is king. However, few of us are lucky enough to attain the Utopia in which punishment is unnecessary and unknown, and it is therefore wise to constantly remind ourselves of the obvious but often overlooked effects of a disciplinary system on working relationships in general. Whilst reprimands and rebukes which are manifestly unfair or badly handled can cause untold harm to good employee relations, the imposition of an equitable and well-administered system will do much to foster and maintain a high level of morale. The employee who, having been reprimanded, declares to all and sundry, 'That was a hell of a rocket — but, at least, the boss was fair about it all. . . .' is a valuable ambassador for management and a potent catalyst for good working relationships. Note, if you will, that the system itself is rarely unfair — it is the practitioners of the system who drop the clangers and cause the trouble.

## Self-tutorial (Part One)

This is a little exercise in which frankness in self-appraisal plays an important part — so, forgive me, I must engage in a small dose of teacher-pupil talk. Apart from the general quiz-type sections in these self-tutorials, the exercises rely for their success on the ability and determination of the reader — to be blunt, his frankness — to critically assess his efforts. This, as a lot of us are aware, is quite a task, and with temptation sitting firmly on our shoulders, it is only too easy to take the line of least resistance — merrily gloss over the various self-tutorials, mutter something akin, to, 'Well, this doesn't *really* concern me' and quickly move on. All right, homily over — let's get cracking!

Please call to mind a recent occasion when it was necessary for you to administer a reproof (or if you are lucky enough to find this impossible, *invent* a situation — think of a subordinate who comes perilously near the point of earning a reprimand and build a situation round that individual). Now jot down on a piece of paper the exact form, the precise wording, of the reproof to suit the occasion — and, if you are recalling an actual event, try to improve on what you said at the time.

Once you have done this — and, remember, you should have recorded the full text of the reprimand — slip the paper into the back of this book and, for the time being, forget it. We will deal with it later on. . . .

## Self-tutorial (Part Two)

Here is a fairly simple checklist which provides a logical approach to this unpleasant business of doling out reprimands. Study it, learn it and, above all, practice it — for unless you do, whatever you utter will be wrong.

1  Establish the facts of the situation — carry out a *full* and *impartial* investigation.
2  Question the employee — this does *not* mean subject him to an inquisition — and listen keenly to his comments and views.
3  Relate the employee's version of the matter with the facts as you know them — and beware of bias or prejudice in so doing.
4  Arrive at a decision and inform the employee accordingly. If a reprimand is justified, explain why — ensuring that the employee is made fully aware of the rule or instruction which has been broken.
5  Issue the reprimand fairly and firmly — and, however trivial the matter, *never* in the general presence of the employee's colleagues. Do not forget 'official' witnesses.
6  Ask the employee if he has anything to say and, if relevant, acquaint him with the procedure for appeal.
7  Whatever you may cause to be engraved in the holy personnel tablets as a record for possible use in the future, treat the matter as closed — justice has been done and, whatever you feel, the employee is entitled to a 'fresh start'.

## Self-tutorial (Part Three)

Read the following dialogue carefully:

*Jones* 'I believe you wanted to see me, Mr Long. . . .'

*Long* 'Yes, I did — come in and shut the door. Wait a minute, whilst I get these things out of the way.' *(Long busies himself with signing various papers and, after a period, puts down his pen and regards Jones with a cool, disapproving stare.)* 'Well, what have you got to say for yourself, eh?'

*Jones (Looks puzzled)* 'Er, I'm sorry, I don't know what you are getting at. . . .'

*Long* 'I think you know very well what I'm getting at — but I'll just jog your memory. . . . Last night, about fifteen minutes before your shift was due to finish, I was on the shop-floor, remember?'

*Jones* 'No, I didn't see you. . . .'

*Long* 'Oh, yes, you saw me all right — but, what is more to the point, I saw *you* and, make no mistake, I didn't like what I saw. . . .'

*Jones (Slightly heated)* 'I don't know what you are talking about!'

*Long (Leans forward in chair and glares at Jones)* 'I'm referring to the fact that you and Jenkins were indulging in a bout of violent and noisy horseplay — treating the place like a kids' playground. . . .'

*Jones* 'No, we weren't!'

*Long (Thumps blotter for emphasis)* 'Don't come the old soldier with me, my son — I saw you both with my own eyes, and I'm telling you here and now, it's going to stop, d'you understand?'

*Jones (Now very heated)* 'There wasn't any bloody horseplay, as you call it — we were just having a bit of a laugh, that's all. No harm in that is there?'

*Long (Adopts a threatening tone)* 'Don't swear at me, lad, or you're for the high-jump — just remember who you are talking to! You were skylarking around, instead of working. Now — you listen to me, I've had just about enough of you and your cronies in that Cutting Room. . . . There's been complaint after complaint from your supervisor. . . .'

*Jones (Outraged)* 'I've never had *any* complaint against me!'

*Long* 'Oh, yes, you have — and don't try to evade the issue. I've made up my mind, I'm giving you a reprimand. . . .'

*Jones* 'Bloody hell, for what, may I ask?'

*Long* 'If you swear at me again, Jones, I'll have you out of here before your feet touch the ground. . . . I've damned well told you once what it's for — I'm reprimanding you for making a thorough nuisance of yourself during the firm's time, and that's that. If there's any more of it, you know what will happen. . . .'

*Jones* 'Does that mean that something's going to go on my record?'

*Long* 'It means exactly what I've said — you're reprimanded, and if there is any repetition, any more mucking about, you know what to expect. . . . Got it?'

*Jones* 'Well, I want to see the production director about this. . . .'

*Long* 'You can see whoever you like, but I don't know what good you think it will do — now, get back downstairs, I've got work to do.'

Completely unrealistic? This may well be true where you are concerned — but, never mind, get a piece of paper and jot down where, in your view, friend Long went off the beaten tracks of good employee relations and discipline procedure. Check your findings with the following list:

1   Long should not have kept Jones waiting whilst he finished his paperwork. This smacks of a ruse to keep the employee dangling on the hook; it is reprehensible and impolite to boot.

2   The invitation to Jones, 'Well, what have you got to say for yourself?' is a crass and, very unfortunately, common opening gambit in such circumstances — it should never be used.

3   'I think you know very well what I'm getting at — *but I'll just jog your memory*. . . .' This is a nasty attempt at sarcasm and is quite unforgivable. Note that Long then continues with his hook-dangling caper, with the words, '. . . I was on the shop floor, remember?' Why, in heaven's name, does Long not tell the man what he is supposed to have done?

4   'Oh, yes, you saw me all right. . . .' A further dose of sarcasm.

5   At long last, the manager describes the alleged offence, which must pose the sixty-four thousand dollar question: why did he not intervene at the time of the incident?

6   'Don't come the old soldier. . . .' This type of retort is a firm favourite of the weak manager and reflects a total lack of basic ability — it is Long who deserves the reprimand.

7   The 'sergeant-major touch' continues with Long's reaction to Jones's swearing, and then, on the available evidence, the manager plunges into a wildly subjective comment on 'complaints'. Note Long's reply to the denial by Jones in this context — and I am sure you did note it.

8   Long then completes a thorough mishandling of a fairly straightforward situation by making an utter mess of the actual delivery of the reprimand — finishing up with a juvenile reaction to Jones's assertion that he intends to complain to the production director. And what a way to dismiss the man from his presence. . . .

What would *you* have done and, much more important, *exactly what would you have said?*

*And the muttering grew to a grumbling;*
*And the grumbling to a mighty rumbling. . . .*

**Robert Browning (1812-1889)**
*The Pied Piper of Hamelin*

# 5

# Defusing the grievance bomb

'Grievance? That's almost a dirty word in my department. . . . Let me give you an example of what I mean — something that happened just recently. Last month, the company announced a new bonus scheme — you know, the kind of thing they do when money is getting tight. There was the usual flourish of trumpets, bags of long-winded explanations and big words — which all boiled down to the fact that if they had their way, we would be earning less money for the same amount of work. Well, naturally the lads were very unhappy about the new proposals, especially those on the jig — which is my baby — and it wasn't long before I had a load of complaints on my hands. Reasonable complaints, you understand — after all, they're not idiots and they could see that the company was obviously trying to pull a fast one, as usual! So, off I went to talk to my boss — he's the production manager, a right 'nana — to see what could be done.

'It was plain that he was expecting me because as soon as I entered the office, he put on that special, boot-faced look — d'you know what I mean? Anyway, I'd no sooner started to tell him that the lads were unhappy about the new proposals, when he cut me off dead and barked something like, "Is this an official grievance?" Well, I ask you — I tried to tell the silly bugger that, as supervisor, it was my job to put him in the picture about the way the men felt, but he wouldn't have any of it. All he would say was that if anyone had a grievance, there was a right and proper way of going about it, and he wouldn't have anything to do with what he called "mass grumblings" put up by a spokesman! I got pretty bloody narked at his attitude and said that the only reason I was there was to *avoid* a load of official complaints — d'you know what he told me? He said that it was *my* job to deal with moans and groans on the shop-floor, that that was what I was paid for and that I was too soft on the men! Well, I just gave up in disgust and told him if that was what he wanted, it was all right by me — and walked out of the office. Next morning, by ten o'clock, he had twelve official grievances on his desk, mine included, from the jig section alone — God knows how many there were from the rest of the factory. I'll tell you one thing — he had a right old time explaining that little lot away to top management, and he bloody well deserved everything he got! They changed the bonus proposals almost immediately, but what a load of cobblers — it could all have been done with a spot of reasonable discussion. . . .'

*(Excerpt from a taped discussion with a works supervisor, whose company just happened to 'go union' very shortly afterwards. I wonder why?)*

Quite plainly, if the production manager in the above account — a management noodle of the first water — had had the good sense to say, 'Right, tell me all about it. . . .' instead of seeking pitiful refuge in the official procedure *and* denigrating his supervisor to boot, things may have been resolved in a far better and happier fashion.

The company chap who seeks to 'say the right thing' when dealing with grievances must, as an essential preliminary, do something about developing a personal technique for solving them. Let me recommend a handy checklist to your attention:

1   *Get to know your people*   An oft-quoted maxim of good management, but for all that, often ignored. All folk are different, and careful study should be given to the individual personalities, attitudes and quirks of behaviour of employees. Does a particular person come into any of the following categories:

    *a*   Those who grumble for the sake of grumbling?

    *b*   Those who are dogmatic, go-by-the-book types?

    *c*   Those who are professional troublemakers?

    *d*   Those who are afraid to air grievances or niggles, however genuine?

    *e*   Those who are out-and-out sheep of the work group?

2   *Be able to sense change*   The manager who keeps his finger firmly on the working pulse of his group will be in a position to sense change, and this is vital:

    *a*   Do the symptoms point to a work problem?

    *b*   Or are they indicative of some social problem, e.g. trouble at home?

3   *Be ready to intervene*   Having sensed or actually spotted that all is not as it should be, the thinking manager will endeavour to assess the nature and

significance of the change and how it is likely to affect the group as a whole. He will consider whether, and how, to intervene and will weigh the possible consequences of such intervention.

4    *The 'nipping in the bud' tactic*   As I mentioned at the beginning of this checklist, all folk are different, and if intervention is to succeed, these differences should be acknowledged by ensuring that any approach is carefully tailored to suit the personality of the individual concerned. Far too many managers take the lazy way out and employ an ill-conceived, completely 'standard' form of approach — *and it just will not do:*

a    Should it be the 'man-to-man' approach straight-between-the-eyes, 'what's wrong — tell me everything'?

b    Or the 'let me be your father' tactic?

c    Or the conversation about everything under the sun, in the pious hope that the employee will blurt out his troubles?

d    Or the 'I'm your friend, you can tell me' approach?

e    Or the 'I'm your manager and need to know' line?

There are infinite variations on the theme of approach, and the sobering truth is that only one form of opening tactic will truly suit each employee and each problem — hence the requirement for careful study of the situation.

5    *Dealing with the presented grievance*   Failure to detect the preliminary symptoms of a grievance will usually ensure that, sooner or later, the thing is presented to the unsuspecting manager in a festering lump — when, cursing his inadequacy at not having spotted trouble in't mill at an earlier and less acute stage, he will be required to think and act very quickly indeed:

a    Bear in mind that the employee may be emotionally aroused — and certainly under some form of stress. Make due allowances for these factors — be patient and tolerant.

b    Help the nervous or embarrassed employee over the hump by carefully timed and friendly interjections — remembering that a careless interjection may do more harm than good.

c    Recognise that a grievance will nearly always loom 'larger than life' in the mind of the chap concerned, and that it is fatal to belittle his problem casually.

d    Hardest task of all — *be a good listener.*

e    Remember that any grievance demands positive action of some form or another — *take it.*

6    *Follow the thing up*   A good fireman knows that apparently dead embers have an unpleasant habit of bursting into flame. The wise manager will always follow up the resolution or treatment of a grievance and, by so doing, not only prevent a possible recurrence but also earn the respect of his employees.

## Carry on, sergeant

I have the misfortune to know one so-called manager who, possessing a positive genius for smelling-out symptoms of grievance in the ranks of his staff, proceeds on every such occasion to prostitute this ability by ducking the issue. The slightest hint of trouble and, wham, he hoists his personal storm-cones and disappears over the horizon at a splendid rate of knots — for this nonentity of a manager *hates facing people*. A practitioner of that dreaded technique, 'management by memo', he will go to any lengths to avoid eyeball-to-eyeball confrontations, and usually succeeds. A product of further education mal-selection and a living example of the criminal ease with which a mediocre teacher may leap over the fence and become an appalling manager, he faces his responsibilities for people by ducking them. By assiduous passing of the grievance buck — 'Just see to So-and-so, Jim, he's got some kind of problem — I have to go to a meeting. . . .' — he has made a major contribution to the maintenance of poor staff relations within his department and is heartily despised by all who know him. There are many such mismanagers — think on't reader, for you surely know at least one such creature.

## Self-tutorial (Part One)

There follows a series of 'closing comments' by managers in grievance situations. Read them carefully and *note down your reactions to them* — you will need the piece of paper later on.

1    'I'm glad that you have approached me on this matter, Jones, and I consider that you have a legitimate grievance. Leave it with me for the time being and I will see what can be done. . . .'
2    'I've listened very carefully to what you have said, and in my view you do not have a legitimate complaint. Take my advice — the situation is not as you describe it, and if you are sensible, you will forget all about it. . . .'
3    'Yes, well, you may have a point. I appreciate your feelings about the manner in which this matter was handled, but as I've tried to tell you it wasn't up to me — the ruling came from upstairs. . . .'
4    'Look, Michael, take a tip from me — you've worked very well since you joined my department, and I have great hopes for your future with the company. I wouldn't like to see you rock the boat over such a trivial matter as this. . . .'

## Self-tutorial (Part Two)

This chapter referred to the need for a manager to get to know his people, and gave five examples of individuals who should be 'pin-pointed'. Using the same piece of paper — remember, you will need it later on — note down *why* it is essential, in grievance terms, to recognise these types:

1    Those who grumble for the sake of grumbling.
2    Dogmatic, go-by-the-book individuals.
3    Professional troublemakers.
4    Those who are afraid to air grievances, however genuine.
5    Those who are the out-and-out sheep of the group.

If we had had more time for discussion we should probably have made a great many more mistakes.

**Leon Trotsky (1879-1940)**
*My Life*

# 6
# Let's have a discussion

'My boss is very fond of the word "discussion" — but the trouble is he doesn't really know what it means. . . . Hardly a week goes by without him calling us all in for a "discussion" and it's always the same — he does the talking and we do the listening.'
*(Comment by a junior manager at a seminar on leadership)*

Just down the road from where I sit writing this stuff, there is a boss (no, not you, Joe) who is liberally tarred with the same brush as the voluble dictator in the above comment — a man who is infected with the curse, not the gift, of the gab. Well aware that he adores the sound of his own voice and that this is a salient personal weakness, he nevertheless succumbs to temptation and snatches the lion's share of any discussion. Since he is also far from being a genius, this crass loquacity has the natural effect of side-tracking and ruining many such sessions — and one fine day someone will say exactly that to his face, and he will deserve it. Too many of us, and especially those who squat in the seat of power, get carried away and make derisory use of so-called discussion — blissfully ignoring the fact that this boorish selfishness is a management crime of near-capital proportions. It behoves us to look at discussions.

For a start, let me tell you a story. Once upon a time, in a technical college, a certain department awaited the arrival of a newly appointed head. In a profession where new brooms are like confetti at a wedding, it is not entirely surprising that the members of the department awaited the arrival of their new boss with some trepidation and a great deal of wishful thinking. The big day came, and the staff assembled for the ritual of the 'opening address' — the young, female members twittering with anticipation, the older, male lecturers intent on preserving an attitude of aloof dignity — but every one of them with slightly bated breath. The new head entered the room, preceded in correct ceremonial order by a painfully obsequious deputy head, and the rites began:

'Firstly, let me say how grateful I am that despite your many duties, you have all managed to attend this meeting. . . .'
*(A dubious opening gambit, since everyone present had been detailed to attend.)*
'. . . my name is So-and-so and, as you are aware, I have been appointed as your head of department. . . .'
*(A blossoming of knowing nods from the creepers in the group.)*
'. . . I'm afraid that as I am a stranger to all of you, it will take me a little time to get to know you individually. . . .'
*(Strong stuff, this. . . . The new head then launched into the standard spiel about not wishing to disturb the undoubted smooth running of the department and the extent to which he would be depending on those present for help and guidance - proof positive that a new broom had arrived and was anxious to start sweeping. Then came the reference to his management style. . . .)*
'I am sure you will all be wondering about the manner in which I propose to manage the department. . . .'
*(Too bloody right - all present sit up.)*
'. . . and this can be summarised in one word — cooperation. I do not believe in management with a heavy hand; we are all adults and expert at our respective jobs. I am merely the captain of the team. . . .'
*(Most of the staff members have heard this guff about 'teamwork' many times before and they are not impressed. However, maybe - just maybe - this time the new chap means what he says. . . .)*
'. . . the last thing I wish to do is to impose unnecessary restrictions on your activities or, for that matter, interfere with aspects of your work which are ticking over efficiently and well. The accent will be on consultation in all matters, and if we encounter difficulties or problems, these will be resolved by discussion.'
*(Yes, some mutter, things are beginning to look hopeful.)*
'I intend to have a chat with each of you during the course of the next week or so — but, please remember, if any of you wish to see me, at any time, I am always available. . . .'
*(And that was that. A brief word of thanks and the head of department walked swiftly from the room.)*

The boss's departure was the trigger for a concerted gabble of conversation, as the staff gave vent to their first impressions of the newcomer. If there was a consensus of opinion, it was one of vague hope for the future. All agreed that the head's address had been remarkably short, and although he had maintained a deadpan expression throughout the proceedings, it appeared that his few words contained more than just a grain of sincerity. Still, it was argued, the future would tell — and, by golly, it did.

The promised chats with individual members of staff duly took place and, almost without exception, were reported by the people concerned as irritating and unrewarding episodes. The head launched each session with a reiteration of his maiden address, and then crowned these comments with a series of exhortations regarding the need for the individual, and the department as a whole, to do better than was apparently the case in the past. The so-called chats were, in fact, monologues, and when some of the staff members attempted discussion, it was made perfectly plain by the head that two-way communication was not on the agenda. During the months that followed, very little was actually seen of the boss — but a great deal was heard. He plainly believed in the efficacy of the written word, for this precluded the need for face-to-face confrontation, and the department was swiftly inundated in a flood of terse directives and memoranda — many of which were couched in critical and sarcastic terms. His promise that he would always be available for discussion turned out to be so much eye-wash, for when he was in his office, he saw to it that he was too busy for casual interruption. Several members of his staff, justly annoyed at the content and tone of memos they had received, bearded the lion in his den by making formal appointments for interview — a right which even this head was unable to refuse. The results were well-nigh disastrous. Backed into a corner by these more spirited members of the department, forced to engage in hated eyeball-to-eyeball challenge, the newly appointed manager revealed himself in his true colours for all to see. Disillusioned and deeply antagonised, the staff turned to obvious ways and means of getting their own back. Voluntary overtime, on which the department relied for a goodly percentage of its work, became a comparative rarity. Lecturers started to inspect their allotted timetables with hawk eyes, pouncing on anything which, however trivial, was not in full accord with their complicated terms of service. General interest in union matters, previously minimal, blossomed overnight, much to the delight of the few militants in the college, who had been trying for years to rally support from within the department. The war-cry was simple and direct, 'We'll see whose rule book wins the day — his or ours.' The sad outcome was that neither side really won the day. Two years passed with varying degrees of unpleasantness; the staff was fed up and thoroughly unhappy — for militancy can be an exhausting business — and the head of department developed some very embittered ideas on staff in general.

The moral to this true story is obvious. The manager concerned possessed a whole battery of faults, but standing high on the list of weaknesses was his fear and dislike of any form of discussion. To make things worse, he had compounded the sin by making a public and utterly false statement that consultation would be the order of his managerial day. Implemented correctly, informal discussion can be the keystone to management success — so let us examine the strategies involved.

## The dangers of the ever-open door

Despite the fact that he is a very busy man, Mr Average Manager often takes a well-intentioned delight in reminding his subordinates that 'he is always available for discussion'. The simple fact is that he is not, and herein lies the rub. Some employees — by no means all of them, for there is a natural reticence to take up such open invitations — arrive at the boss's sanctum, hoping to chat over some problem or other, only to find that the promised ever-open door is firmly closed. It is not that the boss is hell-bent on following that wretched head of department's example; it is merely that the pressure of day-to-day business prevents him from carrying out his good intention. Unfortunately the frustrated employee's reaction is often emotive and illogical: 'Huh, that's the third time I've tried to see him, without success — so much for promises. . . .' I should add that in my experience it is no answer to glibly assert that a manager should set aside a regular period when his door actually will be open to staff — for in practice the dictates and hiccups of business life always put a spanner in such good works. In any event, one is back to the simple fact that, as I have already stated, subordinates do not generally respond to blanket invitations to 'talk things over at any time'. No — it is for the manager, the thinking executive, to take the initiative and ensure that, come hell or high water, he *calls* individuals or groups for informal discussion at very regular intervals.

## Discussions are for discussion

The dictionary reminds us that a discussion is an exchange or comparison of opinions on a given subject — *how* or *what* to do and *why*. Let it always be so. There is no possible excuse for any manager to use the discussion as a vehicle for greedy egotism; solo performances are *out*. The task of the manager, as discussion leader, is not to hog the scene but to define the objects of the get-together (in the case of off-the-cuff meetings, the manager will also be required to *establish* the objects) and outline the main topics in a logical order for discussion.

## *Conducting the discussion*

*The introduction* Operation Break-Ice, call it what you will — the first aim for any discussion leader must be to establish the right 'climate' for the event, and this will vary according to the circumstances involved. All the textbooks I have read on the subject refer to the need to induce a relaxed, friendly atmosphere, and they are right. The more junior members of the group deserve particular attention in this respect, as do the shy and naturally reticent — a stilted discussion is a wasted discussion. Whilst breaking the ice, the discussion leader should take the opportunity to state, or remind people of, the purpose of the meeting:

'I'm glad to see you all — I know that you have a lot on your plates right now, and I will try not to waste too much of your time. John (*referring to junior member of the group*), would you like to sit here (*indicating chair farthest away from old Soames, the garrulous chappie*) — and, Tom, perhaps you would squat over here and take notes for us. . . . By the way, John, thank you for your efforts with so-and-so, I'm grateful for your help. . . . Now — before Maggie brings in the coffee, let me just run over the main points for discussion. . . .'

*Expanding the case*   Once people have settled down and pipes have been lit (the non-smoking discussion leader must suffer Tom's frightful shag), it is necessary for the chap at the helm to mention the important aspects of the subject under discussion and to ask for opinions or ideas. If this valiant attempt at opening the debate meets with a blank wall of silence, it will be necessary for the leader to air his own opinion, thereby encouraging a reaction from the other members. A second tactic is to toss in the odd question to stimulate those present — and it is a good idea to remember basic technique in this context:

| | |
|---|---|
| *NOT* | 'What do you all think of so-and-so?' |
| *AND NOT* | 'Brian, what do you think of so-and-so?' |
| *BUT* | 'What do you think of so-and-so — *Brian*?' |

A simple ruse, but it always pays off to put the question first without naming anyone, thereby jerking all present to attention, and *then* name the person to whom it is directed.

*Exercising control*   One of the finest aspects of an informal discussion is, of course, its informality, but the very absence of constraint means that given half a chance, the subject will be lost in a welter of side issues and tangents before it is off the ground. The discussion leader must ensure that this does not happen and, at the same time, carry out a crafty, individual control of those present — two basic requirements which prompt a double checklist for success:

1   *Control of the subject:*
  a   State and re-state the main objects.
  b   Restrict inconsequential and tangential nattering.
  c   Recap and summarise progress at regular intervals.
  d   Clarify, where necessary, the remarks of others.
2   *Control of individuals:*
  a   Gag (oh, so nicely) the garrulous.
  b   Encourage the innately shy or reluctant.
  c   Extinguish tension when feelings are running high.
  d   Maintain (if only outwardly) an interest in each person present.
  e   Be friendly but firm.

*The conclusion*   The conclusion of the discussion brings the leader face-to-face with his most difficult task, summarising the brute in clear, concise detail and almost always announcing some form of consequence and any associated decisions or recommendations. It is at this point that Tom's job of taking notes of the salient matters which have been raised and chewed over will pay dividends — provided, that is, that Tom was the right choice for this demanding secretarial chore. Do not be rushed into making hasty, off-the-cuff concluding remarks — if the subject-matter has been at all involved, if thought is required, then defer the issue of this vital component until later. But never omit to carry it out, for nothing infuriates staff more than an inconclusive discussion.

## A list of personal sins in discussion

*Sarcasm*   If you want better advice than 'Sarcasm is the lowest form of wit', which it is, I offer the words of Thomas Carlyle for your attention: 'Sarcasm I now see to be, in general, the language of the devil'. The manager who resorts to sarcasm betrays an inherent weakness of character and invites positive and lasting condemnation from all who associate with him — in and out of the discussion circle.

*'Over-disagreement'*   Disagreement is an inescapable feature of discussion, but there are good and bad ways of registering it. There is no need to use words such as 'I violently disagree', for this form of confrontation is intimidating and annoying. It is far better to explain in pleasant terms why you are *unable to agree* with the person concerned. Similarly it is tactically unsound to refute a matter point-blank:

> *NOT*          'That won't work — it's out of the question. . . .'
> *BUT, RATHER*  'It would be fine if we could do it that way — but I ask myself the question, if we did as you suggest, what would be the effect of so-and-so?'

*Heaving democracy out of the window*   If young Willie, the junior staff member, is good enough to sit in on the discussion, he is good enough to enjoy a fair share of the participation. Too many managers pull rank during discussions — sometimes, as we all know, to protect their own inadequacies. A fair say for all should be the keynote, and, remember, the young Willies of this world have a surprising habit of coming up with a heck of a lot of the answers.

*Hiding behind the desk*   A discussion is the time to emerge from behind that damned psychological fortress, the desk. The hermit-crab of a manager, who feels vulnerable and naked without this ridiculous shell, should do his organisation a good turn and allow himself to be gobbled up — for he is fit for little else.

*If you are not a liar, why be dishonest?*   Before passing the message, let me just say, if the cap fits, wear it — and I make no apology for being this blunt. If you are one

49

of those people who finds it hard to admit when you are in the wrong, why not earn yourself an everlasting niche in the managers' Valhalla, and change your spots? A senseless inflexibility of this type is the hallmark of the management rogue, and is *fatal*.

Go to it — have a discussion!

## Self-tutorial

Learn that 'double checklist' for discussions off by heart, not parrot-fashion, you understand, but so that you *know* it:

1 *Control of the subject:*
    *a*  Keep the discussion members familiar with the main objects of the session
    *b*  Keep the discussion 'on course' — minimise casual chatter and 'going off at tangents'
    *c*  Summarise and recapitulate at regular intervals
    *d*  Clarify vague points and issues
2 *Control of individuals:*
    *a*  Prevent the garrulous from hogging the floor
    *b*  Encourage the shy and reluctant to participate
    *c*  Maintain an equable atmosphere when feelings are roused
    *d*  Show an active interest in every member
    *e*  Maintain a friendly, but firm, attitude

When next you lead a discussion — or, for that matter, participate in one — apply the principles you have so carefully learned. *Help yourself by detecting the faults of others, and help others by correcting your own.*

Praising all alike, is praising none.
**John Gay (1685-1732)**
*Epistle to a Lady*

# 7
# A dollop of praise

'. . . I worked for that man for nearly six years, and I can honestly say that I never heard him utter one word of praise during the whole of that time. Once in a blue moon, a pretty grudging 'thank you' slipped out — but praise? Never!'
*(Excerpt from a taped discussion with an office manager)*

'. . . in my opinion, "praise" is an outmoded word. I spend most of my time chasing people, just to ensure that they put in a fair day's work — and, believe me, it's a full-time job. They're only interested in one thing — getting maximum money for minimum effort — and I dare say that it's the same story with everyone here. . . .'
*(Comment by a managing director during a seminar discussion)*

I once knew a director-boss who was too damned nice. A gentleman of the old school, he had followed his father into a non-executive seat on the board of directors of a fairly large company, and for a number of years performed this somewhat innocuous role with great success. Then as a result of an ill-considered decision by the ruling junta, he was rudely pitchforked into full executive status. Loyal to the fingertips, ever-anxious to give of his best and totally unaware of the pressures which were about to engulf him, this benign relic from the age of chivalry found himself struggling with a succession of top-level assignments. He soldiered valiantly on, doing all that a rapacious chief executive demanded of him and a great deal more, until the point was finally reached where the cut-and-thrust of international business took its toll, and he was reduced to a physically ailing husk of a man. However, the company — despite having well and truly extracted its pound of flesh — still required Gentleman John's highly decorative, executive presence on the board, so they did the usual thing and put him out to daily grass. A new 'convenience' appointment was created, and an unsuspecting head office department, which already enjoyed a complete management hierarchy, suddenly acquired the nicest, gentlest and most ineffective head boss that one could imagine. Initially everything in the garden was wonderful, for it seemed that managers and staff could do no wrong. Professing quite correctly that he knew little or nothing about the function of his new bailiwick, the director — who could not bring himself to be anything but 'nice' — praised everyone in sight, again and again and again. Within six months his laudatory currency was totally devalued, and had it not been for the fact that the man was, so plainly and transparently, an innocent in this den of corporate lions, he would have been treated as a nonentity. Truly a case of 'praising all alike, is praising none'.

I know of another boss who is most definitely not a gentleman; in point of fact, he is a full-blown, lying-in-the-teeth, insidious rogue — in short, a 'management millipede' of the first order. (For readers unacquainted with the term 'management millipede', I quote from Capability Goodworth's *Pests and Diseases of the Management Garden* — not obtainable at any bookshop: '*Management Millipedes*, known colloquially as "mini-creepers", are noted for the stealthy manner in which they progress throughout the management garden without being observed. Rarely to be found in their own nests, millipedes spend most of their lives on the crawl, feeding voraciously on the efforts of others. Eradication is difficult, and is best attempted when the pest is impelled by instinct to pause in front of its betters for the purpose of regurgitating the information it has assimilated during the latest feeding cycle. At such times the millipede is virtually defenceless, for it is totally absorbed in holding the attention of its superior and convincing him, by means of squealing sounds and ritualistic movements of the antennae, that the regurgitated material is of its own manufacture. It is often the case that the superior believes this to be true, with the result that the millipede is regarded, quite erroneously, as beneficial to the health and well-being of the management garden. The millipede can normally be recognised by its long, twitching proboscis, the sinuous action of its body as it creeps from place to place and the agility with which it purloins scraps of information from other species in the garden. The pest is known to ascend to great heights if not checked at an early stage of development.') This merry fellow also showered praise on all and sundry but, unlike Gentleman John, did not mean a word of it. Doubtless aware of his many shortcomings, he utilised praise as a vehicle for simple ingratiation, to get his own way with superiors and subordinates alike. Some of his stock phrases deserve mention:

'Bill, you are so good at (*whatever it was*), I wonder if you would do this little job for me. . . ?'
(*Bill finds himself saddled with an exacting task, which has nothing to do with his actual job.*)

'. . . a marvellous result, Jack — that'll take you a long way. . . .'
(*Poor Jack failed to move one iota, either in pay or promotion, whilst under this man.*)

'You've all done extremely well, and I know that the directors will be pleased with the efforts you have made. . . .'
(*Prelude to asking the department to work overtime for the umpteenth occasion.*)

Praise — if I may be permitted to wax a trifle eloquent — is a delicate essence, to be distilled with care and dispensed with forethought. This is *not* to say that it should be treated like gold-dust and only doled out on high days and holidays. We have all suffered under the managerial skinflints who practise this form of parsimony, and we should all be well aware that it rarely works. Remember Frederick Herzberg's research in establishing beyond peradventure that *recognition* is one of the prime motivators to work. [One of the best-known behavioural scientists, Herzberg's books, *The Motivation to Work* and *Work and the Nature of Man* (Wiley), should have pride of place on every manager's bedside table.] I am sure you require little convincing on this point, but just in case you are a Doubting Thomas — why, consider the wife. (Single readers may duck out of this one, or choose some other partner.) Imagine that on arrival home from the office, you are greeted by the little woman wearing a dress that happens to be a certain two years old — but being a conniving brute of a husband, you say, 'Hullo, darling — why, you look simply terrific in that dress. . . .' However drunk she may think you are, or however forcibly she may remind you of the garment's age, her shoulders will straighten up and she will feel a little warm inside — for, dammit, she has been the recipient of praise. People are no less human when at work; they need praise, they thrive on praise and it does motivate them to give of their best — provided it is administered in the right way and in moderation.

## Choosing the right words

Using praise in moderation means, among other things, choosing the right words, words to suit the occasion. If, for instance, having requested Mary, the office junior, to fetch you a second cup of coffee, you greet her with the words, 'Oh, splendid, Mary — wonderful, put it down there, will you?' you may think, if you think at all, that the comment is of little consequence, a mere, friendly thank you. Think again. In fetching the steaming cup, was it necessary for Mary to walk three miles, fight off a horde of bandits or risk life and limb in some other heroic fashion? I fancy not — all that has happened is, one, Mary has fetched you a cotton-pickin' cup of coffee and, two, you have made casual use of the words 'splendid' and 'wonderful'. In fact, you have committed the over-

54

indulgence of making an unnecessary inroad into your word-arsenal — when a friendly smile and a thank you would have sufficed. If one succumbs to the easy habit of casually chucking away such fulsome adjectives, the arsenal will swiftly be depleted, and because they have been used in a casual sense, the words will have lost their value. To put it into a nutshell, treat your word-arsenal as if it were a cash-till; spend wisely and well. Which reminds me, just how much cash do you have in the till? The English language is a very rich bank, and it gives unlimited credit — so make regular withdrawals.

## Cashing a cheque at the word-bank on a theme of praise

| | |
|---|---|
| *well done, first-rate* | 'Well done, Jack, a first-rate job. . . .' |
| *exemplary* | '. . . you have displayed an exemplary attitude to your work. . . .' |
| *admirable* | '. . . a sensible approach, with admirable results. . . .' |
| *worth its weight in gold* | '. . . your contribution to the Open Day arrangements was worth its weight in gold. . . .' |
| *sterling* | 'Your sterling efforts have ensured success. . . .' |
| *grand* | 'There's no doubt, it was a grand accomplishment' |
| *above average* | 'Your performance has been consistently above average. . . .' |
| *phenomenal* | '. . . and your results in the first quarter were phenomenal. . . .' |
| *businesslike* | 'I am pleased with your businesslike approach to your work. . . .' |
| *unflagging* | '. . . your efforts have been unflagging. . . .' |
| *no sinecure* | 'Your task has been no sinecure but, nevertheless, you have. . . .' |
| *go-getter* | '. . . I admire a go-getter. . . .' |
| *enterprising, handsome* | '. . . your enterprising suggestion paid a handsome dividend. . . .' |
| *hive of industry* | 'Your department has been a hive of industry. . . .' |
| *have a way with* | '. . . you clearly have a way with. . . .' |
| *drive* | '. . . you have shown great drive. . . .' |
| *single-minded* | '. . . you displayed a single-minded approach to the problem. . . .' |
| *have what it takes* | '. . . you certainly have what it takes to. . . .' |

And so on, the funds are limitless.

## Individual or corporate praise?

Let us assume that a group of workers under your control has done particularly well at some task or other — in terms of praise, what do you do? One course is to whip the supervisor into your office, deliver some personal plaudits for his ability in managing the affair and then, in passing, tell him to convey your appreciation to the minions who actually did the work involved. This is a popular course of action, mainly because it saves time — but when the achievement has been of a very high order, it is also a lazy and quite improper approach. Picture the obvious sequence of events — the supervisor, having been showered with praise, returns to his flock and hopefully passes on your unit citation. Whilst one or two of the more dedicated workers may experience a figurative blush of pride, it is very likely that the majority, recalling the amount of sweat expended on the task, will indulge in a muted chorus of one word — rhubarb. Give praise where it is due and deliver it in person — by all means, have the supervisor in for a laudatory thank-you, and then go and thank the *workers.*

## Remember, they have memories too

Words of praise, like rockets, stick in the mind, and it is wise to remember the fact. Take, as an example, the oh-so-typical case of the probationary employee who, being painfully aware that he is on trial, will avidly grasp at *anything* which sounds remotely like praise. To this fellow, even the casual exhortation, '. . . there's a good chap', may register as a sign of approbation, an indication that he has been accepted into the fold. Only too often, it transpires that the poor creature is out on his ear — ill-chosen words have led him up the garden path. Lest the reader is colour-blind to shades of grey, I am not advocating that such employees should be treated with verbal asepticism, but rather that when words are chosen, their memories should be borne in mind.

## That stultifying occasion — the presentation

The first warning that it is about to happen again is usually when Mary, do-gooder and organiser-extraordinary — there is one in every office — fixes you with a challenging stare and announces that she is collecting for old George Frobisher's retirement gift. As you part with the necessary sum, you realise with a sinking feeling that, once more, you will be required to perform the ghastly ritual of 'saying a few words' before presenting George with his hard-earned mantle-clock. Picture the typical scene. Be it a gathering in the local pub or an improvised event amid the pushed-back furniture of the general office, the outcome is the same — the moment arrives, someone calls for silence and the dreaded presentation scenario is set. Since the ceremony marks the consignment of George to retired oblivion, it is treated by all present as a cross between a funeral and a Black Mass — the victim is surrounded by a circle of solemn-faced, standing colleagues (the formality of the occasion being momentarily disrupted by an alcoholic snigger from the office junior — who never could behave herself at such important functions), and all and sundry wait upon your valediction. For goodness sake, does it *have* to be this way?

Before considering the wording of your homily, give some thought to the vital business of scene-setting. Contrive, by any means possible, to minimise the 'ritual' aspect — do yourself, and the victim of your kindness, a favour. Try to avoid holding the presentation in the office, for it is virtually impossible to dispel the impression that the event is an *ersatz* affair when surrounded with the paraphernalia of day-to-day business. Have everyone sitting down, for this will encourage informality and relaxed behaviour — after all, the presentation is not a royal investiture. You, as speaker, may wish to stand, but do insist on letting everyone else off the hook. And then sock it to 'em, in a relaxed and 'matey' fashion. I recommend the following checklist to your attention:

1   Do not spend overlong on a recital of George's career with the firm — allude to his length of service and highlight a couple of outstanding occasions or achievements.

2   No manager worth his salt would dream of presiding at a retirement presentation unless and until he was completely familiar with George's intentions after retirement. Refer to these and, if possible, try to emphasise 'how busy' George will be in his new life. Steer away from the 'well-earned rest' theme, for the guy may already feel that he has one foot in the grave.

3   Be humourous, but not at George's expense — for despite his smile, this is not always an occasion that the Georges of this world can truly enjoy.

4   Do not allow your 'few words' to become a protracted monologue.

5   Insert the magic word 'congratulations' in your concluding remark — *not* 'the best of luck', which will only add to George's possible apprehension about his future.

6   Once done, go straight to George and engage him in conversation — have some topic or other ready for use; do not leave him high and dry on the raft of his emotions.

## Self-tutorial

An important requirement often overlooked by managers when composing laudatory comments is the question of 'grading' one's words to suit the particular occasion. Using your imagination to bolster the information provided, compose suitable remarks for the following events:

*(a) Presentation of an award for bravery* George Simpson, 20 years, trainee-machinist in the marine propeller workshop, has been with your company for nine months. Whilst his standard of work has been described by the training officer as 'generally fair', he has received an informal warning for skylarking in the workshop and formal warning following unauthorised absence from work. Simpson is popular with his fellow trainees, but regarded with some disfavour by the chargehands and workshop manager — who deem him slightly work-shy and a potentially disruptive influence in the workshop. During a recent lunch break, a fierce fire suddenly broke out in the deserted workshop and Simpson, who was sun-bathing in the adjacent yard, raised the alarm. He then dashed into the workshop and, at considerable personal risk, removed two fully-charged oxygen cylinders which were threatened by the blaze — thereby averting an undoubted explosion and preventing the fire from becoming a major conflagration. There is no doubt that Simpson's act, which attracted considerable publicity, was extremely brave, albeit foolhardy, and you — as managing director — have decided to award him a cheque for £100 as a token of your appreciation. The presentation is to be carried out in the works canteen, and all employees have been invited to attend.

*(b) Presentation of a long-service award* John Archer, 53 years, chief clerk in the general office, has just completed twenty years' service with the company and is now eligible for the award of a gold watch to mark the occasion. Archer, who joined the company as a progress clerk, has never shown any outstanding ability or desire for swift promotion and, in fact, is regarded as a 'fairly competent plodder'. He is perfectly content with his lot as chief clerk and, health permitting, will probably remain as such until his retirement. His health, however, is a problem — for of late he has suffered from recurrent attacks of bronchial asthma, which threaten to become worse as time goes on. He is a very loyal employee whose conduct has been above reproach, and he has become increasingly worried about the amount of sick leave he has been forced to take during the last eighteen months. Unmarried, with few friends or outside interests, Simpson's work — albeit of a routine and humdrum nature — is his life. He is terrified of losing his job through ill health. The presentation is to be carried out by you, as administration manager, in the presence of all the office staff.

*(c) 'End of probation' interview* Brian White, 17½ years, has just completed his three months' probationary period as a junior clerk in the sales office of the company. White has performed moderately well during his brief service — that is to say, he has done all that was demanded of him, but has displayed little in the way of imagination or personal initiative. Well behaved, of average maturity for his age, opinion is that White will develop into an 'averagely capable' employee of no great distinction or merit. He appears to like his work and despite the lack of flair is obviously anxious over the outcome of his probationary service. You, as

sales manager, have decided to confirm his employment with the company and, during the interview, to encourage him — by means of carefully chosen praise-cum-admonishment — to develop a more lively interest in his work.

How would you be,
If He, which is the top of judgement, should
But judge you as you are?

**William Shakespeare (1564-1616)**
*Measure for Measure*

# 8
# Appraising the hell out of people

The appraisal game started with Adam and Eve and has been complicating our lives ever since. When young Mary, sweet sixteen and waiting to be kissed, trips down the High Street and claps her pretty eyes on a young stalwart across the road, her mental fruit machine clicks automatically into action and presents her with one of a whole variety of conclusions:

> I like 'im. . . .
> A flippin' 'orrible piece of work. . . .
> Wishy-washy — nuffin' to 'im. . . .
> Cor, Doris, look at 'im, wot a luvverly boy. . . .

On the odd, sublime occasion the appraisal fruit machine comes up with the jackpot and triggers the fiery, chemical-cum-mental process of falling in love. On other occasions it presents a bunch of lemons, and in a trice we develop a healthy, or unhealthy, dislike for some soul or other. Most of the time, however, our reactions fall short of these extremes, but — and here is the crunch — we rarely fail to arrive at some form of conclusion. In short we march through life forming instant, almost reflex, opinions of other people — split-second impressions or, to put it a trifle more succinctly, pure and simple 'gut feelings'. Given then that each of us can lay just claim to a lifetime of experience in the art of assessing our fellows, it can come as a bit of a shock, and usually does, when someone like me points a rude finger and says, '. . . and a pretty bad job you made of it too.' So, having galloped way out on a limb, let me explain what I mean.

Imagine, for a second or two, that you are a member of a group of trainees, seated at tables in a typical lecture room — and pay attention to teacher. If I hand each member a tape measure and ask you in turn to measure the length of a certain table, you will all produce, by and large, the same answer. This will be for a very obvious reason — each participant will have used a standard measuring instrument. If, on the other hand, I bring a stranger into the room, invite him to say a few words and then ask each of you for your frank impressions of the newcomer, the individual opinions will tend to vary like the March winds — again for a very obvious reason. The brain, thank goodness, is *not* a standard measuring instrument. It is just not capable of making objective assessments of this nature. We can jog merrily on, forming umpteen opinions of other people, but whether these opinions are correct is entirely another matter.

Let us now consider the nitty-gritty question of appraising people at work. Employment usually begins with some form of appraisal, normally limited to the traditional and horribly subjective interview, and this kind of evaluation continues throughout the entire spectrum of working life. We all, and don't we just, make continuous assessments of our bosses. We inspect our dear old colleagues with a critical eye, mentally listing their weaknesses with, if we dare to admit it, some considerable glee and noting their strengths with more than a touch of envy. And to set the seal on the appraisal merry-go-round, we subject our juniors to constant assessments of their performance and personality:

Good old John, I knew he'd finish the job on time. . . .
As usual, Joan's thinking more about her boy-friend than her work. . . .
That creature is bone idle — he'll have to go. . . .
George would be a good worker if only. . . .
He's late again; that's the third time this week. . . .
I'll have to watch George; he's after my job. . . .

As I have said, the process of appraisal goes on all the time, and despite the alarming consequences of error and inaccuracy, most appointments, promotions and dismissals stem from it. Little wonder that some pretty awful mistakes are made. Little wonder also that many organisations do their best to improve and *formalise* their appraisal systems — but how do they go about it? There is but one way to find out; let us lift the lid of the appraisal stew pot and take a poke at the simmering contents.

## Firstly, a horrendous example of 'formal appraisal'

I wish I could say that this is a fictitious account — unhappily, it is true. Some three years ago whilst doing a spot of consultancy work, I found it necessary to take a close look at a company's computerised accounts centre. This was an isolated outpost of the corporate empire, set in the heart of the countryside where little girl labour was cheap and plentiful — a kind of commercial Colditz. An apt simile, perhaps, for the company's problem was that they could not hang on to their employees. The little girls came, underwent intensive and costly training, had a wee taste of the work involved and, without so much as a thank you, disappeared over the horizon at a high rate of knots. The general manager summed up the situation with a pure cry from the heart. 'I can't understand it, Mr Goodworth. You've seen our accommodation — pleasant, open-plan offices, comfortable furniture, air-conditioning, the lot. We provide free transport from several villages, a staff canteen with very good, cheap food, hair-dos on the premises, excellent pay and goodness knows what else. But they still leave us. . . .'

Obviously, many questions had to be asked, and it was not over-long before I asked, 'What about staff development — what work do you do in this area?'

The response was immediate and enthusiastic. 'Ah, I'm glad you mentioned that! We are very proud of our efforts in staff development. We believe in rewarding good work, both in terms of regular pay reviews and promotion from within the company. *We implement both aspects through our staff appraisal scheme.*'

This is beginning to look good, I thought — but just to be on the safe side, I asked the general manager to describe the system of appraisal in some detail. I was told that each supervisor was responsible for formally appraising his or her team on a six-monthly basis, that the company utilised a 'standard appraisal form' on each occasion and that these important documents were the administrative triggers for increases in pay, promotion and other goodies. I asked to see a copy of the appraisal form and Figure 1 shows what I was given. Take a look at those two little boxes, marked 'Performance' and 'Personality', and consider them in the light of what I had been told by the general manager. The mind boggles — just picture the average supervisor trying to summarise an assessment of an employee within these miniscule spaces and, as I was subsequently informed by the company, ending up with those wholly ridiculous and wildly subjective words, 'good', 'average' and 'poor'. However, worse was to come. The general manager continued with his proud description of the appraisal scheme. 'It works this way, Mr Goodworth — the supervisor completes the appraisal and then passes it to the office manager who, if he agrees with the assessments, hands it to me. I collect all the forms together and send them to my director in London, who decides on any pay increases to be awarded, or whatever promotion is merited. . . .'

I was then told by this general manager that the London-based director had last visited the accounts centre some eighteen months previously, had absolutely no personal knowledge of the employees in question ('Surely that is a good thing?' queried the general manager) and that this senior executive relied solely on the appraisal details when making his decisions. *Appraisal details?* Remember, this was no hole-in-the-wall, two-bit company, but a large,

```
┌─────────────────────────────────────────────────────────────┐
│              SIX MONTHLY STAFF APPRAISAL FORM                 │
│                                                               │
│   Name _____     Branch _____       │
│                                                               │
│   Department _____     Date _____       │
│                                                               │
│                              ┌──────────────┐                 │
│   PERFORMANCE                │              │                 │
│                              │              │                 │
│                              └──────────────┘                 │
│                              ┌──────────────┐                 │
│   PERSONALITY                │              │                 │
│                              │              │                 │
│                              └──────────────┘                 │
│                                                               │
│                                                               │
│   Signed _____     (Supervisor)             │
│   Signed _____     (Department manager)     │
│                                                               │
│                                                               │
│   For HO use only                                            │
│   _____        │
│   _____        │
│   Signed _____     (Director)               │
└─────────────────────────────────────────────────────────────┘
```

**Figure 1**  How *not* to design an appraisal form

nationally-successful organisation, convinced and happy that its abortion of an appraisal system was the answer. What do you think?

## To know or not to know. . . .

Those of you who have been lucky enough to have served in HM Forces will have shared my experience that the omnipotent powers-that-be place great store by formal appraisal systems. The apocryphal story of the commanding officer who wrote of one of his junior officers, 'This officer sets a low standard which he consistently fails to maintain' does scant justice to the research in appraisal which has been carried out by the three armed services. However, it is a curious fact that for many years the Navy, Army and Air Force have been unable to reach tacit agreement on one important aspect of any appraisal scheme — the need or not for the person being appraised to read the report made on him. In the Royal Air Force an officer's confidential report was not, under any circumstances, to be revealed to the eyes of the quaking subject. True, there were certain intimate traits listed in the form which, if they provoked adverse assessment, were required to be notified to the drunk or lecher concerned, but he never clapped eyes on the actual entries — which, incidentally, were always referred to coyly as 'starred items'. The Navy and the Army, presumably with the wisdom of age, permitted officers to have varying degrees of access to that which had been written about them. So it was for many years and, for all I know, may still be the situation. Returning to the present and, more particularly, to the business scene, I am pleased to say that the majority of organisations in commerce and industry favour the 'open book' approach to formal appraisal, when the subject is encouraged to discuss and possibly disagree with the findings. There are, however, the traditional dirty dozen where such democracy and common sense does not prevail — and where the following types of dialogue may ensue:

*Example 1   Sam Plunkett, who has suffered promotion limbo for some time, finally plucks up courage and approaches Marner, his boss:*

Sam   *(With marked diffidence)*   'Er, Mr Marner, I was wondering if. . . .'
Marner   'Yes, Plunkett, what were you wondering?'
Sam   'Well, Mr Marner — er, as you know, I'm overdue for promotion *(A likely story)* and, er, I was wondering whether you have completed my annual report. . . .'
Marner   *(Smiles complacently and gives a knowing nod)*   'Ah, so that's it — yes, Plunkett, you may rest assured — I've finished all the annual reports and they went upstairs several days ago.'
Sam   'Do you suppose you could. . . ?'
Marner   *(Suddenly brusque)*   'Now, you know better than that, Plunkett; rules are rules. Now — what about that job I gave you yesterday; how's it coming along?'
Sam   *(Defeated and wishing he had not mentioned the subject)*   'Yes, of course, Mr Marner. I'm sorry that I, er, mentioned it. I'll get the other papers at once; I think you'll find everything in order. . . .'

*Example 2   Marner, still the manager, happens to pass Joe Wallop's desk, and pauses for a word with him:*

Marner   *(Sotto voce)*   'Wallop — just thought I'd let you know — I completed your annual report this morning. . . .' *(Turns and walks away)*
Joe   *(Startled, addresses Marner's retreating figure)*   'Er yes — thank you, Mr Marner. . . .' *(Thinks)* What the hell did he tell me that for? He sounded pretty grim — I wonder if it's a bad report? No, it must be my imagination; I've always had decent reports — but, I wonder. . . .'

*Example 3    Marner has called George Grimes into his office:*

*George    (Wondering what on earth he has done this time)* 'You sent for me, Mr Marner?'

*Marner    (In magisterial mood)* 'Yes, Grimes, sit down — no, not there, take the upright chair. I think you should know that I've completed your annual report. *(Pauses for effect)* I'm afraid there are certain points that I must bring to your attention.'

*George* 'Yes, Mr Marner?'

*Marner* 'Well, firstly, I had to comment on the matter of your recent absence — over four weeks in total, wasn't it?'

*George* 'Yes, but I was away sick — you had all the necessary certificates.'

*Marner* 'Ah, sickness, was it? Yes, I recall it now — but. . . .' *(Tails off and George is left wondering what Marner actually wrote in the report)*

*George    (Worried)* 'I hope it won't be put against me in the report, Mr Marner.'

*Marner    (Not very convincingly - it is clear to George that the report has left Marner's hands)* 'Er, no — of course not, Grimes. However, more serious than that is the question of your inaccuracies with the ledger — there have been a number of instances during the year when mistakes have been made. . . .'

*George* 'Only on two occasions, Mr Marner — and those were only minor errors. They were corrected straight away, and as you know, there have been many such slips made by everyone in the department — they just can't be avoided.'

*Marner    (Sheltering behind a shield of pontification)* 'Be that as it may, Grimes — these things count, you know. . . .'

*And so it goes on. George finally leaves Marner's office, completely in the dark over what actually was entered in the report and convinced that some points were unfairly made by Marner. George is equally certain that Marner will not be man enough to ensure that the inaccuracies are corrected.*

'Absolute nonsense', do I hear you say? Pause for a second and consider the managers in your own organisation. Unless you are very fortunate and work for a business paradise on earth, if you have more than a half-dozen managers, at least one of them will be cast in the Marner mould. And human nature being what it is, you will certainly have a Plunkett, Wallop or Grimes on the payroll. But, thank goodness, you do not have a 'closed book' appraisal system — or do you?

An old sage of the appraisal world, at whose knee I once sat, would tell me again and again, 'Never forget, me lad, who appraises the appraisers?' So in seeking to establish how best to tackle appraisal, it is necessary to take a long, cool look at the appraiser himself. What makes him tick?

## Playing the appraisal game

One of the in-built weaknesses of any appraisal scheme is the sad fact that the whole caboodle tends to become a bit of a game or contest. The manager, charged with carrying out an appraisal and faced with an intimidating list of characteristics to be scored, may well regard the task not only as an unpleasant chore but, indeed, something of an insult to his ability. In addition he may not know enough about the person he is required to appraise to answer all the 'damn-fool questions' in the assessment list. This may lead him to have serious doubts about the meaning or value of consequent summaries or rating scores. He may be very critical of the manner in which certain qualities are weighted within the appraisal system. Plainly, all these adverse attitudes can endanger the validity and usefulness of the entire appraisal programme:

> 'I used to think that the appraisal system was just another of those paper exercises dreamed up by the people at head office in an effort to justify their own existence — but now I know better. The fact is that they don't trust our judgement any more. They are so removed from the reality of the 'sharp end' where the work is done, that they are completely out of touch with people, and they tar everyone else with the same brush. Instead of just asking me whether I think So-and-so is a good worker or deserves promotion, they try to trap me by wrapping the whole damn thing up in a mass of paperwork — it's amateur psychology gone mad. . . .'
> *(Excerpt from a taped interview with a line manager)*

> '. . . look at some of the items on the appraisal form. I'm required to say what I think of a guy's *features* and, look at this one, *personal hygiene*! What do they expect — a foreman in the bloody paint-shop to smell of attar of roses? Go down the list a bit — look at this — I'm supposed to comment on his 'participation in social activities'. Well, I tell you, *I'm* only interested in one thing — if a man does a fair day's work for his pay, he's all right by me. After fifteen years experience in the industry, I reckon I can sort out the wheat from the chaff — I wouldn't be here now if I'd made a hash of it — and I don't need this kind of nonsense foisted on me. It's a bloody silly waste of time, and our directors must have been mad to let them go ahead — it proves one thing, though; they don't trust their managers any more.'
> *(Excerpt from a taped interview with a works manager)*

## *The heinous crime of leniency or central tendency*

If a manager is critical of the value of an appraisal scheme, it may not be long before his instincts for self-preservation and fair play prompt him to do something about the situation. One very common method of putting a spanner in the appraisal works is, to use the boffins' term, to commit the sin of leniency or central tendency:

'. . . when it comes to the really absurd items on the list — and as you can see from the form, most of 'em are in this category — I play safe and slap the man down as "average". Then when I have to discuss my assessment with him, I just say something about his being "normal — or up to scratch", and that lets us both off the hook. After all, most of us are "average", aren't we?'

'Look — I don't think that you get the point. . . . If the system's bad, and ours is, what on earth is the use of endangering a man's progress by trying to assess him on things you know nothing about? No, give him a good score — I don't mean absolute top marks — and if it cocks up the system, all well and good; perhaps they'll get rid of it. . . .'

'I'm a production manager, not a trick-cyclist. The people who work for me are a pretty good bunch — I've seen to that — and since I'm sure that our appraisal scheme isn't worth a light, I'm not going to risk losing damned good foremen by playing this latest company game. My chaps get a good mark-up and I tell 'em so — to hell with the system.'
*(Excerpts from a taped discussion at a management seminar)*

## The awesome halo effect

It is a feature of human nature that, when attempting to make a complete appraisal of a person, we often permit one outstanding quality to cloud our judgement — the 'halo effect'. It can be said that the ease with which Adolf Hitler swayed and convinced his mass audiences that he was their salvation is a classic instance of the halo effect at work.

## The effect of varying standards

Probably the most common sin committed by organisations when implementing an appraisal scheme is to blithely overcome the important question of training the people who are destined to administer the new baby. This can lead to a whole host of dfficulties, not least among them being the application of varying standards:

'Having finished the appraisal, I discussed it fully with the employee concerned and then passed the report to my head of department. The very next day I was on the carpet in front of my boss — it appeared that he was unhappy with quite a few of my assessments. For instance the subject of the report had displayed some amazing initiative during the year — I reckon he's one of the finest workers I've ever had in the section — and, not surprisingly, I'd awarded him "9 out of 10" for personal initiative. My boss, would you please, who considers himself a dab hand at statistics, informed me that an assessment of nine placed the man in the top $2\frac{1}{2}\%$, or something, of the population. He then went on to tell me that this was not possible! I got pretty mad — after all, I'd discussed my findings with the

man, and he knew all about the rating for initiative — and I wasn't about to change it at this stage of the game. Anyway, I was supposed to record *my* opinions, not those of my boss. . . .'
*(Excerpt from a taped interview with a section leader in a research establishment)*

'I've got a question — what exactly is an "average chap"? I can't get a sensible answer from anyone at the company.'
*(Heard at a management seminar)*

'I'm bloody good — and nobody, but nobody, is going to get a decent appraisal from me, because nobody is as good as me. . . .'
*(The ill-concealed, 'secret' thoughts of a manager-acquaintance of mine)*

## It's the form that counts. . . .

When people go mad over appraisal, anything can happen and usually does. Take a glance at Figure 2, which illustrates an appraisal form introduced some two years ago by an otherwise sensible and successful company. Bearing in mind that the form was intended for the appraisal of supervisory grades, consider some of the items in the list:

*Gestures, Facial expressions*  The mind can run riot with this one. It is not clear whether the first item is intended to pinpoint and condemn the employee who has resorted to the odd, two-fingered exercise — and with this appraisal form there is certainly some temptation. As for 'facial expressions' — well, your guess is as good as mine.

*Poise*  'Look, Jim, you're a good foreman *(Lowers voice to a whisper)* but, old fellow, it's your poise that needs some attention. . . .' Whereupon, the fourteen-stone overseer, ever-keen and ready to enhance his career prospects, takes the hint, turns on one toe and minces out of the office in the finest ballerina fashion.

*Height, Weight, Stamina*  All right, if you happen to be assessing would-be entrants for the next Olympic Games, these items could be relevant. If it is necessary to assess physical fitness for the job, why not say exactly that and no more?

*Participation in. . . .*  This type of item is all fine and dandy for the rarified atmosphere of the officer cadet training unit, but, honestly, is a company really entitled to assess a supervisor's approach to his spare time? No, at foreman and supervisor level, we should be concerned with more relevant issues, like 'relationships with employees' and so on.

*Difficult adolescent history*  'Tell me, Bloggs, when did you last see your father, then?'

## STAFF APPRAISAL FORM

*Employee's name* _____ Department _____

*Appraised by* _____ Date _____

Circle the appropriate rating in each case:

| | | | |
|---|---|---|---|
| *Manner and appearance* | | *Low* | *High* |
| Gestures | | 1 2 3 4 5 | |
| Facial expressions | | 1 2 3 4 5 | |
| Poise | | 1 2 3 4 5 | |
| Dress | | 1 2 3 4 5 | |
| Courtesy | | 1 2 3 4 5 | |
| Height | | 1 2 3 4 5 | |
| Weight | | 1 2 3 4 5 | |
| Stamina | | 1 2 3 4 5 | |

*Social aspects*
  Participation in social activities    1 2 3 4 5
  Participation in local affairs    1 2 3 4 5
  Ability to mix with people    1 2 3 4 5
  Attitudes with other people    1 2 3 4 5

*Personal stability*
  Ability to remain calm under stress    1 2 3 4 5
  General competence    1 2 3 4 5
  Level of personal motivation at work    1 2 3 4 5
  Difficult adolescent history    1 2 3 4 5

*Leadership capacity*
  Leadership experience    1 2 3 4 5
  Motivation to leadership    1 2 3 4 5

*Maturity*
  Personal drive    1 2 3 4 5
  Sense of responsibility    1 2 3 4 5

General comments _____
_____
_____

*Signed* _____ *Appointment* _____

**Figure 2** Another example of appraisal gone mad

'Now, tell me the truth — what dirty habits did you develop as a child?'

Little wonder that the appraisal scheme lasted precisely one month and that its demise was closely followed by that of the so-called personnel manager. Is your organisation — are *you* — appraising the hell out of people?

## A checklist for the appraisal discussion

1    Exactly how *valid* is each part of my assessment?
  *a*    To what extent is it contaminated by subjective weakness or personal bias?
  *b*    Can I support my assessment with *established facts of performance?*
  *c*    Is it a flash-in-the-pan instance, or are there *consistent* strengths/ weaknesses to confirm my assessment?
2    In cases of adverse assessment, have I prepared a *viable* course of action to bring about an improvement in the individual (training, work experience, probationary periods, etc.)?
3    Bearing in mind the personality of the individual concerned, have I an accurate conception of his likely response at discussion — and have I prepared my 'counter-case'? Remember, the session is an appraisal discussion, *not a disciplinary interrogation.*

## A possible approach to appraisal

If there has been a central message or theme throughout this chapter, it is simply that most company appraisal schemes are fraught with a wide and stinking selection of hang-ups and weaknesses. Whenever this is so, the scheme falls into disrepute — and a disreputable scheme ruins morale and is a waste of time and money. Yet some form of appraisal is essential.

A possible way out of this dilemma is the introduction of *self-appraisal* — and just in case a whole regiment of management diehards start foaming at the mouth, let me comment a little more on this form of approach. Firstly, self-appraisals tend to produce surprisingly frank and accurate assessments, and where this is not so, the self-reports are usually couched in such a manner as to make correct interpretation a simple matter. Secondly, a self-appraisal system removes the natural and often well-justified suspicion of appraisal by one's seniors. Thirdly and most important, self-appraisal involves *real participation* by the employees in what, after flippin' all, is a keystone process involving *their* careers, not that of the boss.

Figure 3 provides an example of a typical self-appraisal form — and note, if you will, that this particular scheme is *voluntary*. A voluntary scheme presents certain definite advantages to the wily manager:
1    In the employee's eye, it represents a welcome change from the day-to-day autocracy of working life.
2    Whilst bearing the glorious stamp of democracy — the 'I don't have to do

**Figure 3** A typical self-appraisal form for junior management

---

# THE BLANK COMPANY

CONFIDENTIAL

## Voluntary self-appraisal

Name _____ Department _____

*Notes for your guidance*

1 The object of this voluntary self-appraisal is two-fold:
   *a* to provide a vehicle for the objective appraisal of your working performance during the period under review;
   *b* to provide a basis for the forthcoming appraisal discussion.
2 Two sections of the self-appraisal require numerical *and* narrative assessments. Please complete the numerical assessments by circling the appropriate rating number in each case.
3 If you find there is insufficient space in which to enter narrative comments, please use a separate sheet of paper.

---

*(Continued overleaf)*

## Section 1 — Your job performance

*Please consider the overall effectiveness of your job performance during the period under review.*

|  |  | Low | High |
|---|---|---|---|
| a | How do you rate the *quality* of your work? | 1 2 3 4 5 6 |
| b | Has the *volume* (output) been satisfactory? | 1 2 3 4 5 6 |
| c | Have you tended to solve problems quickly? | 1 2 3 4 5 6 |
| d | Have you tended to solve problems accurately? | 1 2 3 4 5 6 |
| e | Have you been quick to detect inaccuracies? | 1 2 3 4 5 6 |
| f | Have you enjoyed your work? | 1 2 3 4 5 6 |
| g | Are you adequately qualified for your work? | 1 2 3 4 5 6 |

Kindly justify your ratings:

Rating *a*, above _____

_____

Rating *b*, above _____

_____

Rating *c*, above _____

_____

Rating *d*, above _____

_____

Rating *e*, above _____

_____

Rating *f*, above _____

_____

Rating *g*, above _____

_____

_____

Kindly list any training or work experience which, in your view, would improve your overall performance effectiveness: _____

_____

_____

_____

_____


## Section 2 — Your management ability

*Please consider your overall management ability during the period under review.*

|   |   | *Low* | | | | *High* | |
|---|---|---|---|---|---|---|---|
| *a* | Your acceptance of responsibilities | 1 | 2 | 3 | 4 | 5 | 6 |
| *b* | Your ability to organise | 1 | 2 | 3 | 4 | 5 | 6 |
| *c* | Your effectiveness in control | 1 | 2 | 3 | 4 | 5 | 6 |

Bearing in mind that you are appraising your management ability over a period, as opposed to specific instances or occasions, kindly justify your ratings:

Rating *a*, above _____

_____

_____

Rating *b*, above _____

_____

_____

Rating *c*, above _____

_____

_____

Kindly list any management training or work experience which, in your view, would improve your overall ability as a manager: _____

_____

_____

_____

_____

*(Continued overleaf)*

### Section 3 — Your suitability for promotion

*Discounting the factor of long service, please provide an indication of your eligibility for promotion by placing a tick in the appropriate space.*

I am overdue for promotion    \_\_\_\_     I am ready now for promotion \_\_

I am not quite ready               \_\_\_\_     I am far from ready         \_\_\_\_

I do not foresee promotion     \_\_\_\_     I do not want promotion     \_\_\_\_

I am undetermined              \_\_\_\_

Kindly justify your view_____

_____

_____

### Section 4 — Other factors for discussion

*Please consider whether there are any other factors connected with your work which should receive attention during the forthcoming discussion.*

Kindly provide brief details: _____

_____

_____

_____

_____

*Signed* _____ *Date* _____

it if I damned well don't want to' touch — the thinking employee (and this is the lad who matters) will welcome the opportunity presented by self-appraisal. In general those who decline to participate will be the people with very significant weaknesses of one sort or another.

The sole object of self-appraisal is to provoke objective thought on the part of the subject and to provide the basis for a wide-ranging and useful discussion between senior and subordinate. In this context the numerical assessments — see the example — should be regarded with caution by the manager conducting the discussion. Their prime, important purpose is to trigger objective thought on the items concerned, before the subject leaps into narrative print. The theme of the subsequent discussion must be a *mutual* appraisal of strengths and weaknesses, and there must be a determination on the manager's part to identify and implement helpful and realistic courses of remedial action. And — unless you wish to plunge headlong into the fires of eternal damnation — make jolly certain that having determined a course of action, you *do* implement it.

## Self-tutorial

This is a major discovery exercise. You are to imagine that you have been asked to deliver a lecture to a group of senior managers on the topic, 'Appraisal Schemes — Good or Bad'. Using the resources of your own knowledge, the public library (for starters, see the recommended reading list at the rear of this book) and the bare-bones contents of the preceding chapter, prepare a set of speaking notes for the occasion. Once you have completed the task, place your notes in a safe place until such time as you have read and digested Chapters 9 and 10 — and then subject your work to a critical self-analysis.


## NOW — LET US DEAL WITH THE HOMEWORK!

You should have two pieces of paper tucked away:
1   *The answer to Exercise A, Chapter 4 – Your reprimand*
2   *The answer to Exercise A, Chapter 5 – Your reasons why certain employee personalities should be recognised by the manager*


## The reprimand

It was the Roman poet Horace who uttered the immortal line, 'Once a word has been allowed to escape, it cannot be recalled.' For the pedantic reader, what he actually said was, *'Et semel emissum volat irrevocabile verbum'* — so do shut up. Quintus Horatius Flaccus, little wonder they called him Horace, was referring, of course, to the spoken word — and every manager should have the Roman's advice emblazoned on his contract of employment, for he drops more *verbal* clangers than any other variety. The spoken reprimand, alas, is not immune from such contamination, and many managers have gone to the proverbial block as a result of delivering bum reproofs. But on the occasion of this exercise, you have been spared — you *can* recall your words. . . . Read what you have written, weigh the passage word by word and consider — had this been 'for real', would your reprimand have passed with flying colours? Do not kid yourself, for the next occasion *will* be for real!


## The personalities

1   Recognition of 'those who grumble for the sake of grumbling' is plainly essential, for two reasons:
    a   Such employees spread the canker of dissatisfaction among their group, and this must be prevented.
    b   It enables the manager to weigh the validity and importance of grievances presented by such individuals.
2   The dogmatic, go-by-the-book employee's grievance requires very special attention, for unless the manager is careful, he will be felled by the trip-wires of his own company manual. This type of employee may well be familiar with every comma of the regulations — woe betide the manager who cannot match his knowledge.
3   The professional troublemakers — an obvious danger and always a cause for concern to the manager. One ill-chosen or incorrect word and this

species of employee will devote all his considerable energies to bring about the downfall of the speaker — and in these days of legal rights and democracy at work, it can be done.

4    It is essential to spot the employees who are afraid to air their grievances, for it is little short of inhuman to allow a subordinate to suffer an injustice merely because he is shy or scared — and why should an employee be scared anyway? Cultivate, motivate and encourage!

5    The sheep of the group will act like sheep, and an aggrieved example may well be the unwitting agent for a more dominant member of the workforce. This type of employee requires early intervention on the part of the manager.

*  *  *

Well, that is enough of homework and 'doing one's thing' in the daily round — we are now going on to tackle the bigger beasties of doing one's thing before an audience. Stick with it, and the best of luck!

# Part Three
# DOING ONE'S THING BEFORE AN AUDIENCE

**Buddha (5th Cent. BC)**
*Sayings of Buddha – F. L. Woodward*

# 9
# Composing the beast

One of the principal components of almost any public-speaking course is the requirement for each member to deliver a series of practice speeches for the edification of his long-suffering colleagues — and, of course, for the purpose of kindly assessment by the even more long-suffering directing staff. On residential courses it is not uncommon for such tasks to be dished out at the end of a day's work, together with a terse reminder that the victims will be required to do their individual thing in the cold light of dawn on the following morning. When this happens, the evening meal — usually a boisterous and happy affair — assumes an atmosphere more akin to a dentist's waiting room, and a monastic silence descends upon the training centre as, with dinner sitting heavily on their stomachs, the course members seek divine help in the composition of their verbal offerings. On one such occasion, I recall a certain manager-chappie who closeted himself away immediately after dinner and remained in seclusion until well into the small hours, working feverishly on his speech. We — that is, the directing staff — noted this above-average concentration and wondered what the morrow would produce. Well, it produced catastrophe.

The course had been given a free choice of subject for this particular assignment, and when the time came for our hero to deliver his fifteen-minute piece, he dampened the spirits of those present by announcing in a faltering voice that his chosen topic was 'decorating a room'. All and sundry listened with a mixture of sympathy and boredom as the guy stumbled his way through a tedious dissertation on decorating materials and methods — in short, it was terrible. However, worse was to come, for at the end of the eighth minute, the poor bloke dried up; he had obviously come to the end of his laboriously prepared speech. A look of near-panic crossed his face as, realising his dilemma, he sought frantically for some means of prolonging his performance — and that was when Old Nick took a hand in the proceedings. With the fateful utterance, '. . . and now we come to the second wall. . . .', he proceeded to repeat, word for word, that which he had already said. His suffering audience was treated to an identical re-run of the most dull and ill-presented address I have ever heard — his hours of work had been thrown down the drain, a saga of non-composition.

Take, as a further instance of this business of composing a speech, the following cry from the heart:

> 'When it comes to speech-making, my troubles start right at the beginning — you know, thinking-up what the hell I am going to say. Even when the subject is a favourite — something I know backwards — I find that I just sit, chewing a pencil, having a devil of a job sorting out odd details and trying to get the thing into some semblance of order. . . .'
> *(Excerpt from a taped discussion with a member of a course on public speaking who subsequently did very well and grew to like the game)*

Let us dive in at the deep end and examine ways and means, snags and pitfalls of composing the beast.

## Placing the amateur speech in perspective

Think for a moment of the professional or gifted 'natural' speakers of the world — those fortunate people who can lift the worst subject from its salver of mediocrity and by dint of sheer skill with the spoken word, serve up a spicy and tantalising dish of oratory, which will earn the acclaim of any audience. For the run-of-the-mill, amateur speaker, here is the rub. Right at the outset, it must be recognised that, unlike our letters, we are unable to call upon the powers of rhetoric to gild the composition lily. Like it or not, the inexperienced speaker is largely forced to rely on the quality of his composition for success — so great pains must be taken to ensure that it is as effective as possible. Consider, if you will, the essential quality of a good book and, more to the point, the manner in which the author carries the reader through the developing stages of his story. It is not by chance that as the plot unfolds, the reader's emotions are skilfully played — lulled into complacent enjoyment at one stage, jolted into climax at the next, the whole gradually building up to the final denouement of the tale. Obvious though the point may be, many would-be speakers tend to forget that a public address — and most certainly an amateur address — must play on the emotions in exactly the same way. Good composition is the primary key to success.

What, then, in the context of composing a speech, is meant by 'good composition'? It does *not* mean writing out an address in full, glorious detail, for (as I go to some length to explain in the next chapter) a speech should never, ever be read or, for that matter, recited. Good composition is concerned with the detailed arrangement of the speaker's bill of fare, not only ensuring that the component dishes are served in a logical sequence, but also (and just as important) planning for maximum titillation of the audience's interest and emotions.

One of the nastiest pitfalls that awaits the unsuspecting, tyro speaker at the composition stage is concerned with his actual choice of subject. Not long ago, a friend of mine was invited by a Chamber of Commerce to deliver a one-hour address on the subject of 'employment law' and since this was just up his speaking street, he accepted the invitation and, as he frankly admits, regarded the commitment as a 'piece of cake'. After all, what was there to worry about? He knew that he possessed an adequate knowledge of the subject and considered himself to be well briefed for the assignment. On the night before the engagement he made a casual decision to scribble down a few bits and pieces — as he says, an oh-so-nonchalant gesture aimed at swiftly arranging an order of sequence for the presentation. The upshot of this approach was that he tumbled headlong into prize pitfall number one, the coverage minefield. The path to this trap for the unwary speaker is deceptively attractive and wholly dangerous to tread. All that one has to do is choose or accept as an assignment a speaking topic which, by its very breadth, presents little in the way of challenge or potential trouble — and in a trice the victim can be up to the neck in the proverbial. 'Yes, by all means,' he gushes. 'I will be delighted to speak to your members on "Morality". . . .' Then when it comes to the crunch-time of setting ideas to paper, the realisation dawns that the wretched subject is so wide that it is almost impossible to compose an hour of generalities, let alone make the damned thing interesting and entertaining. Beware like fury of the wide subject with its seeming ease of composition — take the wise course and speak on an *aspect* of it. My friend's Chamber of Commerce thing was eventually presented as 'Some Views and Pointers on Unfair Dismissal', but only after he had spent a couple of fruitless hours sweating over a composition of (his words) 'inane and frightfully dull generalities'.

By the way, organisations are very fond of bidding speakers to deliver presentations on wide subjects, usually because the thought of a more specialised address conveys visions of boredom and shuffling feet. Resist such overtures or, if you wish, do the Artful Dodger thing and tell 'em at the beginning of your talk that contrary to announcement and expectation, you only intend to speak on so-and-so. Mention the reason why, and you will win their support.

The reader will find, if he gets that far, that ensuing chapters of this book make monotonous mention of the paramount need for adequate subject knowledge when tackling a speaking assignment. It is not only for the obvious reason that I tend to harp unmercifully on this point — the sober fact is that

83

many inexperienced speakers, either from motives of vanity or a genuine desire to help, accept speaking commitments for which they are hopelessly unqualified in terms of subject knowledge. Do not succumb, for as sure as the good Lord made little apples, Old Nick, usually in the shape of a great, hairy questioner in the audience, will find you out. There *is* such a thing as 'muddling through', and every man-jack in the audience will be aware that that is exactly what the speaker is doing.

The thinking speaker will subject his chosen or allotted topic to a 'validation checklist' along the following lines:

1    Do I possess adequate knowledge of the subject:
    *a*    Sufficient to deliver a fluent and impressive address?
    *b*    Sufficient to cater for unrehearsed 'going off at tangents'?
    *c*    Sufficient to cater for all but the most awkward of questions?
2    Is the subject 'right' for the audience concerned?
    *a*    Will it bore?
    *b*    Will it antagonise?
    *c*    Will it divide the audience?
3    Is the subject 'right' for me?
    *a*    Do I have the status, demeanour and personality to put it over?
    *b*    Do I *believe* in it — or can I lie in my teeth consistently and convincingly?
4    Is the commitment as a whole:
    *a*    Worthwhile?
    *b*    Part-and-parcel of some policy or other — and if so, does my contribution conform with that policy?

Having checked out the subject and made the decision to go ahead with the speaking commitment instead of emigrating to the Orkneys, the next step is to consider the component parts of an address:

1    The introduction.
2    The body beautiful.
3    The conclusion.

## The introduction

Hark back to those magic days in the VIth Form — do you recall old Belcher, the English master, thumping the desk and throwing detentions about like confetti as he struggled to illuminate your juvenile horizon with the light of wisdom? 'Pay attention, you horrible child! The purpose of the introduction is to give a hint of what the essay is all about — to set the scene — wake up, that boy. . . .' Plainly, the introduction to a speech serves exactly the same purpose in life, only more so. If a presentation is to savour the heady delights of success, it is necessary for the introduction, the first few words, to pluck a mighty twang on the audience's interest chords — to make 'em sit up, shut up and really *want* to pay attention. There are a thousand-and-one ways of tackling this opening gambit, but in making his choice, the wise speaker will take three important criteria into consideration:

1   *The audience*   Will they 'accept' the introduction in the manner in which it is intended — will it provoke interest, fall flat on its face or be regarded as a gimmick?
2   *The subject*   Is the planned introduction suited to the subject of the address — will the style 'clash' with the rest of the material; will it be too high-powered and as a consequence overshadow the performance?
3   *Personal skills*   Can I 'bring it off'? — or is the style or form of the introduction foreign to my personality?

There follows a miniature pot-pourri of introductions I have heard over the last couple of years — consider them and form your personal assessment of their effectiveness (as far as you are able, that is, without hearing the speeches concerned). What would you have said in each case?

*A plain-clothes police officer, addressing an adult audience on road safety*
'I am going to talk to you about death — death in its most horrible form. . . .'

*A speaker addressing an audience of managers on unfair dismissal*
'An employer can dismiss anyone he likes, whenever he likes, for whatever reason he likes — but he must be prepared to pay for the privilege. Let's talk money. . . .'

*A police constable, addressing a Women's Institute on security in the home*
'Remember that fanlight you left open at home. . . ?'

*A physical education instructor, addressing an adult keep-fit class*
'I was going to talk to you about the body beautiful — but now that I've seen you, let's talk about the body beastly. . . .'

*A speaker on management, addressing an audience of headmasters*
'Someone once told me that headmasters are the worst managers in the world. I don't think I believed him. . . .'

*A speaker on pollution, addressing a general audience*
'You know, it really is about time that we pulled the chain on this lavatory we call England. . . .'

*A British Rail executive, addressing an audience of commuters*
'Despite 2,166 letters and many, many telephone calls, I remain convinced that tucked away somewhere in British Rail, there is a pristine-clean carriage. I am equally convinced that somewhere, somehow, a train managed to run on time. Let's talk filthy lateness. . . .'

I must add, if only for the record, that it is precious little use setting off a firecracker of an introduction if it is followed by a damp squib of a speech. Having stopped the shuffling of feet, having gained the interested attention of those serried rows of heads — why, give them a body beautiful!

## The body

There is a little more to composing an effective body of an address than merely ensuring that the subject is covered in a comprehensive and interesting fashion — although, mark you, this is of great importance. We must return to this business of 'playing the audience', plucking on their emotions and motivating them to listen. Once again, there is a drill to be followed:

1    Jot down *all* the points and ideas that are relevant to the subject.
2    With the use of a merciless scalpel, eliminate all the material with the faintest tinge of irrelevance (yes, at *second* glance, you will find irrelevancies) and stuff that does not *exactly* suit your approach to the subject, or the anticipated needs and taste of the audience.
3    Arrange the material in a logical order of sequence, bearing in mind that all must build to a crescendo-end — not a deathly, fading away.
4    Bolster weak patches with new points and ideas — remember to examine them critically for their contribution to the whole.
5    Implant in your scheme of things the vital anecdotes and instances — the spice.
6    Examine the result and if you feel really confident that all is well, leave it for a few hours — go and mow the lawn, or be nice to the missus. Then examine it again; you will be surprised how weaknesses will rear their ugly heads.

If one graphed the 'bodily rhythm' of an address, it should look something like this:

Note the manner in which the audience is pitchforked from complacent comfort to some form of 'climax' all along the line. The aim must be to make them forget the hard chairs and aching bottoms, money troubles, wife troubles and goodness-knows-what-all troubles — *get them listening, and enjoying.*

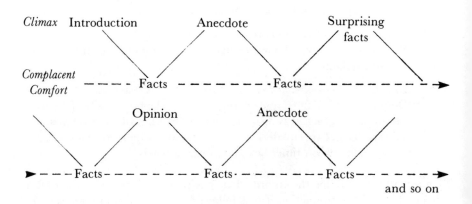

## The conclusion

If the quality of the introduction to an address is important, the quality of the conclusion is *vital*. The average audience will only remember a small proportion of any speech, but, by gosh, they will carry away a lasting and accurate impression of a speaker's final words. Note how the speakers I quoted in the section on introductions concluded their efforts — and once again judge accordingly:

> *The police officer - on road safety*
> 'Like a good police officer, I've noted many of your faces — please don't let me see a familiar face in the kind of mayhem I have described. Stay alive. . . .'
>
> *The manager - on unfair dismissal*
> 'Someone, somewhere is paying a great deal for a dismissal — right now. Will you be next. . . ?'
>
> *The police constable - on security*
> 'So — what about that fanlight, are you still quite happy? . .'
>
> *The PE instructor - on keeping fit*
> 'Would you neglect your car in the same way as most of us neglect our bodies? Let's face it, you may need a major service — or are you going off the road. . . ?'
>
> *The speaker on management - to headmasters*
> 'If you manage as well as you listen — take Sunday off. Thank you and goodbye. . . .'
>
> *The speaker on pollution*
> 'Smell it, see it, taste it, hear it — and before it's too late, *stop it. . . .*'
>
> *The British Rail executive - on British Rail*
> 'Thank you for listening — I must go now, I've got a train to catch. . . .'

It is often necessary for a speaker to conclude his address by recapitulating the main points or an essential part of his presentation, but — unlike teaching — this should not be regarded as an invariable rule. A concluding punch-line may succeed in sending an audience away happy; a repetition of material can make them feel they are back at school, and they may not like the feeling.

Having dwelt for a bit on the business of composing an address, the next chapter deals with the trials and tribulations of *preparation* — and if you think there is precious little difference between the two, read on! But before you do, there is some more work to be done.

A cup of coffee might not come amiss. . . .

## Self-tutorial (Part One)

Remembering the importance of logical, sequential and interesting arrangement of subject matter:
a   Consider your own life history, and compose a factual and entertaining speech about yourself.
b   Now imagine that instead of being the modest violet you really are, you are hell-bent on *selling yourself*. Compose an impressive and persuasive address for the benefit of prospective 'buyers'.

## Self-tutorial (Part Two)

Remembering the importance of the introduction, compose effective and titillating opening remarks for the following subjects:
   The will to work
   A pet hate
   Lavatories
   Adolf Hitler
   A fisherman's tale

## Self-tutorial (Part Three)

Examine your opening remarks for the above subjects in the light of the following requirements — think carefully and amend/change accordingly.
1   *The will to work*   An address to be presented at a meeting of the unemployed
2   *A pet hate*   An address to be presented to a group of psychologists
3   *Lavatories*   An address to be presented to a meeting of the Mothers' Guild
4   *Adolf Hitler*   An address to be presented to an audience of German businessmen
5   *A fisherman's tale*   An address to be presented to (wait for it) an audience composed of members of the clergy

## Self-tutorial (Part Four)

Compose apt concluding remarks for the following subjects:
   The design-mechanics of the brassière
   Fish paste
   Thrills I have known
   Getting away from it all
   Planning for retirement

## Self-tutorial (Part Five)

Now compose apt and striking conclusions for the addresses detailed in Part Three above. Remember that a successful conclusion is seldom the one that offends.

Politics is perhaps the only profession for which no preparation is thought necessary.

**R. L. Stevenson (1850-1894)**
*Familiar Studies of Men and Books*

# 10

# Be prepared, boys — be prepared!

Some years ago, when attending a business lunch, I had the doubtful privilege of being seated next to a man who, believing himself to be the most accomplished of speakers, insisted that everyone was acquainted with the fact. Having announced during soup that he was one of the guest speakers, he then launched into a potted lecture on the art of public speaking which, liberally interspersed with noisy ingestions of food, lasted throughout the main course. However, everything comes to an end and just as sweet was being served, he announced airily, 'Well, I mustn't talk all day — I have a speech to write!' Somewhat bemused, I watched this worthy character as, with complete sang-froid, he proceeded to jot down a series of swift notes on the back of a handy menu. Barely a couple of minutes later, he slapped down his pen and, beaming heartily, proclaimed to all and sundry, 'There — never takes me long, you know! Now, where was I?' Then, would you believe, he started to regale me with an interminable flow of anecdotes, very dull and involved anecdotes, which continued until, at long last, the sound of the chairman's gavel brought the relentless monologue to a halt. Oh, Lord, my loquacious table companion was to be the first speaker — I slumped in my chair and awaited a further dose of his expertise.

It was at this point that Nemesis took a chilly hand in the proceedings. As the man clambered to his feet, he reached for his hastily-composed notes, only to find that the all-important menu, along with sundry other bits and pieces, had gone — quietly whipped away by a zealous and efficient waiter. The result was catastrophic. The self-styled wizard of the public speaking world was reduced in the twinkling of an eye to a virtual nonentity — a flushed, perspiring and wholly inarticulate speaker, whose abject presentation was finally given a merciful *coup de grâce* by means of a hasty interjection of thanks from an embarrassed chairman. If there is a moral to be gleaned from this sad account, it must surely be concerned with the question of over-confidence and, above all else, the vexed subject of *preparation*.

Many non-professional speakers believe with some justification that there is only one thing worse than giving an address, and that is preparing the beast. However, the vast majority of speakers, both professional and non-professional, agree that, chore or not, it has to be done. The extent and style of preparation will largely depend on the type of event and of course on the outlook of the practitioner. The purpose of this chapter is to take a crafty look at some of the advantages and pitfalls which are part and parcel of the preparation game — so if you are ready, let's get cracking.

## Preparing the 'public address'

*The 'get-it-all-down' syndrome and the inevitable result*   When running a course on public speaking, I always start the preparation ball rolling by inviting the course members to compile notes *in their own style* for the first practice speech. The result is always the same; a goodly number write out their intended speech word for word, using pages of paper and expending a great deal of mental and physical effort in the process. Take a peep at Figure 4, which — no names, no pack-drill — shows a typical example of such work. The sad fact is that when the crunch comes, the audience is not confronted by a speaker but by a *reader*, and more often than not, the thing goes off like a damp squib. There are very few people who are accustomed to reading aloud, let alone in public, and it requires little imagination to picture the result. Faults in reading technique — an expressionless, monotone voice, hesitancies, mispronunciations and the like — are compounded by a fear of losing one's place in the text, and the reader becomes so occupied with this critical situation that the poor audience is virtually ignored. In short, the 'speaker' fails to establish any form of rapport with his audience — a vital requirement, of which more anon.

There are several reasons why inexperienced speakers elect to undergo the drudgery of writing out their presentations in full, gory detail:

1   Inadequate knowledge of the subject. Let us not mince words — this death-trap must be avoided like the plague; there is no substitute for subject knowledge, and verbatim notes will *not* save the day.

2   A lack of faith in one's ability to interpret abbreviated notes. I hope to convince you that given subject knowledge, such doubts are groundless — there is a system!

3   A belief that one's vocabulary and powers of expression will be inadequate to the task of translating brief notes into a smooth, interesting and enter-

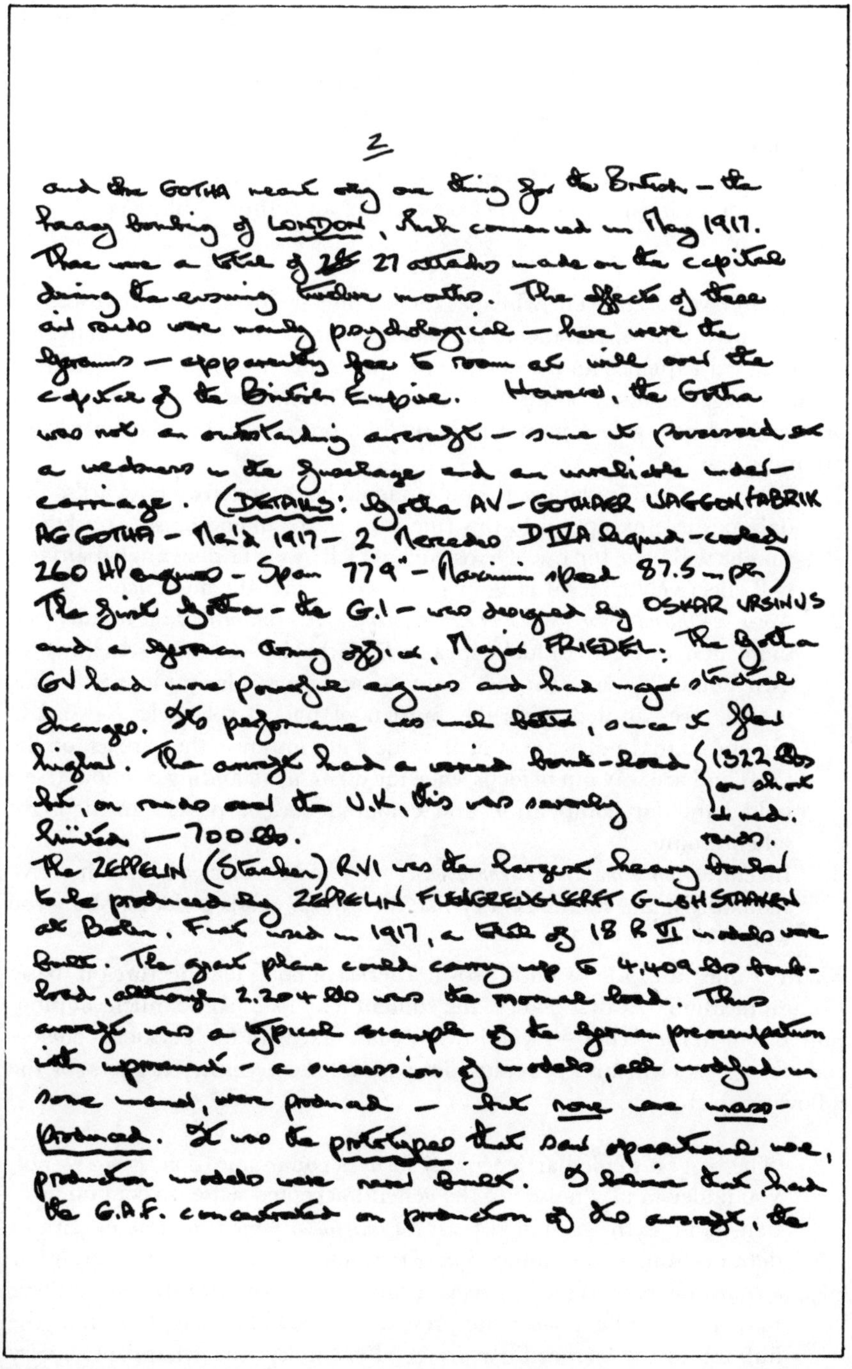

2

and the GOTHA meant only one thing for the British — the heavy bombing of LONDON, which commenced in May 1917. There were a total of 27 attacks made on the capital during the ensuing twelve months. The effects of these air raids were mainly psychological — here were the Gothas — apparently free to roam at will over the capital of the British Empire. However, the Gotha was not an outstanding aircraft — since it possessed a weakness in the fuselage and an unreliable undercarriage. (DETAILS: Gotha AV - GOTHAER WAGGONFABRIK AG GOTHA - Maid 1917 - 2 Mercedes DIVA liquid-cooled 260 HP engines - Span 77'9" - Maximum speed 87.5 mph) The first Gotha - the G.I - was designed by OSKAR URSINUS and a German army officer, Major FRIEDEL. The Gotha GV had more powerful engines and had major structural changes. Its performance was well better, once it flew higher. The aircraft had a varied bomb-load {1322 lbs on short distance raids. lb, on raids over the U.K, this was severely limited — 700 lbs. reduced.

The ZEPPELIN (Staaken) RVI was the largest heavy bomber to be produced by ZEPPELIN FLUGZEUGWERFT GmbH STAAKEN at Berlin. First used in 1917, a total of 18 R VI models were built. The giant plane could carry up to 4,409 lbs bomb-load, although 2,204 lbs was the normal load. This aircraft was a typical example of the German preoccupation with improvement - a succession of models, all modified in some manner, were produced — but none were mass-produced. It was the prototypes that saw operational use, production models were never built. I believe that had the G.A.F. concentrated on production of this aircraft, the

**Figure 4** An example of a slippery stepping-stone on the path to speaking disaster — part of an address written out in full

taining flow of speech. This can be a very real fear, but once again it can very often be groundless — more of *this* anon.

4    Plain ignorance — the intending speaker has never had occasion to think about preparing or making a speech, and imagines that a full script is 'the thing to have'. It isn't.

So — away with sheaves of paper, long hours of writing and the dreadful spectacle of an inexperienced speaker reading an address. Abbreviated notes are the answer.

*Short, sharp and succinct*   The wise speaker will prepare his notes with two aims in mind: firstly, to provide a means of checking that the presentation is delivered in a planned sequence and, secondly, to equip himself with a series of 'instant memory triggers' at key points in the address. The method by which these aims are achieved is largely a matter of individual preference, but there are some ground rules:

1    For ease of manipulation, the notes should be compiled on postcards. The only possible exception to this rule is when the intending speaker knows that he will have the use of a rostrum, which by virtue of its angled surface, will effectively conceal large pages of notes from the audience.

2    *Notes are intended for swift and easy reference*   All too often and usually in a moment of crisis, an unlucky speaker finds that he is unable to decipher his own notes. Those with poor sight — and particularly those who, like myself, are saddled with the burden of bifocal spectacles — should remember that notes are of little value if, for instance, they are left on the table and are way out of focus when the user is in a standing position. Use a bold hand for compilation and coloured inks or pencils to highlight salient points.

3    Invent a *simple and easily remembered* 'code' of abbreviations and directive symbols. Again, methods vary like the March winds — let me show you what I mean. . . .

Figure 5 illustrates the second card in a series of notes for a lecture on 'Basic Communication'. At first glance, the content may look like so much mumbo-jumbo, but to the writer — who is wholly familiar with his 'personal code' — the message is clear and provides him with all the necessary triggers for the following spiel:

'The biggest single barrier in any form of communication is *noise* — not, you understand, "noise" in the general accepted sense. In communication, noise is the technical term for *any factor* which interefes with or detracts from a communication between transmitter and receiver. *(Show overhead transparency No. 5.)* As you can see from this transparency,  there may of course be *actual* noise present — a crackling telephone line, the hubbub of the factory floor are good examples. Or as happens so very often, the transmitter employs words which are not familiar to the receiver — who, as a consequence, cannot understand the communica-

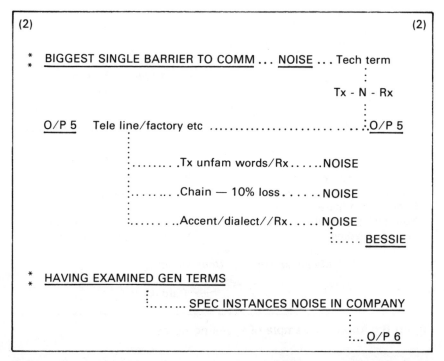

* BIGGEST SINGLE BARRIER TO COMM ... NOISE ... Tech term
*
                                                                                              Tx - N - Rx

O/P 5    Tele line/factory etc .........................O/P 5

                    ........ .Tx unfam words/Rx ......NOISE

                    ......... .Chain — 10% loss...... .NOISE

                    ....... ..Accent/dialect//Rx. .... NOISE
                                                                                          ..... BESSIE

* HAVING EXAMINED GEN TERMS
*
                    ........ SPEC INSTANCES NOISE IN COMPANY

                                                                                          ... O/P 6

**Figure 5** An example of speaking 'triggers' — speaking notes composed on small cards for handy reference and ease of manipulation

tion, and this lack of understanding constitutes *noise*. Another form of noise — remember, we are using the technical term — occurs when a verbal communication is passed along a chain of several people, and as sure as God made little apples, the rule of '10% loss' comes into play. This simply means that as each person in the chain receives and transmits the message, a percentage of the original communication is lost or distorted. As a final example of noise in communication, think of the transmitter who is blessed with a strong accent or dialect — it may be a joy to hear but terribly difficult to understand, and in such circumstances *noise* will rear its ugly head. This reminds me of the sad story of Bessie, the tea-girl. . . *(Recount Bessie gag.)* 'Having examined communication noise in very general terms, *let us* look at some more specific instances of communication difficulties within the company. . . . *(Show overhead transparency No. 6.)*'

Figure 6 shows an alternative format for speaking notes, which, although not my personal cup of tea, is employed with great success by a colleague when lecturing on his various subjects. He tells me that the system provides a ready supply of information on lecture sequence and memory triggers — as indeed in this example, which deals with the development of a central theme, 'The Cultivation of Memory'. He commences his address by expanding on the items

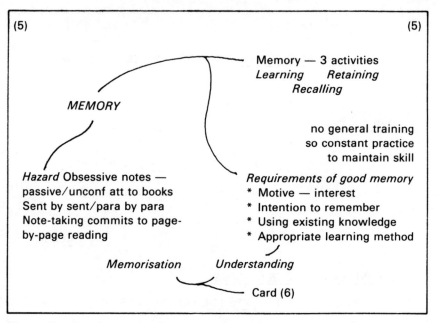

**Figure 6**  Another example of speaking notes

mentioned in the top right-hand corner of the card, and then proceeds in a clockwise direction 'round the wheel'. Notice, as with the previous illustration, that the card is clearly marked with its serial number; this is essential if muddles are to be avoided — Sod's Law dictates that one fine day the speaker will drop his cards.

*More on the question of subject knowledge*  Remember that the need for adequate subject knowledge extends beyond the required ability to present an address, for on most occasions the speaker has also to cross the Rubicon of questions from his audience. Whilst there will always be the odd time when a speaker, however expert, is stuck for an answer, it is absolutely essential that the extent of one's knowledge is sufficient to cope with the normal run of questions to be expected from an interested audience.

## Preparing the 'committee report or address'

Everything that I have offered thus far applies to the preparation of an address or report to a committee-type audience, but this type of minefield contains some additional perils for the speaker — and he would be wise to take them into account.

*Weighing up the opposition*  Instead of confining one's thoughts about probable opposition to sentiments such as, 'I'll bet my bottom dollar that Jones will disagree — he always does' or 'The old man is bound to object to something or other', the speaker's presentation should include a tactical appraisal of the situation:

1    What *exactly* is likely to be So-and-so's objection?
2    What form is this opposition likely to take?
3    How effective is it likely to be?
4    How may the opposition be countered or overcome? *By factual argument?* If so, is the planned argument logical and persuasive, and have all possible side-issues been taken into account? *Or by outright rejection?* If so, is the planned rejection sufficiently logical and devastating — and again are there side-issues to be taken into account?
5    How will other members of the group react to a particular person's opposition?
6    Exactly how important *is* the issue involved — how far am I prepared to go in its support, and in any event do I have right and logic on my side, *or am I kidding myself?*

*Preliminary manoeuvres and skirmishes*   Completion of the tactical appraisal will almost invariably bring the intending speaker to the point where he considers what can be done *before* the meeting in question to further his cause. Consider the following checklist:

1    Exactly who are the best people to approach — and why? Will I gain more than merely a sympathetic ear?
2    Can I depend on them for support — and to what extent?
3    Will they talk about my approach to others — and to what degree and effect?
4    Exactly how should I make the approach?
5    Does the issue really warrant a behind-the-scenes approach?
6    The paramount question — what *is* my standing with these people — without deluding myself, *do I enjoy sufficient respect or popularity to ensure that my approach is worthwhile?*

Whilst hardly a meeting goes by without the nominated members indulging in prior discussion of some sort or another, the cautious person will recognise that this apparently harmless pastime can be fraught with danger. Committee meetings, or any other events which entail the prospect of an individual being required to perform under the nose of his boss, bring out the worst in people. It is at such times that the struggle for personal survival in the company pecking order is likely to influence decisions, and all too often a fervent promise of support given at a pre-meeting discussion undergoes a marked transformation when crunch-time finally arrives:

'Well, yes, Mr Chairman — it's true that I agreed *in principle* with Jack's proposal when he spoke to me last night, but now that I've heard your comments, I'm bound to admit. . . .'

'But, John — when we spoke to each other before the meeting, I didn't realise that you actually meant so-and-so. . . .'

'Sorry, Peter — but when we discussed this, I had no idea that there would be so much opposition at the meeting. . . .'

The average boss has a handy vocabulary with which to indict those unlucky souls who are thus dropped in the mire by their defecting allies — trouble-maker, rabble-rouser, kite-flier and so on. Therefore, before engaging in preparations for pre-meeting manoeuvres and skirmishes, remember the check-lists and let common sense dictate the answers.

## The infernal business of rehearsal

The inexperienced speaker who fails to rehearse his presentation is asking for trouble — unfortunately the poor chap who decides to do things the right way may well find trouble:

'I'm not a good speaker at the best of times — in fact, the mere thought of having to face an audience scares me to death, especially if it has something to do with the company. Last year the local Sixth-Form College held a kind of careers convention, and I was nobbled at pretty short notice to give a presentation on our management trainee scheme. Normally this is the personnel manager's pigeon, but on this occasion the lucky blighter was away on holiday and I got the job. Well, things were pretty hectic at the time, and apart from collecting a mass of details on the scheme from the personnel section, I didn't have a chance to do any preparation until the night before the event. No — that's not strictly correct — I guess the truth is that I kept putting the damned thing off. Anyway, that evening I tucked myself away in the dining room, and using the company brochure as a guide, roughed out about three pages of notes. Then I read the whole thing through—and that was when I began to get really worried. My so-called exposition of a wonderful career opportunity sounded as dull at dishwater, so — don't laugh — I decided, almost in desperation, to have a pukka rehearsal. There I was, tramping up and down the dining room, declaiming to thin air, trying to look and sound enthusiastic — when the wife, hearing the din, came in to see what was going on. Trust the missus to inject a grain of sense into the proceedings — in no time flat, she had me pretending that *she* was the audience, and off I went again. To cut a long story short, the re-run seemed to be much better, and my wife said that it all sounded very interesting — so, feeling a bit more hopeful, I called it a day.

'You can probably imagine the rest of the story. I turned up at the school far too early and feeling anything but optimistic — in fact, I was little short of terrified. There were several speakers and we all sat in the usual kind of semi-circle — on a damned great stage which seemed miles above the audience, facing goodness knows how many youngsters. The

headmaster told me that I would be the second speaker, but what he *didn't* tell me was that the first guy on the list was a born natural — you know, the kind of speaker who has an audience in the palm of his hand from the word go. Smooth, witty, debonair — you name it, he had all the attributes. By the time my turn came, I had been reduced to an abject state of nerves; there was simply no way I could even approach this chap's level of expertise. Still, it had to be done and I ground my way through the speech as well as I could. I made one or two wisecracks — which had sounded pretty good the night before — but instead of the hearty belly-laughs which had greeted the previous speaker's 'funnies', all I succeeded in raising was the odd titter. I reckon the whole ghastly episode could be summed up by saying that it passed off in an atmosphere of polite attention — the headmaster had his beady eyes on everyone, and they were under orders to listen, or else. It ended with the head calling for the traditional round of applause; 'twas almost clapping by numbers, and I remember feeling very glad that the managing director had not been present to witness it all. . . .'
*(Excerpt from a taped discussion with a company accountant)*

What, then, of this rehearsal game? Let us take a quick peep at some of the salient features of the rehearsing minefield and, where possible, come up with some recommendations.

*Talking to thin air*   Many inexperienced speakers succumb to the apparent need to rehearse a presentation 'out loud', but because they fear making a fool of themselves, elect to do this in the privacy of an empty room. Hold on though — *is* it the fear of embarrassment or, more to the point, the fact that criticism will create a hiccup, an unwelcome delay, in the process of getting the rehearsal out of the way — and out of mind — as soon as possible? Whatever the motive, talking to thin air is strictly for the birds; it will do more harm than good. The unpleasant truth is that solitary rehearsal — apart from sending you blind — almost always produces an irresistible urge to 'overact the part', to indulge in mannerisms and forms of affectation which are blatantly artificial and larger than life. This pitfall must be avoided at all costs, *for the key to effective speaking is to be the person you are, not someone you are not.*

*Talking to the mirror*   Go on, admit it, it happens. Quite a few of us engage in this form of solitary rehearsal — and it is a killer. Never, ever give in to the compulsion to rehearse in front of a mirror, for the practice will lead, once again, to the invention and use of a whole series of ghastly and completely artificial mannerisms. The careful cultivation of what appears to be a most effective facial expression will, in fact, turn out to be something more akin to a Quasimodo-like leer. The practitioner may deserve the inevitable result, but the poor audience certainly does not.

*Rehearsing in front of the missus* At first glance this may appear to be a harmless and even beneficial form of rehearsal, but there is a potential snag. The little woman, God bless her, realising that her great lump of a husband is making a pig's breakfast of his address, will often allow loyalty to sway her judgment:

Husband  (*Very hopefully*)  'Well, that's it, Doris — what do you think. . . ?'
Missus  (*Bored to tears, but worried for her man*)  'Wonderful, dear — I liked it very much. Shall I make the cocoa now?'

Of course some of us are endowed with a slightly different kind of help-mate — but the effect is the same:

Husband  (*Again, very hopefully*)  '. . . what do you think?'
Missus  'I say, you don't really intend to talk to them like that, do you. . . ?'

*More on the business of acting a part* When the inexperienced speaker thinks about presenting an address, his mind will often turn to pure and juicy fantasy, and in the best Walter Mitty tradition, he will dream of holding an audience spellbound with the sheer eloquence of his oratory. Now it may be fairly harmless for little Willie to engage in fantasies about hypnotising an audience with his compelling rhetoric and awesome gestures, but it becomes an entirely different kettle of fish if Willie tries it 'for real'. If there is one lesson to be learned about the speaking game, it is the hard fact that speaking is speaking — *not acting*. Leave the cooking-up of gestures, poses and mannerisms to the professionals, and whatever you do, forget trying to emulate them.

*Rehearsal is about timing* Given adequate subject knowledge and well-prepared notes, rehearsal should be concerned with the timing of a presentation and precious little else. It is absolutely essential for an intending speaker to check and possibly amend the duration of his address, and this can only really be done by what I term an 'armchair run-through'. Select a quiet spot away from the television, the kids and the missus; note the time and *go through the thing at the requisite speed*. It is well to remember that, invariably, the chosen speed of delivery will in fact be much faster than imagined — *so make a conscious and continued effort to go slowly*. Allow deliberate and seemingly over-long pauses between sentences — and at other points in the address where a 'pause for effect' is deemed beneficial. If, when the run-through is complete, you find that the presentation falls short of a crucial, required duration for the real thing, do not make the fatal mistake of imagining that everything 'will be all right on the night'. It won't be. You will find that the shortfall at rehearsal of, say, three minutes will have expanded 'on the night' to a horrible six or seven minutes, and Sod's Law will have triumphed again. Be realistic and add more material, but please beware of the Jabberwock — adding more material does *not* mean padding the wretched thing out with meaningless and ineffective rubbish.

Remember also that after-dinner and similar addresses require the timing treatment — have you never suffered from some of the interminable monologues dished out on such occasions? Ten minutes can be a hell of a long time — say it in five.

## Self-tutorial (Part One)

The following information was noted when an industrial site at the Abbey Trading Estate, Ramsey, Cambs., was investigated by your company's project team with a view to constructing a new factory at the location for the manufacture of aircraft in-flight recorders and other lightweight electronic components for the aircraft industry.

*Your task* From the information supplied, compile speaking notes for the delivery of a suitable presentation to senior management entitled 'Review of the Ramsey Situation'. For the purposes of this exercise, you should not take the timing of the address into account.

1   There are no rail facilities at Ramsey.
2   Three-star hotel accommodation at Huntingdon (11 miles).
3   Electricity supplies are available at the site.
4   Direct access to site from B1040.
5   Site situated on clay subsoil.
6   Male unemployment in the area is 7.5 per cent, mostly unskilled and semi-skilled.
7   Ramsey-Peterborough 12 miles.
8   Nearest seaport, Kings Lynn 38 miles.
9   Rail, including heavy goods, Peterborough.
10  Four-star hotel accommodation at Cambridge (25 miles).
11  Water mains and sewers laid to site.
12  No gradients to site.
13  Ramsey population 5700.
14  Limited public transport in area.
15  Moderate supply of unskilled female labour available in area.
16  Good selection of building firms capable of factory construction in area.
17  Site situated 13 miles from A1(T) via Huntingdon.
18  Gas available at site.
19  Site not in a development area — no government grants possible.
20  Seaport at Kings Lynn handles vehicles, general cargo.
21  Skilled operatives would require to be transferred from London factory.
22  B1040 via B605 to Peterborough, and via A141 to Huntingdon.
23  Moderate housing in area, if Peterborough, Huntingdon included.
24  Nearest airport Cambridge.
25  Hostel accommodation would be required for London workers pending house acquisition.
26  Several coach firms in area for contract work.
27  London (78 miles) via Huntingdon A1(T).
28  Possible hostel accommodation at Cambridge.
29  Inter-City service Huntingdon BR — Kings Cross.
30  Council house accommodation possible at Huntingdon.

Having prepared your speaking 'triggers' from the above information, be brutally frank with yourself and check them for *logical sequence* and (in case you have forgotten) *ease of manipulation*.

## Self-tutorial (Part Two)

## A GENERAL QUIZ ON THE PRECEDING CHAPTER

### Answers

### Questions

1 What are the two aims of speaking notes?

1 To provide a means of ensuring that the address is presented in a planned sequence, and to equip the speaker with a series of 'memory triggers'

2 For ease of manipulation, speaking notes should be compiled on —

2 Postcards

3 Can there be any exception to this rule?

3 Only when the speaker *knows* that he will have the protection of a rostrum — then notes can be of larger size

4 When preparing as address to a committee, what prime factor should be taken into account?

4 *Weighing up the opposition!*

5 What is the prime purpose of a presentation rehearsal?

5 *Timing* the thing — a crucial requirement. Fail to time accurately and you are lost

6 What are the three S's of good speaking notes?

6 Short — Sharp — Succinct!

7 Name one method of dealing with opposition at a committee.

7 By factual argument — or you could have said, by outright rejection

8 What form of preparation does 'factual argument' entail?

8 Ensuring that the planned argument is logical and persuasive, and that all possible side-issues have been taken into account

9 What about 'outright rejection' — what tactical preparation does this entail?

9 Ensuring that the planned rejection is logical and devastating, and again taking all possible side-issues into account

Nobody is on my side, nobody takes part with me:
I am cruelly used, nobody feels for my poor nerves.

**Jane Austen (1775-1817)**
*Pride and Prejudice*

# 11
# The dreaded
# heebie-jeebies

'There is absolutely nothing to worry about — it'll be all right on the night. . . .'

'Remember, you are not alone — the finest actor in the world suffers from butterflies in the tum. . . .'

'M'dear chap, you *know* you can do it. . . .'

'I honestly don't know what you are making all the fuss about. . . .'

There is one thing for certain, if you do not have a number of such hollow phrases scudding about in your memory, you are either a consummate extrovert — in which case, what the devil are you doing with this book — or you are enjoying a convenient bout of amnesia. Faced with any form of 'public speaking', the vast majority of us would willingly trade a small fortune in return for a panacea for that worst of speaking ills, the onslaught of nerves. Let us wallow in a spot of masochism and picture the scene:

Everything is fine and dandy in Mick Carter's little world — the job is going well and the boss is pleased, he's finished the damned wallpapering in the lounge and the wife, bless her, is on speaking terms again — when, wham, a bolt from the blue shatters his contentment and casts him into Stygian gloom. Poor Mick learns with a mental shriek of horror that he is next in line to deliver a speech at that oratorical holy of holies, the Rotary lunch. Despondency rapidly changes to dread as he recalls the suave urbanity with which last month's speaker addressed the membership — there is absolutely no way in which he can match that so-and-so's expertise — dear God, the whole thing will be an awful shambles. In desperation, Mick considers a range of possible excuses; the flu, perhaps, or a vital commitment at work, a sudden bereavement, a trip abroad — but it is all to no avail, for Mick is saddled with a solid-gold conscience and, come hell or high water, he just has to go through with the wretched speech.

As the days pass and our hero's assignment with fate draws inexorably closer, he alternates between bouts of totally unrewarding rehearsal and unsuccessful attempts to rid his mind of the whole matter of the impending trial — the 'don't think about it and it will go away' syndrome. But it doesn't, and to cut a long story of private agony short, Mick eventually finds himself seated at the Rotary table, fiddling with Rotary chicken and trying, with a numb sense of failure, to cope with the lump of lead which sits firmly in the pit of his near-convulsing stomach. . . .

Enough of that bilious stuff. One hard and immutable fact of public speaking life is, quite simply, that there is no cure, no all-embracing panacea, for the willies. So what is the purpose of all this waffle? A good question, and do take heart, for there is a worthwhile answer. Whilst there is no perfect cure for pre-speaking nerves, there are a number of sure-fire part-cures or, to be more precise, *factors* which, if taken into careful account, will go a long way towards ameliorating the effects of the butterfly bug. So without ado, let us proceed to grasp as many straws as possible and, would you believe, construct a life-raft for survival in the war against nerves.

## A little knowledge is a dangerous thing

The intending speaker who suffers the burden of inadequate knowledge of his subject invites disaster in the first round of his battle against the jitters. This may seem to be a very trite observation, but think on't. Whilst we bounce the golden rule, 'know thy subject', back and forth with monotonous regularity, the fact remains that countless speakers — some on the odd occasion, some on many occasions and politicians on nearly every occasion — pronounce and pontificate on things they know little about. If, and you must believe this, the vast majority of speakers suffer from nerves, it follows that the uninformed chappie incurs his fair share of the galloping heebie-jeebies — the only difference is that the poor soul cannot hope to lessen the affliction. The fear of being tripped up, of having one's lack of knowledge exposed for all to see, is in itself a prime ingredient for a hefty attack of nerves. Couple this with a general apprehension over speaking in public, an innate shyness or what-have-you, and come what may, the victim is doomed to suffer the full and ghastly panoply of *irreducible* nerves. So — the first lesson, obvious though it may be, is to kill off one strain of the butterfly bug at source by simply knowing one's subject. Then, and only then, will the speaker be in a position to tackle the several other factors which contribute to nerves.

## Getting to know the beast

*Recognise the fear of 'general exposure'*   Public speaking entails, in essence, 'standing alone' and becoming the cynosure of all those horrible eyes, the focal point of gloating attention and the target for goodness-knows-what criticism and ridicule — or so the intending speaker, up to the hapless ears with *'bacillus nervosa'*, tends to believe. Is he correct? Will he be the subject of a merciless scrutiny, with every actual or imagined imperfection of clothing, stance and physical make-up examined and found wanting? Well, if it is his intention to address the local Women's Institute dressed only in long-johns and a top hat, brandishing a rawhide whip in one hand and a hard-porn magazine in the other — yes, he may certainly be correct. If, on the other hand, he is just another Mr Average and people in the street do not stop to gawp at him as he walks by, the overwhelming odds are that he is grossly incorrect in his assumption. Public speaking is not a question of being generally exposed but rather a question of being *generally in command*, and whilst this should promote some careful thought and bags of preparation, there are precious few grounds for actual fear. This brand of pre-speaking nerves is a psychological backlash from our primitive past, when tribal instincts were the order of the day and it was downright dangerous, if not suicidal, to 'stand alone'. In today's faintly civilised world, with the possible exception of political meetings and the chief executive's command get-together, human beings tend to remain human beings when listening to one of their fellows, and they are mostly preoccupied with just that — listening. If the intending speaker finds it hard to dispel the dreadful thought of all those beady eyes looking at him, he should remember that most people do this because it points their ears in the right direction. Even if boredom sets in, perish the thought, and people fail to listen, they do not embark upon a visual inquisition of the speaker; they merely daydream.

*Recognise the audience for what they are*   The first and worst advice I ever received on the subject of pre-speaking nerves was to think about the impending presentation in terms of addressing a field of cabbages. 'That's right, my boy', intoned the misguided mentor. 'Think of 'em as cabbages, treat 'em like cabbages, and you won't go wrong.' I am glad to say that I was suffering from a major onslaught of butterflies at the time and I found it quite impossible to follow this particular oracle's advice — with the result that although my nerves continued unabated, when the occasion finally arrived, I did not make the fatal mistake of 'talking down' to the audience. They are *not* cabbages; *neither are they ravening, blood-seeking monsters hell-bent on the kill* — they are a perfectly ordinary

103

collection of human beings and, bearing in mind the unique command position of the speaker, should be treated as such.

The speaker who quantifies his fears, instead of floundering aimlessly in a sea of misgivings, will recognise that his audience will be composed of individuals. Some will be interested in what he has to say and will show it; some will be disinterested and even apathetic — and again will show it. Some, with strong feelings ranging across the entire spectrum of interest, will remain impassive, and, who knows, one or two may even drop off to sleep. The speaker who has something of value to say, and who recognises his audience for what they are and not what he imagines them to be, is well on the way to accepting pre-speaking nerves as a peculiar and unavoidable form of sheer excitement — lay back and enjoy it!

*Recognise the dangers of compulsive rehearsal*  An acute attack of the jitters, usually of the type that manifests itself in actual physical pain, often compels the unfortunate speaker to engage in a frenzy of rehearsal — thereby triggering a vicious circle of the very worst order. Desperately seeking an escape from his anxiety maze, the victim takes refuge in the old and sometimes misleading adage that practice makes perfect, and plunges headlong into a series of interminable and entirely counter-productive rehearsals. The most trivial errors assume major proportions, and inevitably a state of near panic ensues. Once again, it is absolutely vital that the intending speaker conducts a dispassionate examination of the reasons for his fear — when, on very many occasions, he will realise that compulsive rehearsal is strictly for the birds and most certainly not a solution to his troubles.

*Recognise the perils of acting a part*  Plainly, the entire fabric of this affliction we call 'nerves' is permeated by one root cause: the conviction that one's personality or general make-up is inadequate to the task of delivering a public address. Some folk, anxiously seeking a way round the problem, come up with the foolhardy decision to 'act the part', either by attempting to copy the gestures and mannerisms of a more proficient speaker or, probably worse, by inventing a character. Rehearsals, instead of being used for the correct purpose of checking content presentation, timing and whatnot, are devoted to terribly amateur and ludicrous acting exercises — and the intending speaker is well and truly on the slippery path to disaster. Some years ago I had the misfortune to witness a classic example of this type of thing, when the speaker concerned had obviously decided to cast himself in a Churchillian mould — and the result was little short of bad pantomime. He was a scrawny chap, endowed by his Maker with a very prominent Adam's apple and a high-pitched voice, and there he was, trying to screw his thin face into a semblance of the British Bulldog look and attempting, totally without success, to produce Winstonian growls from a piping larynx. The ghastly thing was that shortly after he had started his presentation, he realised the enormity of his tactical blunder — but it was too late.

The moral is obvious — never allow an onset of butterflies or anything else, for that matter, to persuade you that mimicry and invention will improve a speaker's personality. They won't.

## A look at 'on-stage' heebie-jeebies

Thus far I have attempted to highlight some aspects of *pre*-speaking nerves, but what of the presentation itself? Tossing convention to the four winds, I would like to start by disposing of one particularly hoary old belief: namely, that in the case of inexperienced speakers, nerves do *not* vanish in a puff of smoke once an address has commenced. Yes, I know that one hears the traditional cry from the heart, 'I felt terrible beforehand, but once I had got going, everything was fine!' — but, believe me, the jitters are there, all the time, up to their nasty little tricks. The fact is that once the nervous speaker has started his spiel, his attention is distracted — he no longer has the time to *think* about his butterflies. Remember also that such comments are invariably made immediately after the event, when the subject is almost euphoric with relief that the damned thing is over and done with — it is relief, itself, that is talking. No, nerves continue throughout the presentation; it is merely that in many cases they go under-ground, forming a woefully efficient fifth column which is primarily responsible for many of the gaffes and errors which occur. But back to the start of the address. . . .

*An effective opening palliative for nerves* For many speakers the worst part of the proceedings is the first few seconds; that is to say, coping with the deadly hush of audience anticipation or, as sometimes happens, wondering how best to deal with and break through the general hubbub of a less caring group. For those speakers who suffer 'opening qualms', I strongly recommend the following drill:

1    Make a slow, deliberate entrance (or stand up in a leisurely, controlled manner).
2    Take time to visibly and slowly adjust to the surroundings, and if using notes, take time — even when it is unnecessary — to 'adjust' them.
3    Take a pleasant and leisurely look at the audience — allow the eyes to take in the whole scene — and pay particular attention to those who are holding any form of conversation.
4    If at a rostrum, for instance, take time to remove your watch and place it within view.
5    When *you* are ready — why, think about starting!

When carrying out this opening drill, always remember that the accent is on 'taking time'. To the nervous speaker a seemingly interminable pause will, in reality, only constitute a few seconds, so *really* take time.

*Just a wee dram to steady the nerves* Speaking as an ardent devotee of God's own, twelve-year, finest malt, it hurts me more than a little to say that whilst a drop (or two, or three) works wonders for the nerves, the same drop (or two, or three) taken immediately before a speech may have a pretty devastating effect — an effect which, like drinking and driving, will probably remain unnoticed by the speaker but be painfully obvious to others. So, nervous speaker, beware of the jabberwock and refrain from slurping too much of that delectable claret.

*Fighting the fidgets*   Probably the most widely encountered characteristic of a full dose of speaking heebie-jeebies is the unconscious compulsion to fiddle and fidget. We have all witnessed the coin-jangler, whose pearly words of wisdom are punctuated by clanks and clangs as he carries out a concrete-mixing job on a half-pound of loose metal in the trouser pocket. We have been fascinated by the cuff-jerker and sleeve-twitcher and, above all, by the trouser-hitcher — the poor guy who is convinced that Mother Earth's gravitational attraction will have the pants off him in a flash unless he engages in a constant tug-of-war. There are many varieties of '*homo fidgetans*' — take, as a further instance, the Dave Allen syndrome, when the hapless speaker has obviously been invaded by a plague of ants. Then there are the knee-benders, the pencil-pointers, the head-nodders and the agonising leg-twisters, who always succeed in giving the impression that they have a desperate need for the cloakroom.

What on earth does one do? At one public-speaking course, run by a suave chappie who had obviously had his nerve-ends pulled at birth, the advice was quite simply, 'Conquer fidgeting by standing to a relaxed position of attention'. Have you ever tried to stand at a relaxed position of attention when delivering a public address? The truth is that fidgeters are born to fidget, but, for goodness sake, try not to do it too much! The nervous speaker should rid himself of loose change in the trouser pocket, wear those old-fashioned things called braces, check beforehand that his flies *are* as decorum dictates and, above all, remember that normal clothes stay normal, even when speaking in front of an audience.

*Don't be a hypnotist. . . .*   It sometimes happens that a nervous speaker, having commenced his address, is wont to scan the audience in an anxious search for a friendly pair of eyes. Having located two such luminous orbs, he then proceeds to address himself to their owner throughout the entire presentation, to the total exclusion of the rest of the audience. Lord be praised, he has found a pal in his time of need. The poor fellow concerned, wondering what on earth he has done to merit such undivided attention, is either mesmerised by the speaker's unbroken gaze or just plain annoyed. The remainder of those present, since they are being virtually ignored, are not kindly disposed towards the speaker and break into a multitude of fidgets and whispers — and the damage is done. Be ruthless and stamp on this nervous characteristic right from the outset. Remember that each and every member of the audience is entitled to, and expects, his fair share of the speaker's attention — and, by jingo, if it is not forthcoming, there will be trouble.

*The agony of verbal tics*   The nervous habit of punctuating an address with innumerable 'ers' or regional equivalents, such as the dreaded words 'you know', can succeed in infuriating some, if not all, of the audience. My personal and current affliction is beginning every second sentence with the word 'now', and it is a positive curse. The only possible way to effect a cure is to remind oneself continually that the habit is there, and must be conquered. Now — what's next. . . .

*More on the question of being 'in command'* It is vital for the nervous speaker to recognise the immense, tactical advantage of being 'out front'. Whatever his qualms and whatever the occasion — heckling and hostile meetings excluded of course — the speaker has open access to a potential command situation, and he should not allow his nerves to tell him otherwise. This is not to say that he has a licence to be rude, overbearing or act the sergeant-major, but rather that he uses all the speaking talents at his disposal to steer the event and the audience in the direction he chooses, at the pace he sets and in the manner he prescribes. *This is what public speaking is all about* — nerves will tell you otherwise, and should not be believed.

*Verbal diarrhoea* 'I don't want to be doing this, but I'm stuck with it — let's get it over as quickly as possible!' Many a nervous speaker thinks thus, and the scene is set for yet another audience to be smothered in an avalanche of verbal debris. The usual outcome of galloping willy-nilly through a presentation is that mistakes and clangers increase ten-fold, and as a consequence nervous tension approaches a shrieking crescendo, the speaker feels like a stretcher-case and the audience suffers the torture of the damned. More of this anon — for the moment, suffice it to say that the fatal temptation to hurry the thing along must be resisted at all costs; it invites disaster.

## To sum up and sweeten the pill

As I intimated at the beginning of this tale of woe, there is no complete cure for nerves, and in one important sense this represents a tremendous advantage. A dose of nerves means that the bloodstream is enjoying more than its usual share of adrenalin — and adrenalin, remember, is the five-star producer of that vital stuff, *energy*. Do not fritter away this marvellous commodity on wringing hands, getting into a flap or calling on your God, but, far better, use the additional energy at your disposal to *strengthen your presentation*. Get in there and floor 'em!

## Self-tutorial (Part One)

This is going to take a little bit of doing, but stick with it! Firstly, prepare an address on *one* of the following subjects:

What I'd do in the house, if I had my way. . . .
My personal failings and weaknesses
Why I'm a difficult person
Family life

Now — having carefully chosen an appropriate time (*not* when the family is watching a favourite television programme or when you are in bad favour with them), *announce without warning* that you are going to deliver an address on so-and-so — *and stand at the end of the room and do exactly that.*

## Self-tutorial (Part Two)

The ideal way to live with nerves is to get used to them. Prepare an effective address on a relevant and interesting topic for one of the following audiences:

The Boy Scouts (or Girl Guides)
The Combined Cadet Force (or Air Training Corps, Sea Cadets, etc.)
The local youth club
The local church fellowship
Or some other, local youth organisation

Then, contact the organisation concerned and offer to go along and give the address. They will welcome your gratuitous assistance.

De l'audace, encore de l'audace, et toujours de l'audace!
Boldness, more boldness, and perpetual boldness!
**Georges Jacques Danton (1759-1794)**
*Speech, 2 September 1792*

# 12
# Surveying a sea of faces — and winning

A requirement to speak in public can come about in one of two ways. It can be a planned event, known well in advance or, horror of horrors, it can be the 'sudden death', the commitment that hurtles over the poor victim's horizon in thirty seconds flat. To the inexperienced speaker the planned event is bad enough, but the unexpected invitation — or as is so often the case, the inescapable command — to get up there and do one's impromptu best is far worse. This chapter sets out to provide some hope and, if the gods smile on us, a spot of help to meet both of these contingencies.

## The planned event

### Reconnaissance pays off

A good general never enters battle without surveying the terrain, and the speaker should always try to inspect the venue of a planned presentation before the event.

*Acoustics can kill* Some years ago I was asked to deliver an address to an audience of motor traders (and, believe me, audiences don't come more hard-headed than that), and although I had been given ample notice of the event, I failed to take the trouble to spy out the land in advance. There was no real excuse for this, but plenty of reasons — the venue was miles away, the weather was awful, I knew my subject pretty well and, surmounting everything, I was clear up to the gunnels with burgeoning self-confidence. On turning up at the appointed hour — no, I did not even bother to arrive early — I discovered that my *tour-de-force* was to be presented in one of those time-scarred, Victorian monstrosities known as a 'public hall'. You can imagine the type of place I mean — dark, dank corridors leading to an even darker hall, nooks and crannies moribund with a century of undisturbed grime, a creaking, wooden-planked stage which made one's footsteps sound like the Four Horsemen of the Apocalypse and, you've guessed it, the whole ghastly place endowed with the acoustics of Kings Cross Station. Having been introduced — which was a bit of a misnomer, for in the all-enveloping gloom of this mausoleum, I could only discern a third of the audience — I commenced my presentation. Then it happened.

As I pronounced my fifth and sixth words, the first and second bounced back at me with almost undiminished volume — I was at the mercy of an almighty and unrelenting echo. I spoke at the ceiling (I couldn't see the damned thing, but I spoke at it), I spoke at the audience, I spoke to one side and then the other — all to no avail, for that echo was everywhere. What made things worse was that whilst I had to bear the brunt of this devilish reverberation, by some further acoustical quirk, half the audience could not hear a word I said. So the moral must be — check out the acoustics and, when checking, ensure that the seating is positioned as it will be when you deliver your address, for this can make all the difference in the world.

*Is the stage set to your advantage?* A preliminary visit — provided of course that His Majesty the caretaker has laid out all the bits and pieces — will enable you to assess the pro's and con's of your *speaking position*. The presence of an angled rostrum can be of great comfort, a hidey-hole for voluminous notes and a Rock of Gibraltar shield between you and the audience — but is it situated in the best position for your address? Are there any other 'props' that need your attention? A friend of mine was once saddled with giving an address at a hotel, and although he inspected the venue, he failed to attach any significance at all to the long, cloth-covered table at the rear of the room concerned. Halfway through his presentation, a bevy of hotel staff suddenly trooped in with trays of crockery and started to lay out all the gubbins for coffee-break — 'Well, as I was saying, ladies and gentlemen (*tinkle, rattle*), the object of the expedition (*rattle, crash*) was primarily concerned with (*crash, tinkle*). . . .' Yes, check *all* the props, and plonk your foot down with some firmness if anything requires changing.

*Get some information on the audience* A planned presentation often permits the good tactical advantage of learning something about the prospective audience. Will it be a group of intellectuals, a band of shop-floor workers, an audience of hard-core opponents to whatever it is you intend to dish up? What will be the general circumstances in life of the audience? Remember the certain Secretary of State who, when addressing a group of Newcastle unemployed, concluded his informal spiel with the sterling words, 'Well, I don't know about you chaps — but I must go, I've got work to do. . . .' The intending speaker must concern himself with level and style of delivery — for, plainly, twenty rows of eggheads may not take so kindly to the brand of rollicking humour and blunt speech perhaps better reserved for lesser (and more human) mortals.

Will the audience be conscripted for the occasion or will they be volunteers? If the latter, could it be possible, Lord help us, that they will have *paid* to get in? If so, you had better be good. . . . Will the audience be largely male or female, young or old? Last but not least, what size of audience is destined to hear your sterling words? There is little use going to all the trouble of planning an effective presentation if you are completely in the dark over the size of the audience — an informal, 'intimate' approach will work wonders with a small band of listeners, but you try it in a vast hall with an audience in the hundreds. Style of delivery, volume, extent and type of visual aids (for which, see Chapter 15) will all be dictated by the size of the audience, so give much thought to this very important consideration.

## Comes the appointed hour

*The question of dress*   It is difficult to give better advice than the oft-repeated words, 'dress for the occasion'. But dress is an essential weapon in the speaker's armoury, and it merits more than four words of homily. In these days of casual wear and freedom of individual expression — which, funnily enough, has resulted in the emergence of an army of identical blue jeans — the dictates of dress do not press as firmly on the speaker's perspiring brow, but there is still a need for a modicum of caution. First impressions count, and linger. I recall attending a dinner at which evening dress was the order of things — marvellous affairs, these, great gaggles of elderly gentlemen with pot-bellies, up to the ears in starch, looking and walking like king penguins — when this business of first impressions reared its ugly head. One speaker must have patronised Liberace's tailor, for he turned up in quite the most dazzling, lace-bedecked, Palladium-style outfit I have ever seen — with the immediate result that an almost audible quiver of outrage rippled through the assembled throng. The guy's speech was very good, but the damage had been done — the man was a 'damned upstart', etcetera and so on. I should add that he was not in the least bit worried by the stir he had caused — bully for him — *but he was a professional*. The inexperienced speaker could well have been dismayed by the very tangible atmosphere of disapproval. Dress for the occasion. . . .

*The all-important opening*   The time has come, the introduction is over and you are on your feet. Hopefully you have followed my earlier tip and have gone through the leisurely business of adjusting notes, wrist-watch and whatnot — now you merely have to open your mouth. I am not a very original thinker, and when wondering what to mention at this stage, I blush to admit that the words, '. . . unaccustomed as I am to public speaking . . .' crossed my mind. However, I

111

am quite convinced that no one would dream of committing this hackneyed gaffe — or would they? Just in case, and for the perishing record, let me say that this form of apology and all other forms of apology *are entirely verboten, forbidden and just not done.* The speaker who, at the start of his address, offers an apology for his lack of skill is handing his audience an open and tempting invitation for the gathering to start looking for faults — and look they will. The effective speaker will waste no time on preliminary chit-chat; he will give a pleasant thank you (and I mean just those two words) to the person who introduced him and, without further ado, will launch into his spiel.

*An adjustment of volume*    A frequent hallmark of the inexperienced speaker is his failure to adjust the volume of his voice to suit the requirements of the audience. Adequate volume is not only essential to the success of a presentation, it is the essence of good speaking manners — and no amateur can afford to be rude. Fortunately there is a method for ensuring that one speaks loud enough to suit any occasion, and I would like to recommend it to your attention. The drill is very simple; before commencing the address — or, at the latest, during the first few sentences — take a quick peep at the rear wall of the room or hall and, in the mind's eye, picture it at a position half as far away again as it actually is, *and then speak to that position.* So if the hall is, say, 60 feet in length, the speaker with an eye (or ear) for volume will be speaking to suit an imaginary distance of 90 feet. Take my word for it, it seems to work.

*Keep 'em all in view*    I make no apology for repeating my earlier advice on the question of scanning *all* of the audience *all* of the time. Every single person present is entitled to the benefit of your gaze, and it is lazy and tactically foolish to ignore anyone.

*The question of asking questions*    If the occasion is suitable and the subject warrants it, the audience should be encouraged to ask questions. Since a public address is not a seminar, it is usually best to deal with questions at the end of a presentation, and it is a sound tactic to make this quite plain from the word go. In fact, it is possible, by careful choice of words, to make the point about questions *and* impress the audience at the same time:

> 'I will welcome your questions at the end of the session and look forward to any comments you may care to make. It will be refreshing to have a spot of two-way discussion — so let's have your queries, and since I'm a big boy now, if I don't know the answers, I'll jolly well say so. . . .'

Note, if you will, that the speaker has acknowledged possible weaknesses of knowledge, but he has *not* apologised.

When question time arrives, be a little crafty, and without giving the impression of being a crawler, greet the odd question — even of the inept variety — with a slow, understanding nod and such words as, 'That's quite an interesting point. . .'. The tactic of treating members of the audience as if they are making valuable contributions to the session, which they may well be, is a powerful string in the bow of the canny speaker.

*Don't subject 'em to a lingering death*  Many inexperienced speakers find it difficult to 'switch off' at the end of a presentation, and as a consequence audiences find themselves subjected to bottom-wriggling and tedious sessions of listening to utterly tortuous perorations:

> 'Well, er, thank you, ladies and gentlemen, that is about all I have to say. . . .' *(Thank God, breathes a tired audience)* 'I, er, seem to have finished earlier than I, er, intended — perhaps there is someone who would like to ask a question. . . ?' *(Not on your Nelly)* 'Oh, well — in that case, I had better, er — thank you all for listening to me — I, er, hope that I've made everything clear. . . .' *(Visibly wrenches himself from the audience's hypnotic glare)* 'Er, thank you again — and, er — goodbye. . . .' *(Sits down with a bump and a clatter, red of face and perspiring overall)*

And so on.

It seems to be a horrible fact of speaking life that the worse the performer, the longer it takes the poor creature to say his piece, shut up and sit down. There is absolutely no need to preface this simple bending of the knees with a great rigmarole of staccato and awkward 'winding-down' phrases. If the speaker feels — or, Lord forbid, knows beyond a doubt — that his offering has failed, no amount of trying to make friends with the audience at the end of the fiasco will help his cause. Good *or* bad, the clean break is the answer:

> 'That's all I have to say — thank you for listening'. *(And sit down)*

## The impromptu event

I need hardly mention that where inexperienced speakers are concerned, the best way to deal with impromptu addresses is to avoid them. However, life is not like that, and sooner or later (and always sooner than one thinks), there comes the dreaded and inescapable moment. So — prepare for it, for there is a way.

When attending any function that carries the slightest risk of being required to deliver an impromptu address, select in advance a simple message or thought which is wholly appropriate to the occasion, for example:

> *Harry's retirement dinner*  'Some people profit from retirement.'

Having selected the message, think up another way of saying it:

> 'Some folk retire, switch off and quickly fade away.'

Then give the message a further twist:

> 'A happy few — those with imagination and a yen to achieve — look upon retirement as the "great beginning", a licence for opportunity.'

Now add a punch-line:

'Harry is one such person.'

It merely remains to prepare a couple of reasons why dear old Harry is the retirement hot-shot of the year, and, bingo, you have an adequate skeleton for an 'impromptu' speech. If shoved into the hot-seat, you will be in a position to deliver a short — remember, always short — and effective address.

Of course, there will be occasions when one has not been able to undertake any preparation, however minimal, but the drill is still the same. Swiftly choose a simple message, and then:

Deliver it
Give it the first twist
Give it the second twist
Deliver the punch-line
Add a couple of supporting reasons
Wish thanks, encouragement or good luck as appropriate
And *sit down*

## The grand art of toasting

It sometimes happens that having been conscripted into attending a formal shindig, an inexperienced speaker is required to pay in blood for his *coq au vin ordinaire* by proposing, or replying to, a toast. A common result is that the poor victim sits through several courses of apparent mish-mash in an agony of apprehension, shooting his cuffs every tenth second and wishing that he was dead. The wish is seldom, if ever, granted and — like the great, big saw — the dreaded moment comes nearer and nearer. But it need not be a dreaded moment, for much of this very real fear is born out of ignorance of the toasting game. The speaker who gets to know the procedure on such occasions will find himself basking in that sterling side-product of knowledge, confidence. Let us try to work the oracle.

### Proposing a toast

The really formal session will entail the services of that major-domo of ceremonial lick-spittling, the toastmaster. The task of this imperious and awe-inspiring functionary is to call the rabble to order and organise the speaking. When the time arrives, usually at the coffee stage, the toastmaster — readily identified by his John Peel tails and, more often than not, half-hundredweight of medals — checks that the speaker is ready for the fray, calls for order and, in ringing tones, announces the speaker's name:

*Toastmaster* *(CRASH goes the gavel)* 'YOUR ROYAL HIGHNESS, Your Excellencies, my LORDS, Ladies and Gentlemen, PRAY SILENCE FOR Mr Montgomery SPLATT, who will propose the toast of. . . .'

The wily speaker who has not bothered to memorise the correct form of address for the gathering can thus take heart, for he has only to repeat the toastmaster's words to be entirely correct:

> *Speaker   (Rising and calmly surveying the assembly)*  'Your Royal Highness, Your Excellency, my Lords, Ladies and Gentlemen, it is my very great pleasure to. . . .'

To *what?* Take heart, for there is a procedure:

1   The speaker stands up and completes the correct form of address.
2   He then proceeds with the phrase, '. . . it is my very great pleasure to propose a toast to our honoured guest, Ted Grunt.'
3   The speaker should now say something nice about friend Grunt and, if possible, make his comment suit the occasion. The accolade should be brief; two or three minutes can be a hell of a long time.
4   Finally, the speaker concludes the business by issuing the executive word of command, '. . . and I now ask you to rise and join me in the toast to TED GRUNT.'

If there is no toastmaster present, the speaker will have the additional task of calling for silence and, of course, ensuring that he delivers the correct form of address, for which some preliminary enquiries may be necessary.

## Wedding toasts

The wiles of Bacchus should not be permitted to disrupt the order of toasts at a wedding:

1   An old friend proposes the toast to the bride and groom.
2   The groom replies on behalf of his wife and himself — to the usual accompaniment of leery grins and ribald comment.
3   The groom then proposes a toast to the bridesmaids.
4   The best man replies.
5   The best man then proposes a toast to the parents.

## Replying to a toast

The reply to a toast is a fairly straightforward affair and should be moulded on the following pattern:

1   Give adequate thanks — taking care not to gush forth with over-fulsome thanks — for the wishes expressed in the toast.
2   Express pleasure, where relevant, at being invited to participate in the gathering.
3   If required, wish all good luck and success to the people or organisation concerned.
4   If the occasion demands and your wit permits, tell a short story relevant to the event — remembering that *your* joke-of-the-year may be *their* ancient history.

**Self-tutorial (Part One)**

## A GENERAL QUIZ ON THE PRECEDING CHAPTER

**Answers**

**Questions**

1  Why is it dangerous for a speaker to apologise for his lack of skill or knowledge?

1  Because an audience, being human, will tend to react against the weak member of the herd, and look for the speaker's faults and weaknesses

2  How may a speaker 'adjust for volume'?

2  *(a)* Assess length of the room
*(b)* Add 'half as much again'
*(c)* Adopt a volume suited to the new 'imagined length'

3  Why is a preliminary inspection of a speaking venue essential to the success of the occasion?

3  In order to assess:
*(a)* The acoustics of the venue
*(b)* The seating arrangements (adequacy, tactical positioning, etc.)
*(c)* Arrangements 'on the stage'

4  Why should a speaker (and, note, this does not apply where lecturers or instructors are concerned — for which, see later in this book) refrain from making long-winded concluding remarks?

4  Simply because his message — his subject — is *over and done with* and protracted farewells will *not* gild the lily; they will make things much worse

5  What is the drill for delivering an impromptu address?

5  *(a)* Select and deliver a chosen message
*(b)* Give the message in another form
*(c)* And another. . . .
*(d)* Apply one form of the message to the proceedings — the punch-line
*(e)* Give a couple of supporting reasons — or expansions of the theme
*(f)* Give closing thanks or good wishes

## Self-tutorial (Part Two)

Practise the 'impromptu speech drill' by applying it to the following subjects —
remember, you need three message 'versions', some form of punch-line, and a
couple of supporting reasons or facts:

Your favourite hobby or pastime
A strongly-held political conviction
A favourite hate
Marriage

Make a point of completing this exercise *verbally* — for this will help to cement
your experience when it comes to the real, impromptu thing.

The gallery in which the reporters sit has
become the fourth estate of the realm.

**Thomas Babington Macaulay (1800-1859)**
*Historical Essays*

# 13

# Speak to the Press —
# not on your life!

One of the finest ways to set Mr Manager's nerves tingling — to thoroughly
upset his executive metabolism and convince him that he is a candidate for the
corporate chopping-block — is to require him to speak to the gentlemen of the
press. With the notable exception of those slightly terrifying and amoral
androids from the public relations office and, of course, certain members of
senior management who do it for kicks, we do not exactly relish the thought of
acting as 'company spokesman'. Little scenarios tend to come to mind:

*Managing director* 'John, there's a chap from the press coming at ten o'clock
about the Williams affair — I'd like you to deal with him, please.'
*Manager - shortly to be Manager, RIP* 'Er, yes — certainly, Brian. I'll get on to
it right away. . . .'
*Managing director* 'Good — but hold on a minute. Remember, we want to
take the usual company line — an investigation is currently under way,
and until the findings are known, we have no comment to make. Watch
points, there's a good chap — we can't afford another blow-up in the press
after last month's fiasco. . . .'
*Manager (Nods wisely as expected of him)* 'No, indeed, Brian — I'll do
exactly as you say. Now — if you'll excuse me. . . .' *(Scurries away to do his
master's bidding)*

*The next morning – same scene, same people, different climate*

*Managing director   (Purple with fury – brandishing newspaper)* 'You've seen this? What the hell is going on? I told you quite clearly — yesterday, in this very office — there was to be *no comment!*

*Manager   (Sadly perplexed and quietly hysterical)* 'I cannot understand it — I didn't *make* any comment. . . .'

*Managing director* 'Then how, may I ask, do you explain this glaring head-line, "Company spokesman fails to deny allegations", eh?'

*Manager* 'But that's just it — you told me not to make any statement — and I didn't. . . .'

*Managing director* 'My God — am I surrounded by idiots? Can't you even see what you've done? You've succeeded in making the company look thoroughly guilty. . . .'

*Manager* 'But, surely. . . .'

*Managing director* 'But nothing — I absolutely refuse to spell it out for you. I gave you a simple job to do, and look at the result! For goodness sake, get out of my sight!' *(Manager retires to oblivion, kissing anticipated promotion farewell)*

\*   \*   \*

*Arthur Carruthers, managing director, seated at the breakfast table, remains transfixed as – with egg-spoon poised in mid-air and yolk dripping on his trousers – he reads a newspaper report.*

### 'HUNTINGDON HITLER' SACKS GIRLS AFTER OFFICE PARTY

A managing director who dismissed seven female office workers from his company at Huntingdon, because they held a pre-Xmas office party was ordered yesterday to pay them a total of £2,300 compensation. But after the industrial tribunal, he said, 'They call me the Hitler of Huntingdon, but I don't care. I am not going to have drinking orgies in my company, whether it is Christmas or not. I have told my workers they can have parties in their own time, but not mine.'

Mr Arthur Carruthers, who told the tribunal that he strongly disapproved of 'young girls in advanced states of inebriation', agreed under cross-examination that the seven workers had only consumed one glass of sherry each, but stated, 'One thing can lead to another, if you know what I mean'.

Mr Rory French, area official of the General and Municipal Workers' Union, told the tribunal, 'We have, in Mr Carruthers, an extraordinary and positively Dickensian example of a boss who, in some miraculous way, has survived the demise of the dark, satanic mill and still contrives to wield his bigoted axe.' When asked by our reporter about the union official's views, Mr Carruthers said, 'You people are all the same; you are trying to make something out of nothing.'

> *Carruthers* *(Addressing his wife with spluttering voice)* I'll sue them — that's what I will do — it's a disgrace, a scandal. . . . What are you laughing at?'

## Acting as the company spokesman

Like it or not, a manager's responsibilities extend beyond the perimeter of his day-to-day operations within the four walls of his company — for in accepting a slice of the corporate cake, however meagre that portion may be, he assumes two further obligations:

1 A duty to protect and enhance his company's image at all times.
2 A share in the organisation's social and moral responsibilities to the community at large.

From time to time, certain of us are required to discharge these obligations by dealing with the press, and provided the ground rules are followed, this need not be the horrific business it is sometimes painted.

*Developing an eye to a situation* It should be remembered that the facts of a matter as they appear to the company or the people involved are not always the facts that a journalist will want or print. Hence the inexperienced spokesman (and the similarly undiscerning boss) may be vastly put out when a grandly announced and significant company event fails to make the headlines — particularly if a story about young Susie, the office girl, and her collection of boa constrictors, is spread all over the front page. However much the pontiffs of senior management and their acolytes may disagree, the reporter sets out with one aim in mind — to find out and print that which will attract the reader's eye, to pinpoint and publish *news*. It therefore behoves the company spokesman to climb inside the skin of the journalist and view a situation with the reporter's eye, not his tunnel-visioned own.

*Learn the style* Journalists write in a certain way, and the manager who wishes to prepare himself for encounters with the press will study the very individual styles employed by the newspapers with which he is likely to come into contact. He will then gain at least an inkling of *how* to say his piece to ensure accurate reporting and a minimum wielding of the editor's blue pencil.

*Get to like 'em, they're only human, after all* Watch any television news programme and the odds are that sandwiched between gory shots of the latest killing and hospital scandal-of-the-week, one's tired old eyes will be greeted with yet another example of television's most tedious and banal news item. I refer, of course, to those countless occasions when slightly frayed and desperate news reporters attempt to waylay politicians and titled adulterers in a usually vain effort at extracting off-the-cuff and juicy statements. A goodly proportion of

120

these so-called public figures deliver their 'no comment' replies with a degree of over-the-shoulder rudeness that belies their station in life and does them little in the way of personal credit. Sadly, there is a tendency for the inexperienced company spokesman to emulate this graceless attitude and deal with reporters in a po-faced, condescending manner — to treat them as if they were faintly smelly members of some off-beat and uncultured hoi polloi. A grain of courtesy costs nothing and can pay handsome dividends when speaking to reporters — for, remember, *they* may have the last laugh.

## Dealing with the impromptu occasion

Firstly, be honest — exactly how often does the impromptu occasion arise? The manager who returns red-faced from the industrial tribunal, muttering vengefully that he has been ambushed by reporters — the irate boss who, having made half of his work-force redundant, fulminates over the attentions of the local press, cannot in all honesty claim that they have been made the unwitting victims of a surprise encounter. Any company man worth his salt — which, of course and by all that is holy, means *you*, reader — will recognise any event which is likely to attract the eye of the press and plan accordingly.

However, there are always exceptions and any one of us is liable, probably when least expected, to be halted in our tracks by the ominous words, 'I'm from the Daily Gargler — do you have any statement to make on so-and-so. . . .' It is at such times that many a company innocent recalls the television shots of the high-and-the-mighty spitting those magic words, 'no-comment', and out they come, often with scant regard for the potential consequences. However stressful the time, however pressing the occasion — *pause and think hard*. Picture, if you can, the *whole* of the report as it may appear; consider the situation in its entirety, not merely the words you are about to utter. How will that terse line, 'a company spokesman declined to comment', fit into the general pattern of things — will it make the company look as guilty as hell? If you feel that you are totally unqualified to act as spokesman on behalf of your outfit, for goodness sake, *say so* and impress upon the reporter that under no circumstances are you to be regarded as such — but say it nicely. Remember also that having refused the dubious honour of spokesman, anything you say 'on the record' will be labelled as your personal opinion — and your boss may well view this as heresy. Note the handy value of the instruction, 'this is off the record', and its vital corollary, 'this is *on* the record'.

## Dealing with the press conference

In the context of this humble treatise, the term 'press conference' is probably a bit of a misnomer, for it implies mighty gatherings with newsmen from all points of the compass awaiting pronouncements from on high. All fine and dandy, but this kind of corporate cabaret will be stage-managed by the denizens of the public relations department. I am concerned with the downtown, across-the-tracks meeting with the press, the occasion when old Joe Higgins, doyen reporter of the local rag, is invited around for a noggin and a natter. Do not run away with the notion that I am belittling the low-key press conference by referring to it in this manner, for it is a supremely important occasion — after all, Joe could decide that the news is good enough to be 'put on the wire' and, bingo, fame at last.

The basic rule for any press conference is to present the news item, whatever it may be, in writing *and to be fully prepared for the questions which it will prompt*. There is absolutely no excuse for the manager who, having arranged a meeting with the press, finds himself facing unexpected questions and the heart-stopping prospect of having to provide off-the-cuff answers. Lest you doubt this pontification, consider the following checklist — a drill, if you like, for the planning of a press conference:

1 Is the news ready *in all respects* for publication, or are there 'grey areas' of doubt or contention? Reporters are adept at winkling out such aspects.
2 If there are grey areas, but notwithstanding, the decision is taken to go ahead, have *all* potentially awkward questions been taken into account — and answers prepared?
3 Have possible side issues been considered — and again have all possible questions been taken into account?
4 Has the press release been prepared correctly and in accordance with the style of the media for which it is intended?
5 Have the supplementary 'fact sheets' been prepared — i.e. history of the organisation, aims and objects, other background information which may be requested?
6 Have all the managers concerned with the conference:
   a thoroughly prepared their answers?
   b allocated responsibility for dealing with specific areas?
   c taken advantage of a pre-conference conference?
7 Are they all personable, friendly, expert guys?
8 Who is going to be boss?
9 Will the planned 'hospitality' be suited to the occasion? Bad or contentious news will not be helped by an over-liberal flood of whisky; it will merely confirm the reporters' fears.

## Self-tutorial (Part One)

There are very few company chappies who can place their hands on their hearts and state that they have never, ever been involved in some form of unpleasant disciplinary matter. Think in terms of one such occurrence and imagine that you have been tasked with the preparation of a press conference on the subject. Compose a suitable press release to be handed out at the conference (if in doubt about the mechanics of composing a press release, jolly well get a book from the library and find out how to go about it), and jot down all the 'awkward' questions that in the circumstances might be asked.

Then note down your answers.

If you wish to check your work, get a friend to act the role of reporter — hand him your press release and ask him to put as many nasty questions as possible . . .

## Self-tutorial (Part Two)

A practical exercise, this — one that could pay off. Visit your local newspaper and get to know the editor and his reporting staff. Remember that the local press-boys are always keen to learn of events and developments in local industry and commerce — try to come up with a project of some sort or another and report on it for them.

It's my opinion, sir, that this meeting is drunk.

**Charles Dickens (1812-1870)**
*Pickwick Papers*

# 14
# Meetings — and how to keep one's end up

'George, I'm glad that I've caught you — I wonder if I can have a quick word, it's rather urgent. . . .'

'So sorry, old chap, it'll have to wait — I'm already ten minutes late, I must dash. . . .'

Having uttered the classic words with an apologetic smile, George vanishes up the corridors of power in a puff of smoke, to play a further round in that greatest and most revered of organisation games, the meeting. Meetings are the life-blood — or as some may say, the thrombosis — of any organisation, and like it or not, commerce and industry cannot pretend to exist without them. It must be admitted, of course, that large chunks of certain outfits exist *because* of meetings — beautifully engineered, Quatermass-like hierarchies that use meetings to conceive and incubate infinitely effective methods of self-perpetuation. As an example, I call to mind that doyen of committees in the world of further education, the academic board. Junior only to the august board of governors in the technical college scheme of things, it shoulders the grand responsibility of 'advising on the planning, coordination, development and oversight of the academic work of the college'. Anyone worth his organisation salt knows that another name for an advisory committee is a castrated committee, and thus nobbled, the academic board soldiers on, rubber-stamping the efforts of others and solemnly ensuring, by means of a proliferation of sub-committees and working parties, that it defers sufficient items on each agenda to guarantee its perpetuity and wholly on-the-surface effectiveness. Lest you doubt that meetings are the spice of organisation life, take a crafty peep at local government, the civil service, any company — *your* company.

## Why meetings, anyway?

Why do pigs fly? Meetings are used, or so we are told, when it is found necessary to bring a number of different opinions and brands of expertise to bear on a particular project or problem. Whilst acknowledging the old adage which reminds us that a camel is a horse designed by a committee, we are urged by the management pundits to remember that meetings are prime vehicles for the transmission and swopping of advice and communication. We are also informed that meetings are a prime link in the chain of management life, that they provide a vital training ground for the participants — making them aware of the problems of others and, hey ho, giving them a first-class opportunity to solve them. Lastly, and this titbit is inscribed on the very tablet of organisation religion, we are told that meetings are the nestbed of corporate judgement, teamwork and wisdom. So — that is why we have meetings. . . .

## Is everything in the meeting garden wonderful?

Well, if it was, not only would the camel look a slightly different animal, but — to mention just a few examples — the National Health Service might be doing a bit more about health, school-leavers might be able to spell, the Ombudsman would be in the dole queue and, glorious thought, a legion of human blow-hards would be face down in the dung-heap. No, meetings have disadvantages. They are the stamping ground of that great order of management chivalry, the Buck-passing Brigade, and they are the seedbed of compromise. Meetings gobble up time like mad and prevent managers from doing what they are supposed to do — manage. They encourage irresponsibility, in that individual members can shift the blame for rotten, personal decisions — '. . . wasn't my doing, old fellow — I'm afraid it was a committee decision. . .'. But meetings are here to stay, so we had better see what makes 'em tick and, more to the point, examine ways and means of coping with the beastly things.

## The formal meeting

### The mighty rules of order

The rules of order which are adopted for the regulation of almost any meeting under the sun have sprung from that fountain-head of meetings, the English Parliament. Over the centuries and despite the immeasurable volume of hot air which has been generated in that hallowed place, there has emerged an imperishable system for the conduct of meetings — and woe betide the company chap who remains in ignorance of the holy law.

*Chairing the Chair*    The Chairman, the Shahanshah of the meeting, occupies the Chair — not an ordinary, common-or-garden chair, you understand, but *the* Chair, the *office* of the Chairman. The Chair, God bless its hand-carved legs, preserves decent order in a meeting and regulates its procedures by swatting recalcitrant members over the head with the rules of order.

When the Chairman's rear end is reposing on the Chair, he must remain completely impartial at all times and not engage in controversy. If the temptation is too much and he wishes to frolic or indulge in argument, then he must lever himself out of the Chair, thereby quitting his office in the twinkling of an eye, and assume the lowly mantle of an ordinary member. The rules of order require that the Chairman be addressed as 'Mr Chairman' or, of course, 'Madame Chairman' and not, as some would have it, as, 'Bill, you old cuss' or 'Mary, poppet'. In more formal circumstances, such as the bi-monthly meeting of the Slopthwaite District Council General Purposes Committee, the members will look straight at the Chairman and, figuratively speaking, wipe him off the face of the earth with such expressions as, 'If the Chair will forgive me . . .' or 'Through the Chair, I would like to say . . .'. This rather quaint custom of addressing a piece of furniture instead of the guy who is perched on it is, in fact, founded in good sense, for it strengthens and supports the rule that the Chairman, when in office, is sacrosanct and above mere human frailties. The rule has a further advantage in that when things get rough and members decide to vent their spleens on the Chairman, it can be fairly said that the Chair is getting it in the neck, and not the poor incumbent. All of which, of course, leads to a checklist for would-be chairmen:

1    Be impartial as a judge — refrain from speaking for or against a controversial motion.
2    Ensure that members behave themselves — do not permit them to engage in cross-conversations or argument; have everything addressed 'to the Chair'.
3    Be friendly (remember, you will not be Chairman for ever) — but be firm.
4    Be prepared to say to anyone, 'The Chair calls the speaker to order.'
5    Stick to the agenda like glue (more about this anon).

*Rising to the occasion*    The rules of order dictate that no member of the meeting may speak unless called upon or 'recognised' by the Chair. This business of rising to be recognised used to mean exactly that — a hasty clambering to the feet — but in these more enlightened times, it is usually sufficient (provided of course that the Chairman is looking your way) to give a languid wave of the hand. However, courtesy and the rules also dictate that only one speaker may perform at a time, so the fellow who is burning to pitch in with his verbal masterpiece may have to wait for recognition.

*Taking the floor*    This very British expression — heaven help the student of the English language — means simply that, having been recognised by the Chair, a member has the right to speak without interruption. (Or nearly always so, for there are certain privileged or emergency exceptions. For example, a member may interrupt a speaker on 'a question of privilege' — when, say, his character is being impugned or he cannot hear the speaker. He may legitimately interrupt on 'a point of order' — to remind the meeting that the speaker has transgressed the rules of order. Other examples include registering an appeal against a decision of the Chair — 'rising to a point of information' — when the member wishes to query that which the speaker has said — but the query must be sufficiently urgent as to warrant interruption — and to register an objection to a particular point or motion.)

The golden rules for taking and holding the floor are as follows:

1    Speak shortly and succinctly — observe any time limits that may be set.
2    Take care to avoid personal attacks on fellow-members — for despite the daily examples set by our beloved politicians, such chincanery is taboo, unless and until one has been personally impeached.
3    Let everything you say be relevant to the occasion.
4    Refrain from using language that is unsuited to the occasion.

*Putting motions*    The business of making, or putting, a motion could not be more simple:

George        *(Hand aloft)*  'Mr Chairman. . . .'
Chairman      *(Formal version)*  'The Chair recognises Mr Finch.'
              *(Informal version)*  'Yes, George — you have the floor. . . .'
George        *(Starts with a brief explanation)*  '. . . and I therefore move that so-and-so be done. . . .'
Chairman      *(Formal version)*  'Mr Finch has moved that so-and-so be done. Is there a seconder to the motion?'
              *(Informal version)*  'You've all heard George's motion — is there a seconder?'
Another member    'I second the motion.'
Chairman      *(Formal version)*  'It has been moved and seconded that so-and-so be done. Is there any discussion?'
              *(Informal version)*  'Fine — does anyone wish to comment?'

Note the requirement for the Chairman to refer a motion, once made and seconded, to the meeting for discussion. This formality is often the signal for all and sundry to plunge into violent and sometimes totally irrelevant debate — a testing-time for any Chairman. Every meeting has at least one member who has been vaccinated with a gramophone needle, and he must eventually be silenced, nicely but effectively. The Chairman will also have to cope with the frantic exploration and expounding of side issues and pet themes — there's a pretty job, but it has to be done.

*The sacred order of business*    The order of business — the list of items to be considered during a meeting — is set out and enshrined within that well-known document, the *agenda*. The format and content of an agenda will largely depend on the degree of formality of the meeting concerned, and it is likely that a completely informal meeting will proceed, or attempt to proceed, without one. Here is a fairly typical list of the contents to be found in an agenda for a formal meeting:

1  Apologies for absence.
2  Reading of minutes of the previous meeting (read by the secretary).
3  Matters arising from the previous minutes.
4  Reading of correspondence received (read by the secretary).
5  Opening comments by the Chairman.
6  Matters adjourned from the last meeting, if any.
7  Financial and other reports (treasurer's report, reports by sub-committees and working parties, etc).
8  Any election of officers to the committee.
9  Making, seconding and discussing various motions, when prior notice has been given.
10  Date of next meeting.
11  Any other business (see below).

The second point at which many meetings are liable to go completely haywire is when they arrive at the *'any other business'* stage of the agenda. Once again, the poor old Chairman may have to strive mightily to maintain order and sanity in the proceedings, remembering that 'any other business' is intended purely and simply as a means whereby *minor matters* can be raised. This section of the agenda is not a passport to freedom for artful Joe Bloggs to drop the bombshell of the day, for matters of importance should always be notified in advance. Note that by the time 'any other business' rears its head, most members of the meeting will be wriggling on their bottoms and anxious to get on with some real work. They should be allowed to do so.

## Speaking the language

To be successful at meetings, one has to speak the lingo. Here is a checklist of the most commonly used terms:

*Ad hoc*  Commonly misinterpreted as meaning 'casual', *ad hoc* means, in fact, 'special purpose'. Thus an *ad hoc* committee is not a random collection of bodies gathered together for some vague task, but a committee formed for a specific purpose.

*Addendum*  An amendment that tacks words on to a motion.

*Amendment*  This is a proposal to alter a motion by adding or deleting words. An amendment must be proposed, seconded and put to the meeting for acceptance.

*Casting vote*  This is a second vote usually allowed to the Chairman when, like Solomon, he can convert a stalemate vote into a decision. It is worth noting that some organisations hold the view that if the feeling against a motion is so strong that half of those voting are against it, the Chairman should use his casting vote to defeat the motion — thereby preserving the *status quo*.

*Closure* This is a motion submitted with the (usually desperate) object of ending an interminable or unwanted discussion.

*Co-option* The power given to a committee to allow others, usually with specialist knowledge, to serve on the body.

*Dropped motion* Simply a motion that has to be abandoned because there is no seconder or because the meeting wishes it to be dropped.

*Ex officio* A grandiloquent way of saying 'by virtue of office'. Hence an *ex officio* member of a committee attends the meetings by reason of his office, his position in the organisation.

*In attendance* People who have no right to be present at a meeting are said to be 'in attendance'. This does not refer to gate-crashers but, for example, to the secretary to the committee.

*In camera* Behind closed doors, in private.

*Intra vires* Within the power of the body concerned.

*Kangaroo closure* More power to the Chairman's elbow — the right of a Chairman to hop from one amendment to another omitting those which, in his wisdom, he considers to be trivial or time-wasting.

*Lie on the table* A document is said to 'lie on the table' when a meeting decides to do nothing about it.

*Nem. con.* Well, who would want to say '*Nemine contradicente*' when '*Nem. con.*' will do? It means 'No one contradicting'.

*No confidence* Things are taking a nasty turn for the worse when this term gets bandied about — the Chairman who aggrieves a substantial majority of the members may be ousted by a vote of 'no confidence'.

*Proxy* One member who acts for another, or the document that entitles a person to attend a meeting and vote on behalf of another.

*Quorum* A quorum is the number of persons required to be present for a valid meeting, and should be spelled out in the regulations of the committee concerned.

*Reference back* A favourite dodge of committees that wish to avoid a difficult issue is to 'refer the matter back' to some working party or other for further details. The practice must have originated in local government. . . .

*Resolution* A motion that has been carried.

*Sine die* Adjourned '*sine die*' — postponed for an indefinite period.

*Ultra vires* The opposite to '*intra vires*', meaning beyond the power or authority of the committee concerned.

## Informal meetings

Informal meetings will have few, if any, set rules of procedure and, of course, the term covers a multitude of sins. Essentially, an informal meeting is either a *discussion* (and we have covered this aspect in Chapter 6) or that instrument of management ecstasy, the *command meeting*. Now the pundits tell us that command meetings are called by managers for the dual purpose of obtaining information from subordinates and conveying the precious stuff to them — but all too often the accent falls on that magic word, 'command'. It is totally reprehensible for a manager to call a meeting of staff for the purpose of issuing instructions unless those who attend are permitted a fair opportunity to air their own views and recommendations. The reader who doubts this should canter straight back to Chapter 3, without passing 'Go' and without collecting £200. A sad extension of this failing is the command meeting called by the manager-coward who, having made some kind of a decision, wishes to shift some or all of the responsibility to the broad shoulders of his subordinates. Such a rapscallion will permit bags of opinions to be aired at the meeting, but the gesture will be completely hollow — for, whatever may be said, his mind is made up. Then at a later date if things go wrong as a result of his arbitrary decision, he will be in a position to console himself and others by calmly blaming his juniors for having failed to anticipate all the snags. Nasty. . . .

There is one type of informal meeting that deserves special mention, and that is the *sales meeting*. Let us imagine that the old-established firm of Spratweed and Belcher Limited wish to increase sales of their well-known cough lozenges, Phlum-Lumps. Let us also imagine, for a brief instant, that you, patient reader, are the sales director at S&B and that you have convened a sales meeting for the purpose of determining how to foist additional loads of Phlum-Lumps on an unsuspecting public. How effective will it be, do you think, if you open the meeting with, say, the words, 'The sales of Phlum-Lumps this year have been very disappointing, and I require your proposals for an improvement in this sad state of affairs'? The probability is that such a statement will be largely ineffective, because it fails to provide a sufficient definition of the problem. Your salesmen need to be stimulated into objective thought by the provision of, at least, some views on *why* sales are down — was it simply a case that the sales target was unrealistic, has a competing product entered the field, have there been fewer colds this year and an overall decrease in the sale of cough lozenges? An efficient and comprehensive review of the situation will encourage the members of your meeting to come up with their own, objective views and recommendations — for the problem will have been defined. Your next task as sales director-cum-chairman of this informal meeting will be to ensure that each proposer has an ample opportunity to say his piece before the matter is thrown open for discussion. You will be very busy at this stage for in addition to controlling the discussion, you will be noting down the salient details of each proposal and, from the points made in discussion, gathering together the bare bones of an evaluation of each suggestion. Your notes could well take the following form:

| | Proposal | Course of Action | Evaluation |
|---|---|---|---|
| 1 | Up-date the ads and packaging (BJ's proposal) | PR agency to produce new presentation | Possible cost £50,000 — high, but worthwhile |
| 2 | Change the name (HT's proposal) | PR to produce new presentation | Phlum-Lumps a household word — not on |

| 3 | Lower the price (My proposal) | Consult Production to see if possible | Good PR needed if adverse public reaction to be avoided — but remains good possibility |

and so on.

Having ensured that the group has explored all the avenues, you will conclude the meeting with a summary of all that has transpired and, since you are the sales director, some words of encouragement for your team.

Salesmen are very often the ballerinas of the business world — up in the air with the heady delights of success at one moment and down in the depths of gloom at the next. They are also and very naturally the first people to sense when they are being *given* a sales spiel. For these two reasons sales meetings should be handled with great care — remember the volatile nature of the average salesman and, above all, do not try to 'give him the gears', for you will earn his instant dislike.

## What are you like at meetings?

Being human, one of our favourite pastimes at meetings, is 'watching the other fellow'. Nasty little thoughts cross our minds:

> . . . just look at that idiot, Cribbins — dropping clanger after clanger. . . .
> . . . for goodness sake, why does she go on so. . . .
> . . . I'd never dream of saying a thing like that. . . .
> . . . he's obviously bucking for promotion. . . .
> . . . who does he think he's trying to impress. . . .

Bearing in mind that this is a universal game, it might be a better idea to give a thought to what *others* are thinking about *you*. So with hand on heart, take a long, cool look at yourself. Do you, for instance, exhibit the faintest resemblance to any of the following characters?

*The belligerent bulldozer* Often a 'self-made man', whatever that may mean, and inordinately fond of reminding everyone that 'he has come up the hard way'. This type is basically insecure and will attempt to cover the weakness by trampling underfoot anyone who dares to question his views. Usually of late middle-age, he tends to regard younger and more proficient colleagues with fearful suspicion, and if there is the faintest risk of being cornered in a discussion, he will resort to the well-worn ploy, '. . . of course, it's experience that counts.' Seldom a natty dresser, he is inclined to wear the same old suit day in and day out, a threat to the dry-cleaning trade and those unlucky souls who are destined to sit next to him.

*The eager idiot* This worthy, sometimes distinguished by an over-earnest expression, thinning hair and a constantly bobbing Adam's apple, is a bit of a menace at any meeting. Seldom proficient at his job and usually incapable of making any original contribution to the business in hand, he will strive to impress his colleagues — and, more particularly, the chairman — by the use of very transparent chicanery. His box of tricks includes arriving very early at a meeting, carrying armfuls of useless boomph, fixing every speaker with an intent stare and nodding furiously at every word, constantly interrupting with inane queries, and filling reams of scribbling paper with completely worthless notes. The eager idiot appears to favour ill-cut, brown suits underlaid with cardigans knitted by the little woman, and he sits through almost any meeting in a lather of nervous perspiration.

*The academic*    The only thing wrong with this character is the fact that he is unable to speak simply and succinctly about anything. Wrapping his over-active tongue smoothly and lovingly round such favourite words as ethos, homogeneity and infra-structure, he will complicate and prolong the most basic of issues — for in his erudite book, all conversations, and certainly all meetings, provide an ideal opportunity for academic discussion and debate. A disturbing individual who, at the flick of a verbal wrist, will provoke and annoy less gifted and infinitely more practical colleagues.

*The inarticulate sheep*    That's right, there is at least one of these impotent hobgoblins at every meeting. Scared stiff of expressing his own opinion and hellbent on going with the wind, he will agree to the execution of his own grandmother if it entails 'not making waves'. Watch him carefully as, faced with two powerful members who are arguing opposing points of view, he frantically endeavours to spot the winner — poised in the meantime on painful horns of dilemma, lest he should make a fatal mistake and toss a 'yes, I agree' in the wrong direction.

*The Jekyll-and-Hyde merchant*    This is the sinister professional in the art of treachery — the 'colleague' who, oozing friendship and sworn support prior to a meeting, calmly proceeds to slip a dagger between his unwitting comrade's ribs at the appropriate point on the agenda, and does it with a smile. Are you a corporate turncoat?

*The gas-bag*    The guy (or gal) with verbal diarrhoea, who goes on and on — and bloody on. To this hideous character a meeting represents one thing, a captive audience, and, boy, will he or she take advantage of it! Silenced only by the Chairman's gavel — preferably straight between the eyes — he waffles on and costs the organisation a fortune in terms of wasted time and energy. If, perchance, you find that people are constantly finding something urgent to do when you are in the middle of a chat, then it is likely that either you suffer from halitosis or, yes, you are a gas-bag. . . .

No resemblance at all, do I hear you say? Who is kidding whom?

## In conclusion

If you are looking for a simple recipe for keeping one's end up at meetings, I can do no better than offer the following:

Think up your piece
Say it simply
Say it succinctly
And shut up.

## Self-tutorial (Part One)

## A GENERAL QUIZ ON THE PRECEDING CHAPTER

**Answers**

**Questions**

1 What are the golden rules for good chairmanship?

1   *a*   Impartiality
     *b*   Efficient implementation of the rules of order
     *c*   Maintenance of a friendly, but firm, attitude
     *d*   Efficient control of the order of business

2 What is meant by 'taking the floor'?

2 Having been recognised by the Chair, exercising one's right to speak without interruption

3 What, if any, are the exceptions to the right to speak without interruption?

3 When an interruption is made:
     *a*   on a question of privilege
     *b*   on a point of order
     *c*   rising to a point of information
     *d*   to register an objection

4 What is meant by interruption on 'a question of privilege'?

4 When, say, a member cannot hear or understand the speaker, or when his character is being impugned by the speaker

5 What is meant by interruption on 'on a point of order'?

5 When the speaker has transgressed the rules of order

6 What is meant by interruption on 'rising to a point of information'?

6 When a member wishes to query anything which has been said by the speaker

7 What is meant by interruption to 'register an objection'?

7 When a member wishes to object to a particular point or motion

8 May a member interrupt a speaker in order to register an appeal against a decision of the Chair?

8 Yes, he may

9 What, normally, are the first three items on the meeting's order of business?

9   *a*   Apologies for absence
     *b*   Reading of minutes of the previous meeting
     *c*   Matters arising from the minutes

10 And the last two items?

| | |
|---|---|
| 10  *a*  Date of next meeting<br>    *b*  Any other business | 11  What is the meaning of 'Nem.<br>    Con.'? |
| 11  'No one contradicting' | 12  What is the meaning of 'Sine die'? |
| 12  Postponed for an indefinite time | 13  What is the meaning of 'co-<br>    option'? |
| 13  The power given to a committee<br>    to allow others, usually with<br>    specialist knowledge, to serve on<br>    the body | 14  What is the name of the paper<br>    which sets out a meeting's order<br>    of business? |
| 14  The agenda | |

## Self-tutorial (Part Two)

Beg, borrow or steal copies of current minutes from the office and examine them closely. Select at random various propositions, and from the dry information on the minutes, decide exactly how *you* would have spoken on the proposals. Use the following pointers as a yardstick:

1   Have you composed an effective introduction?
2   Is the body of your proposal wholly informative, short and succinct?
3   Finally, the 'formal proposal' — is it couched in telling, crisp terms?

## Self-tutorial (Part Three)

Using the same minutes, select a resolution and, using your imagination, compose a suitably telling argument which might have been offered *against* the proposal. Then ask yourself the following questions:

1   Is the argument crisp and to the point?
2   Does it anticipate side issues and deal with them effectively?
3   Does it pose questions in the minds of your imagined audience, and have you got impressive replies ready?
4   Is the argument complete?

Human history becomes more and more a race between education and catastrophe.

**H. G. Wells (1866—1946)**
*The Outline of History*

# 15
# It's not all chalk and talk

## A letter to a training manager

Dear Kenneth,

I was very pleased that as a result of your recommendation to the Chief Executive, I spent last weekend at your general managers' course on employment selection. In fact the skill of your department in timing my invitation to arrive on the Friday morning enabled my wife to share my pleasure, for it gave her the opportunity to chat over the telephone with various relatives as she cancelled our planned, but utterly unimportant, trip to Cornwall. I recall that just before we departed from the training centre late on Sunday evening, you asked course members to supply you with feedback on the weekend's activities, and I do hope that this letter will be of some help to you in planning future events.

Your decision to employ the 'total immersion' technique was absolutely capital, and I do not think that anyone could have chosen a more secluded venue for the course. In today's world of concrete and a shrinking countryside, it was quite refreshing to discover that the training centre was situated at least ten miles from the nearest main road — and the four miles of heavily rutted lane which led to the rendezvous merely added zest to the journey. Incidentally your decision that the inaugural dinner should commence promptly at 7 p.m. on Friday evening clearly took into account that we general managers are very busy on this last full working day of the week, and even though the drive for each participant was only in the region of 65-70 miles, I am sure that we all appreciated this most thoughtful timing on your part. I really must apologise, of course, for the fact that I contrived to miss dinner and only arrive during the Chief Executive's speech; this was entirely due to my carelessness in failing to discover prior to my journey that the map, so kindly provided with the joining instructions, was largely illegible. I expect that the other six members who arrived late for the same reason will be tendering their individual regrets.

It was exhilarating to be told at the conclusion of the Chief Executive's speech that the course would start straight away, particularly since it was then only 9 p.m. and the evening was still young. When you informed us that the first session would consist of impromptu, ten-minute lecturettes, with each participant being handed his topic on a slip of paper, I must admit that I entertained some initial doubts. However, I am glad to say that my fears proved groundless, for the topics had obviously been chosen with great care. I much enjoyed being asked to speak on 'the economic use of human waste', and I hope that my rather staccato, two-minute delivery was not too much of a disappointment. It was certainly very amusing to watch old Mr Bretherton become so tongue-tied with his topic, 'liberation for the gay', and I thought that he feigned embarrassment in a most expert and convincing manner. As you know, the 18 lecturettes were followed by your short briefing on the following day's programme, and I was really impressed with the amount of detail you managed to pack into those 90 minutes. One lesson which I learned from this first evening of the course is that I am obviously out of condition for, much to my disgust, I found it very difficult to stay awake during the last session.

You asked for comment on the standard of accommodation at the centre, and in reply let me say that I found my room to be entirely adequate. There was, of course, the fact that a hot water cistern, situated on the other side of the wall adjacent to the head of my bed, gurgled incessantly throughout the night — but even this minor distraction served a useful purpose, in that I managed to get bathed, shaved and dressed long before my alarm clock, always an unreliable instrument, went off at 7 a.m. It was a nice change to be ready for breakfast, scheduled for 8.30, and the staff were certainly quick on their feet. My boiled egg arrived promptly at 8.55, and I enjoyed a satisfying meal before joining the course at 9.00. I found the lecture room to be slightly on the small side, but I am sure that it was my innate clumsiness that prevented me reaching my seat without a struggle. The horseshoe seating arrangement was a welcome change from the usual classroom layout, and my position at the left-hand end of the horseshoe proved to be of great personal advantage; firstly, the position of the overhead projector at my elbow meant that I was able to read direct from the transparencies, instead of looking over my shoulder at the screen, and, secondly, since I was seated nearest to the lecturer, the haze of cigarette smoke in the room failed to inhibit my view of the various speakers.

As you know, the first day of the course was largely taken up with the seven lectures delivered by Mr Ogilvy, a freelance lecturer in management hired by you for the occasion. I found him to be a quite fascinating character, who, in addition to being well-versed in the subject, managed to keep all of us entertained with his attractive stammer and remarkably complex facial twitches. The fact that he has never actually engaged in the business of selecting employees enabled him to present a fresh and unbiased view of the problems which face management in this field, and I am sure that we all listened to him with great attention. His dissertation on the non-statistical combination of test scores was of particular significance to me, and struck right at the heart of my never-ending problems in selecting good typists, clerks and counter assistants. Mr Ogilvy's opening statement to the effect that we, as practising managers, knew nothing about employee selection plainly succeeded in warming us to him and, of course, utterly convinced me that my 25 years in management had been largely misspent. I look forward to studying the 13 books recommended by Mr Ogilvy as essential reading, and I am sure that these will enable me to fully comprehend the 72 pages of lecture handouts kindly supplied by him.

Dinner on Saturday evening was, for me, a highlight of the course. Apart from the fact that as a vegetarian — I believe I mentioned this to you early in the day — the meal of liver pate, roast venison and angels-on-horseback proved something of a challenge, I was deeply impressed by the manner in which the waitresses ensured that the meal progressed at a leisurely and relaxing pace. The 25 minutes' interval between courses not only meant that our digestive tracts suffered minimal strain, but also prevented us from being forced to kick our heels whilst awaiting the evening exercise at 9 p.m. With regard to this final session of the day, I must apologise for falling asleep during the practice interviews.

Sunday morning's film programme was a pleasant surprise, especially since all 4 films were of American origin. There is no doubt in my mind that the problems and solutions depicted in these films are exactly those which I encounter in my day-to-day experience, and I am truly grateful that you did not elect to show us a series of parochial and probably irrelevant British productions. It was unfortunate that by some mischance you were unfamiliar with the operation of the projector, but the various intervals between and during reels gave us ample opportunity for discussion.

The afternoon sessions on the theory, administration and scoring of selection tests were of true value. There is nothing like a practical approach to a subject, and I much enjoyed actually completing 14 tests of general and specific ability. It was certainly not your fault that this section of the programme overran slightly — as you remarked at the time, any training programme needs to be flexible — and anyway it was Sunday. To be frank, I was a little dismayed at the group's lack of cooperation at the final debriefing session, which took place at 7 p.m. I can only assume that the paucity of questions during this open forum reflected our complete understanding of that which had been put over during the course, and I must compliment you accordingly.

I thoroughly enjoyed the course and eagerly await the next opportunity to attend one of your functions. Unfortunately this may not be for some time, as my wife has seen fit to leave me and I am therefore forced to spend the weekend looking after my children.

Yours sincerely,
George

P.S.   You expressed a wish to have a look round my branch at some convenient time — may I suggest that you pop over next Sunday — at around 6.15 a.m.?

Whilst I must come clean and confess that George's letter is a product of my evil imagination, it does contain a selection of the very real and quite horrible mistakes regularly committed by managers who set foot on the training road. I am quite sure (at least, I think I am) that *your* presentations will involve none of these clangers — so without further ado let us get down to a few brass tacks.

## Know your onions

A training officer, lecturer, teacher — or poor old Fred, nobbled for the first time in years with the task of instructing a group of employees in something or other — must know far more about his subject than he is required to impart. If Fred delivers a lecture or piece of instruction that sweeps him to the limit of his knowledge, he invites disaster in two nasty forms:

He will be thoroughly floored by disconcerting and unanswerable questions from that creature in the back row.

He will stand in imminent risk of being labelled for all time as an unconvincing and ill-qualified mentor.

Unfortunately the proud possession of a well-stocked brainbox is not the only qualification for an effective trainer, and the hallowed company habit of conscripting the first 'expert' to come along to do this or that job of instruction often results in some pretty painful and tedious affairs. A large lump of subject knowledge is but one of several vital ingredients in the training mix.

## So you know it — but can you show it?

The trainer who grinds out knowledge with the monotony of a hurdy-gurdy, with no sense of motivation and little perception of the 'feel' of his trainee-audience, will swiftly discover that he has anaesthetised a goodly proportion of his unlucky victims.

There is absolutely no escaping the fact that in seeking to impart knowledge effectively and well, *personality* counts. Having said that, I have decided to omit from this chapter all the traditional gubbins on personality development and 'projection' — for I take the view that no amount of textbook preaching can hope to achieve any significant change in the personality of the reader. By and large, we are firmly stuck with the innate and highly complex features of our own personalities. The ability to motivate trainees to learn, to implant fire in the bellies of those who face our efforts, is very much a heaven-sent skill. Courses in instructional techniques can build upon a vocation and provide the mechanical knowledge necessary in a good trainer, but unless he possesses that magic personality-mix, he will be little more than an animated teaching machine. In view of the other chapters in this book, I should add that it is one thing to don a book-learned veneer and 'act out' a role as a *speaker* in various situations, but it is quite another thing to imagine, even for a moment, that one can act out a *training* role. If you believe, as you should, that effective training and education are vital functions of the working world, then that belief must surely embrace the conviction that those who deliver the education and training goods must be the right people for the job. It is my belief that you, reader, will *know* whether or not you possess the personality for the job by the reactions of those with whom you associate and a pure and simple gut-feeling. Enter your private confessional and ask yourself, does your name come naturally to the lips of whoever-it-is when there is a training job to be done? Do people listen, really listen, when you expound, and do they go away with that fire in the belly? Do you relish the thought and the actual job of imparting knowledge to others? If the answer to all this is a truly genuine 'yes', then read on for some very basic tips on how to embellish your proficiency. But please be honest with yourself, if you cannot stand the training heat — *get out of the kitchen.*

## Know your people

One of the most dangerous assumptions for the inexperienced trainer to make is that having achieved success with one presentation, the law of averages will ensure that ensuing sessions are greeted with similar success. There is a special provision within the limitless clauses of Sod's Law to ensure that this will not be so. The thinking trainer (lecturer — call him what you will) will take out part-insurance against this risk by carefully examining the composition and likely attitudes of any group with which he is to come into contact. I recommend the following checklist:

1    What is the status of the group:
    *a*    In terms of their jobs?
    *b*    In terms of intellect?
    *c*    In social terms?
2    Is the group a conscripted bunch or will they be attending by choice?
3    What will be their likely attitudes, in terms of morale and motivation?
4    Are you known to the group:
    *a*    As a respected colleague or senior?
    *b*    Or are you an unknown outsider or distant senior?
5    How relevant is your subject:
    *a*    In terms of the group's actual needs?
    *b*    In terms of their general interest?

The answers to the above points will provide some valuable help in assessing the approach to the assignment concerned (method, style, etc.).

## The lecture — training tool or spanner in the works?

Whilst the lecture has an important place in the training scheme of things, far too many managers make it their automatic choice of training method. This is probably because the intending trainer falls prey to the tempting advantages offered by the lecture:

1   It is the easiest way of handling a number of people — 'sit down, shut up and listen' can be a convenient way out.
2   Once he has prepared his subject, the lecturer can regurgitate his material with comparative ease — 'once more unto the spiel, dear friends' — what could be better?
3   There is no apparent need for equipment to be used (oh, yes?), or for the speaker to indulge in 'fancy techniques' — pure essence of chalk and talk.

Sadly, however, the lecture has significant disadvantages as a training medium:

a   It offers little or no scope for participation by the group, and individual participation is the biggest spur to the retention of knowledge.
b   Passive learning invites saturation and boredom — the glazed-eye syndrome.
c   As a general rule, skills and techniques cannot be taught by the lecture alone.

If it is decided that a lecture will best suit a training requirement, remember to ensure that concise, well-produced handouts are distributed immediately after the session — not beforehand, please, if you wish to avoid inattention and the rustling of paper (to say nothing of premature release of your secrets). Pay particular attention to the use of visual aids, for which see later in this chapter, and note that earlier chapters on the preparation and delivery of public addresses are plainly relevant.

## The seminar or discussion

The essential requirements for this type of training activity are a number of people who possess similar levels of knowledge of the topic concerned, albeit at a basic level, but who can bring to the session the advantages of varying backgrounds and experience. Since the accent is on individual participation, it is necessary to limit the size of the group and pay some attention to its composition — remember the pre-session checklist. The activity can take several forms:

*The 'straight discussion'*   Since I have already dealt at some length in Chapter 6 with the pros and cons of the discussion, suffice it to make two points:

1   In the training context, it is even more important for the discussion leader

to keep a steely eye on the planned objectives of the session.

2    There is a fairly widespread belief that the discussion approach to training is too esoteric for the likes of operatives and other shop-floor employees — yet another snide dig by the uninformed at the so-called *hoi polloi*. One fine day, such bigots will realise that intelligence is not the sole prerogative of the white-collar brigade. If the *subject* is right for discussion, then, believe me, the guys and gals at the sharp end will cope — and keep the discussion leader well and truly on his toes.

*Case studies*    In this form of discursive training, the group is supplied with information on a given situation and is tasked with finding a satisfactory answer to the problem by means of discussion and analysis. It is a fairly common and satisfactory practice to split the group into smaller syndicates; then — by means of report-back sessions — a number of solutions can be considered and discussed by the group as a whole. Good case studies require much detailed, preparatory work — all too often groups find that the study contains insufficient information or is poorly expressed, with the result that the exercise loses realism and impact.

*Role-play exercises*    Role playing involves members of the group in acting the parts of given characters in a situation, and herein lies the rub. Individuals of a cheerfully extrovert nature will vastly enjoy themselves (and, unless restrained, act larger than life), but those who dislike disporting themselves in such amateur dramatics will not enjoy the process. The role-play exercise and the participants have to be very good if the session is not to assume a high degree of artificiality.

*Business games*    Much longer in duration and more involved than role play exercises, business games require expert planning and preparation — to say nothing of implementation. A number of hole-in-the-wall firms have climbed on to the business games bandwagon, with the result that the market is saturated with poorly produced, shoddy 'kits'. If you wish to buy business games off the shelf, be prepared to spend a lot of money for the genuine article, and do check with great care that the goods suit your precise requirements.

## Visual aids

Visual aids add the essential spice to any presentation, provided they are of good quality, relevant and used in moderation. Let us just remind ourselves of what is available:

*Film projectors*    One of the cardinal sins of training is to show a film merely because it fills a gap in the planned programme or, worse still, because the trainer imagines that it will save him saying anything. A further cardinal sin is to make a poor choice of film, and this is a very common occurrence in management and supervisory training. Good British films, although on the increase, are still pretty thin on the ground — but do think twice before acquiring, say, an American film which, although relevant in subject, may be completely foreign to the hard-headed taste and established practice of a British group. Never, ever show a film immediately following a meal break, unless, that is, you wish the soundtrack to be drowned in a cacophony of snores.

*Overhead projectors*   The much loved stand-by of the trainer, the overhead projector, with its dual facility for the projection of large transparencies and 'projection as one writes' by means of felt tip pens and acetate scrolls, is an extremely useful visual aid. Transparencies on a variety of subjects can be purchased commercially and of course can be home made. I might add that a poorly drawn transparency is a thing of horror — do not succumb to this easy and awful way out; buy or cajole the services of someone with an artistic touch.

*Slide projectors*   Despite all the claims of the manufacturers, I have yet to be convinced that a slide projector, including the back-projection variety, can be used successfully in other than a semi-darkened room. Whilst they are necessary for the projection of photographic transparencies (35 mm, 2 inches square, etc.), I have never indulged much in their use, and, for my money, I prefer the overhead projector.

*Epidiascopes*   The name smacks of the Victorian era and my dictionary definition is even worse — 'an optical lantern for the projection of images of both opaque and transparent objects'. All of which is not quite fair, for the epidiascope can be a very useful visual aid. As indicated in the definition, its main advantage is the ability to project pictures of solid objects — provided of course that the object concerned is not a double-decker bus. Epidiascopes are freely available and most will accept 'book-sized' objects for projection, but again they are best used in a semi-darkened room.

*Closed-circuit television*   No self-respecting training establishment would be seen dead without its CCTV, for in addition to its uses, possession of this electronic bag of tricks adds considerable status to the place. The main value of CCTV is probably the facility to record selected television programmes for subsequent and repeated showing at a later date — provided, always, that the law of copyright is not infringed. The use of CCTV in filming role-play exercises and the like is an undoubted advantage, but only if the apparatus is used with care and discretion. Too many trainers are so taken up with their new toy that they callously disregard the feelings of the shy or the sensitive trainees, forced to watch their own indiscretions and clangers on the silver screen for all to see.

*Tape recorders*   Valuable for the brief and 'dramatised' illustration of selected points, the tape recorder can be an effective tool in the hands of the thinking trainer.

143

*Felt and magnetic boards*  A modern and slightly gimmicky extension of the blackboard, felt (or flannel) and magnetic boards are useful for the 'building up' of an illustration as a lecture proceeds. Felt boards have an unpleasant habit of voluntarily jettisoning their bits and pieces right at the climax of the talk, so I tend to play safe and opt for the magnetic variety (magnetised, self-adhesive tape can be purchased for use with illustrations made from card).

*Charts and diagrams*  These are virtually self-explanatory. Again care should be taken to ensure that they are well produced, free from ambiguity and entirely relevant to the occasion.

## Let's have a guest speaker

Finally, a cautionary tale. Very recently a friend of mine called Jack had occasion to run a management seminar on a particular aspect of employee relations, and, because the programme had to include some pretty turgid material, he decided that it would be a good idea to use the services of an accomplished guest speaker. After a bit of a search he found the ideal chap, an acknowledged expert in the subject and, just as important, an eloquent and entertaining speaker. The man's terms were favourable and the necessary deal was made — everything seemed set fair for a first-class seminar. Then two days before the event, misfortune struck and my pal heard that his guest speaker had succumbed to an attack of flu and would not be able to attend as arranged. Jack was left with a gaping hole in his programme, which had to be filled pretty damned quickly. Several telephone calls later, he was still without a substitute, and in some desperation he sought advice from a government department that had dealings in the field concerned. Jack was very relieved to find himself talking to a most helpful individual, and even more relieved to learn that, yes, indeed, a specialist in the subject was actually on the staff of the department and that he would be pleased to arrange for the expert's attendance at the seminar. In reply to Jack's tactfully phrased question, the civil servant emphasised that the man concerned was in great demand at such functions and, yes, he was a lucid and most entertaining speaker. Oh, joy, problems over, Jack thought, and swiftly made the necessary arrangements.

Along came the appointed day and about five minutes before the seminar was due to kick off, with all the delegates sitting present and correct, Jack was informed that the man from the Ministry had arrived. He sped off to greet him. There was only one person waiting in the reception area — a sad little man, sitting in a hunched position, with watery eyes darting hither and thither as he nervously clenched and unclenched his scrawny hands. Jacks tells me that his heart sank to his boots as he approached the man — it couldn't be, surely this was not the guest speaker? He was sure that his voice betrayed his utter dismay as he asked the newcomer whether he was Mr So-and-so — and then it happened.

The thin, colourless lips parted and according to Jack there emitted the most mellifluous, baritone voice he had ever heard. This scraggy figure of a man was the owner of a voice in a million, and as it transpired he succeeded in holding every member of the seminar spellbound for four magic hours. Little wonder that he was in great demand, it was a privilege to listen to him — and I should know, for I was one of the delegates. So, where is the moral of the tale, do I hear you ask? Simply this, bearing in mind the immutable provisions of Sod's Law, the next time *you* book a speaker blind, how do you think it will turn out?

## Self-tutorial

*Note* For the purposes of this exercise, you will require a copy of the Employers' Guide to the Employment Protection (Consolidation) Act 1978, available free of charge from any office of the Department of Employment or HMSO.

Please imagine that, as training officer to your company, you have been requested by your managing director to ensure that *all* the employees (see below) receive adequate instruction, commensurate with their status, in 'Employees' Rights at Work'. Your boss is additionally concerned that management and supervisory grades should be equipped with sufficient knowledge of the subject to ensure that the company is not embroiled in complaints to an industrial tribunal arising from management ignorance of the law. The personnel involved are as follows:

    12 senior managers
    25 middle managers
    32 supervisors/foremen
    35 office workers
  180 skilled operatives
  190 semi-skilled operatives
    52 unskilled workers

There is a training room at your disposal, with desk-seating accommodation for 20 persons, and you have a complete range of audio-visual equipment. The works canteen can also be utilised for general lecture purposes, with seating accommodation for 250 people.

Your exercise task is as follows:

*a*   Determine the syllabus of training applicable in each case and produce training programmes for the relevant groups. Your programmes should include the titles of each syllabus item, the method by which each item will be presented, the estimated duration of each item, the audio-visual aids to be utilised in each case and notes on the provision of any handouts, etc.

*b*   You should then select an appropriate programme item and prepare detailed speaking notes for the implementation of this section of the syllabus.

*Further note* It may appear at first glance that this exercise involves one hell of a lot of work for precious little return — teacher not standing at your right shoulder and all that jazz. However, there are some benefits to be derived from your industry and they include:

1   Valuable familiarisation with the Employment Protection (Consolidation) Act — and no manager can afford to lightly discard that little lot.

2   Some practice in the business of looking objectively at training programme design and implementation.

3   Some more practice in the preparation of adequate speaking notes.

If the reader is lucky enough to work for an organisation with a training officer on strength, I am sure that this worthy will cast a kind eye over your efforts and provide come constructive criticism. So — why not get down to some work?

There was things which he stretched, but mainly he told the truth.

**Mark Twain (1835-1910)**
*The Adventures of Huckleberry Finn*

# 16
# On being a good candidate

It comes to most of us in time — the urge or the dire necessity to find another job. In the case of an acquaintance of mine, it happened to be dire necessity. At 9.15 on a wintry morning, he was an enthusiastic and apparently successful company executive, sitting happily in a well-paid job with bags of prospects and the comforting thought that everything in the garden was lovely. A minute later on that notable day he was out of work. The victim of a quick bullet, fired from the hip by a financially pressed boss who had clearly seen too many Westerns, he remained unemployed for several months — and learned some of the stickier facts of life. One lesson which emerged from this chap's painful experience was simply that good executive or not — and since he was sacked, he could not have been considered that good — he was singularly ill-equipped to cope with that final hurdle in the employment stakes, the interview. The aim of this chapter is to highlight some of the difficulties experienced by him, and in so doing provide a ray of hope for the many executives who find themselves in a similar position — sitting, metaphorical cap in hand, on the wrong side of the desk.

Once in a blue moon, fortune smiles on the brave and our first and only application for a job results in that magic piece of paper, a call for interview. Sadly, however, this is not usually the case and we share the depressing lot of my friend who, having received one reject note after another, wonders if he will ever strike lucky. Although it may be a bit difficult to convince someone who has just completed his 40th application without success, the fact remains that sooner or later a call for interview will pop through the letterbox. An anxious shuffle through the mail and there it is, nestling coyly between the second reminder for the school fees and a further letter from the bank manager — an envelope bearing the hoped-for postmark. Instant euphoria! The wife (who has borne the brunt of the tension with a stoic calm) receives a long overdue kiss, the kiddies realise that it is safe to stop whispering, the cat emerges from its hiding place and suddenly all is right with the world. However, a few hours later when the letter has been read and re-read, the mood of happy achievement is gradually replaced by one of more sombre, contemplative hue. The job-seeker descends to earth with a bump as he realises that the battle has scarcely begun, the major bout is yet to be faced.

It is at this stage that many applicants undergo the torture of the damned, the trial of waiting for the fateful day, for the appointed hour to arrive. Much worried thought will be given to the question of how best to conduct oneself at the interview, and the whole event will be rehearsed again and again in the applicant's mind as he tries to cater for each and every contingency that may arise. This is all good stuff, for it makes sound sense to practise one's mode of presentation and try to anticipate snags and pitfalls. Make no mistake, there is some very real work to be done.

## Know thine adversary

It is one thing to sally out for an evening on a blind date, but quite another to gaily attend for an interview without knowing as much as possible about the prospective employer. There is not only the important question of whether the organisation will suit the applicant's requirements — working conditions, environment, company image and so on — but in addition there is the absolutely vital consideration of doing everything to lessen the odds at interview. Consider, if you will, the unknown factors:
1    The size of the short-list.
2    The quality of the other candidates.
3    Whether or not our hero is considered to be one of the best prospects on the short-list.
4    The full requirements of the job — seldom, if ever, spelled out in the published detail.
5    The selection policy of the firm.
6    The quality of the interviewer.
7    The content and style of the forthcoming interview.
Faced with this panoply of 'unknowns', is it wise to add to the list an almost total ignorance of the organisation concerned — with the possibility that this may be construed as lack of interest at the interview? Of course not, the determined applicant will learn all he can about the firm before the interview takes place — in short, do all that can be done to get to grips with this stranger, and not risk pinning faith on a blind date.

148

## Interview tactics and gamesmanship

What about the dreaded interview or, more to the point, *the unknown character who will conduct it?* Is there anything that can be done to maximise one's chances of success, rather than just sit back and hope for the best? Yes, by golly, there is.

First of all, in planning the tactics to be employed at the interview, it is wise to remember that very few employers give any sort of consideration to the need for training their executives in interviewing techniques. The selection of employees has always been regarded as one of the more commonplace requirements in the manager's day-to-day activities, a purely routine chore which, despite overwhelming evidence to the contrary, warrants little or nothing in the way of professional training. The inevitable result is that most interviewers fail to recognise the basic fact that information about the candidate filters through the highly subjective screen of their own views, needs and prejudices. The determined candidate will familiarise himself with the characteristics of some of these factors, for they represent weaknesses on the part of the interviewer by which he may profit.

*The halo error*   A common failing in which an interviewer may tend to judge a candidate in terms of a general attitude towards the subject's personality as a whole. A classic example is the manager who, requiring a secretary, is faced with a candidate possessing everything, but everything, in the way of physical attributes. Well aware that the acquisition of such a beauty will make him the envy of every full-blooded male in the organisation (let alone thoughts of a more personal and direct nature), he tends to overrate the girl's very limited typing ability. The gorgeous legs and the etceteras have had their halo effect.

*The logical error*   An inexperienced interviewer is very often inclined to arrive at similar assessments in respect of qualities in a candidate that *seem* logically related. Hence the applicant who gives every indication of being a quick thinker may be assessed as intelligent. Similarly the unfortunate candidate who possesses a 'foxy' countenance — say, with a rather pointed nose and eyes that tend to glance swiftly hither and thither — why, he may be pronounced as being 'on the sly side'.

*The mirror-image error*   This weakness relates to the interviewer whose creed is simply, 'I know I am good — therefore for the candidate to be good, he must be like me.' This quaint breed of interviewer may often be detected by the obvious delight shown by him on discovering that the candidate shares his enthusiasm for a certain hobby — or, more ridiculous, had the good sense to follow a similar career pattern.

*The contrast error*   The sinister opposite to the mirror-image syndrome, the interviewer tends to assess others in the opposite direction to himself in given qualities. The usual reason for this failing is self-preservation; the man fears for his job and is determined not to breed competition.

At this point, the reader is fairly entitled to react in a somewhat caustic manner: 'All right, so I've had a mini-lecture on interviewing weaknesses — exactly how the hell does this help me in projecting myself at interview?' Bear with me a little longer, for — before we get to the meat in the sandwich — there is some more groundwork to be covered. It is necessary to take a glance at the question of interviewers' attitudes, to gain an insight into some of the more common postures adopted by interviewers — which again can be traded upon by the thinking candidate.

*Aggression* Many interviewers — and indeed many companies — believe that an element of stress should be introduced in the selection process. Some insurance companies and many marketing organisations, when seeking to recruit 'thrusting, highly motivated salesmen', subject interview candidates to an almighty and very aggressive grilling session, declaring that the stress interview is a necessary means of sorting out the wheat from the chaff. Some interviewers, notable those of the Colonel Blimp variety, are aggressive by nature — their wives suffer and, not surprisingly, their interview candidates suffer.

*Domination* A classic attitude — that distributor of headaches, the boisterous, hearty type who swamps the poor candidate in a spring-tide of bonhomie. Death to the retiring or shy candidate and a menace to all, this zestful pachyderm of the interviewing jungle will dominate every session until, finally, his coronary carries him off.

*Argument* We have all met this type of chap at some time or other, and unfortunately many of them carry out interviews — the irritating, usually little, person who cannot let the time of day pass without arguing the toss. Every comment made by the candidate will evoke the same kind of response, 'Oh, but are you quite sure? I don't think that. . . .' Or 'I can't really agree with you . . .' and so on, *ad infinitum*.

*Insistence on showing authority* Usually the badge of the self-made man or the incompetent and as a consequence displayed by a large number of interviewers, this failing can be highly irritating to candidates — who are forced to sit back and suffer the interminable monologue of success, struggles against overwhelming odds, infinite ranges of responsibility and the like.

*Losing control of the interview* A 'minus-attitude', if you like. The depressing spectacle of the man who, innately shy or nervous, should never be allowed to interview is known to us all. The session, instead of developing into a friendly, steered discussion, becomes a ghastly, spasmodic and stumbling failure. The candidate is ill-at-ease and annoyed, and the interviewer undergoes his all-too-familiar form of anguish — the interview is lost.

Now we come to the meat in the sandwich — what, in the light of this recital of failings and adverse attitudes, can the candidate do that will possibly help his case? Well, as with so many things the task is easily defined but, make no mistake, extremely difficult to carry out. Normally at interview the candidate's attention is focused on but one objective — the single-minded aim of impressing the interviewer with every word he utters and thus to pass muster and emerge as the successful candidate. Obviously this is a laudable aim — but there must be more. In striving to achieve the objective, the candidate should not direct *all* of his faculties to the task of providing the 'right answers'. A goodly proportion of his mental armoury must be devoted to the vital and difficult task of *assessing the interviewer* — seeking out and, as far as is possible, identifying the type of failings and attitudes I have described, and others. Only by carrying out this conscious assessment will the candidate manage to trade upon and profit by the interviewer's weaknesses — which brings me to the second difficult aspect of the task.

A candidate who overplays his part in reacting to the weaknesses he has detected will invite disaster. The overall strategy must be 'slowly, slowly, catchee monkey', and the recipe is, quite simply, bags of practice. No, not at interview but every day and at every opportunity, in general chit-chat and serious conversation, practise detecting weaknesses such as I have described and learn the art of subtle interview gamesmanship. Lest the reader is inclined to emit an impatient snort and mutter something like — 'This really is too basic for words — when is he going to stop trying to teach me to suck eggs — doesn't he realise that I'm an experienced man of the world?' — I had better add a brief homily. Having put several hundred managers of all shapes and sizes through interviewing and selection mills, having listened to many of them snort in similar, derisory vein, and having seen how they tend to come apart at the seams when either interviewing or undergoing interview, then, being beastly frank, this ain't such basic stuff. So if there are sceptics in the house, take the word of this 'ere veteran: learn how to impress by trading on the inherent prejudices and views of others, and learn how to do this in a skilful manner.

1  Ensure that the right amount of 'agreement' is displayed — without being pronounced a toady or creep.
2  Produce the right amount of argument to signify a questing and mature outlook — without being pronounced as merely argumentative.
3  Display the right amount of counter-aggression — without being labelled as bloody-minded.
4  Listen attentively to the interminable speaker and interject with the right comment at the right time — thereby bringing him to a halt without upsetting the applecart.
5  Respond to the dominating speaker in such a way that he is not annoyed at the stand being taken against him.

## Starting off on the right foot — an opening gambit

There is yet another human failing to which most interviewers are prone, the 'first-impression syndrome'. A candidate sets one tiny foot inside the room and, wham, the interviewer's mental computer has done it again:

> 'I like him. . . .'
> 'I don't like him. . . .'
> 'I'm uneasy about him. . . .'
> etc.

There is absolutely no doubt that this split-second reaction, the much researched first impression, tends to colour an interviewer's judgement during the course of the interview. This being so, it is essential that the candidate does all that he can at this time to turn the situation to his advantage — and here comes the second homily. Sit a manager behind the immensely comforting protection of his own desk or even let him take part in any of the activities of normal business life — and by and large he will be an averagely confident cuckoo, possessing all the know-how of executive airs and graces, and using them to advantage. Pluck this same, averagely confident cuckoo out of his accustomed environment, label him 'candidate for interview' — and watch how, all too often, he becomes a shallow, ill-at-ease shade of his former self. The name of the candidature game is *gaining the initiative* — right at the instant when the interviewer's fruit machine is clacking away at his first impression. The ingredients for the opening gambit are obvious: the purposeful advance into the room, the pleasant and brisk self-introduction, the confident manner with which the candidate moves the proffered chair to a better position, the man-to-man look, and so on.

## Answering the questions in the right way

A trained interviewer will ask very few direct questions, those which prompt a mere 'yes' or 'no' answer. He will have the interviewer's 'magic six' firmly engraved on his heart:

> What. . .?   Why. . .?   Where. . .?   When. . .?   Which. . .?   How. . .?

He will know that questions commencing with these words guarantee results — the questions will be open-ended and the candidate will provide him with the information he seeks. More often than not, however, the interviewer will have received no such training, and if the wily candidate is to maximise his chances of success, he must watch out for weaknesses in questioning technique.

*Direct questions*  A few direct questions are necessary, particularly at the commencement of an interview. If, however, a candidate finds that he is being deluged with them, and this does happen, he should help the poor, misguided wretch by volunteering information. This is not to say that the candidate should indulge in lengthy monologues — fairly short spiels should be handed out for the interviewer's easy digestion. A word of warning, do not allow the interviewer to wallow in direct questions by roaming through the application form or c.v., merely confirming the information already in his hands. This type of interviewer will fail to recognise that he, in fact, is the spanner in the works and will interpret the candidate's limited responses as 'taciturn' or 'not forthcoming'.

*Standard-revealing questions*    These are questions which are couched in such a way as to reveal, voluntarily or involuntarily, the interviewer's own feelings or prejudices or those of his organisation:

> 'You know, Mr Williams, the one thing I cannot abide is the chap who makes little or no use of his spare time — tell me, what do you do with yourself in your leisure hours?'

> 'We feel that the successful applicant for this post must be willing to accept much arduous work at various locations throughout the country — how do you feel about long absences from home?'

Plainly, if the candidate is asked questions of a standard-revealing nature, he would be wise to fall in line with the disclosed view or attitude — unless, that is, such agreement would be prejudicial to his interests. The candidate should also guard against being pronounced as a yes-man. Remember, slowly, slowly, catchee monkey. . . .

To provide a general lesson in the art of answering questions is very difficult. We are all blessed with vastly differing personalities, and strive though we might to improve our technique, such improvements are bound to be limited by the strictures of our individual make-up. For instance it is all very well to say that a candidate should not be garrulous at interview, but how many people know whether they are garrulous or not? Even if they are aware of the characteristic, how many leopards are actually capable of changing their spots? The art of being a good interview candidate has much in common with that of the successful actor or public speaker; if the 'mental mix' is right, all is well.

One useful tip in answering questions at interview is to ensure that each answer contains something 'new'. Many candidates furnish replies, sometimes very long-winded replies, that provide little or nothing in the way of fresh information. This habit of regurgitating information already supplied in the application documents can result in the candidate being labelled, at best, as unimaginative and, at worst, shallow in activity and outlook. The point is best illustrated by some examples:

> *Interviewer*    'I see that your personnel specialism is union negotiations — how do you regard that activity?'
> *Candidate*    'Well, I quite liked it at my last job — I found the work challenging.'
> *as opposed to*
> *Candidate*    'Well, I received a kind of baptism by fire at my last job — I had only been there 3 months when I was faced with Phase 2 pay disputes

and during the ensuing couple of years spent more time sitting at the negotiation table than I seemed to spend at my own desk. A hectic time, but the cut-and-thrust provided a challenge. . . .'

*Interviewer* 'I see that fell-walking is one of your leisure pursuits — tell me a little about this.'
*Candidate* 'Well, it's just that, over the years, I've grown to enjoy outdoor activities — and I find fell-walking good exercise and very relaxing. . . .'
*as opposed to*
*Candidate* 'It really all started when I managed to get some local youths interested in the sport — I think I mentioned that I lend an occasional hand with the Sea Cadet Corps — and we formed a fell-walking club. This gives the lads a spot of strenuous activity in the open air and provides me with all the exercise I need! We usually manage a 10 or 15 mile stretch every month or so, weather permitting. . . .'

*Interviewer* 'Tell me about your job as credit controller at Brown Ltd.'
*Candidate* 'Well, I was in charge of all credit arrangements — vetting and authorising credit applications, and responsible for ensuring prompt payments. . . .'
*as opposed to*
*Candidate* 'I was directly responsible to the financial director for all credit customer arrangements, and controlled a department of 12 employees, including 2 credit managers. On joining the company, I was tasked with the reduction of the credit period from. . . .'

## 64,000-dollar questions

Nearly all interviewers have certain favourite 'key questions' which they regard as essential to their version of the selection process. By far the most common in this rather odd collection is the traditional:

> *'Tell me - why do you want this particular job?'*

This question deserves highlighting for not only is it used with monotonous frequency, but tremendous importance is attached to the manner in which candidates reply to its ominous content. The average interviewer is quite convinced that the quality of the response will reveal the candidate's innermost thoughts and depth of character — despite the fact that, patently, there is no single, correct answer to the beastly thing. The thinking candidate, well aware that the interviewer is probably seeking an answer that reeks of sweet moderation, will say what he hopes the inquisitor will wish to hear — and it will probably be far removed from the literal truth:

*Interviewer* 'Tell me, Mr Jones, why do you want this particular job?'

*The literal truth* 'Because this is the only damned interview I've managed to get in 15 applications — because I'm desperate for work — because I've got a massive overdraft and umpteen bills that I can't pay — because if I don't land this job, I'll be up to my neck in trouble. . . .'

*The actual reply* 'Well, to begin with, I know a little about your company and its reputation as a good employer — and your advertisement gave me the opportunity I was seeking. The job specification is, in my view, ideally suited to my qualifications and experience, and what you have told me serves to confirm my initial thoughts — the post offers interesting and challenging work to someone with my background. . . .'

There is another favourite in this collection of oddities:

*Interviewer* 'Mr Brown, this post requires, more than anything else, a man who is an efficient and able man-manager. Tell me, how do you fit the bill?'

*The literal truth* 'If you were half as good a manager as I am, you wouldn't ask such damn-fool questions. There's nothing holy or special about your job — it just pays more than my last one and I'm going to use it as a stepping-stone to something better just as soon as I get the chance. I can eat it. . . .'

*The actual reply* 'Speaking candidly, I think I'm a good manager, especially where people are concerned, and I feel that this is reflected in my career achievements. I'm very much aware that I am by no means perfect — but I'm confident that your organisation will give me the opportunity I seek to build on my capabilities. . . .'

A last word on these 64,000-dollar efforts — never question the question. However provoked, it would be application suicide to throw such mud on the interviewer's *tour de force*. Just provide a carefully composed reply, remembering that gamesmanship and sweet moderation are the keystones to success in this final round of the match.

## A bag of dirty tricks

The interviewing tribe contains just as many rogues — in fact, far more — than any herd of elephants. Every now and again, a candidate will find that he has been pitchforked into the presence of one of these scoundrels, and if he has any perception at all, he will begin to think that the selection world has taken leave of its senses. I refer, of course, to that small but dangerous band of megalomaniacs who fondly believe in salting the interview with devious tricks, convinced that such knavery will test the candidate and lay bare his weaknesses of character and personality. One such charlatan, a typical quack of the interviewing trade, is the unfortunate and impressionable man who, during World War 2, passed through the hands of what was then known as a War

Office Selection Board. Equipped with a hazy recollection of what transpired at the WOSB, he decides that he also can introduce science into the selection process, and in no time flat he is a rogue interviewer. His younger counterpart is the equally dangerous and mentally immature manager who has clearly watched too much television and who again has decided to harness science as an aid to swift and efficient selection — with the same appalling result. Whilst, thank goodness, one does not encounter these blighters very often, it is wise that job-seekers should know of their existence. What kind of amateur villainy can be found in their scran-bag of dirty tricks?

*Rascality with chairs*   This simple but Machiavellian dodge consists of having two chairs facing the interviewer's desk — a hard, upright office chair and an obviously comfortable easy-chair. The interviewer will wait with bated breath to see which chair the candidate will elect to use and by dint of some mental process known only to the perpetrator, will attach deep significance to the choice. A variation on this theme of chairs involves the use of one seat only, a chair so low that the unfortunate candidate, if he does use it, finds that his chin is virtually resting on the interviewer's desk. Presumably in this case the interviewer is waiting to see how the candidate reacts to the situation, when — in some magic and mysterious way — he will be assessed accordingly.

*The 'powers of observation' nonsense*   This trick is introduced by the interviewer suddenly announcing, 'I'm terribly sorry, old chap, but I've just remembered something I simply must attend to — would you mind if I asked you to step into my secretary's office for a minute?' Naturally the candidate does as he is asked, and after a short interval he is invited to re-enter the interview room — to be greeted by Colonel Blimp asking him how many pictures he observed on the walls of the outer office or some other rubbish. This 'powers of observation' trickery is usually reserved for the younger candidate, for plainly the more mature applicant would make some very forthright comments — or would he? Only recently there was a letter from an interview candidate of some maturity published in a management magazine, in which the writer related how the personnel director-cum-interviewer resorted to a similarly banal trick. On entering the interview room, the candidate noticed a document lying on the floor in front of the interviewer's desk — and picked it up. This particular candidate got the job — and was informed, very proudly, by the personnel director that one factor that had mitigated in her favour was the voluntary retrieval of the piece of paper. Gawd help us, it was a plant, another attempt at selection quackery.

These rogues will go to almost any lengths to think up new tricks with which to bedazzle themselves with their inventive genius. Some will prepare devious and totally invalid written questionnaires and tests that purport to assess the candidate — and will place total reliance on the results. Others will concentrate on the 64,000-dollar question aspect, asking ridiculously inane questions aimed at some form of assessment or other. They are a menace, nothing less and —

although this is little comfort to the candidate caught up in their trickery — they should not be countenanced.

Enough of all this — take heart when you enter the application stakes and the very best of luck!

## Self-tutorial (Part One)

One of the secrets of success at interview is the *ability to anticipate questions* — particularly those of the 64,000 dollar variety. Imagine that you are attending an interview with the Devil incarnate, and compose effective replies to the following horrors:

a    What factors influenced your choice of . . . as a career?
b    What, in your view, is your best qualification for this type of work?
c    What are your career objectives in the short term — say, in the next five years?
d    And what are your long-term career objectives?
e    What do you consider has been your best accomplishment, and why?
f    If you were able to change your career without any difficulty, what choice would you make, and why?
g    How good are you as a manager?

## Self-tutorial (Part Two)

Some interviewers, who should know better, take the lazy way out by posing that devil of a question, 'Tell me about yourself'. Compose that which you regard as a suitable reply — and try it out on a good friend, get him to criticise your effort.

When we apply it, you call it anarchy; and when you apply it, we call it exploitation.

**G. K. Chesterton (1874-1936)**
*The Scandal of Father Brown*

# 17
# Happy days with shop stewards

'Today's shop steward will be gone tomorrow and in his place will be a skilled, tough professional who, unless we are very careful, will meet and beat the manager at his own game.'
(*Comment by a personnel director at a management meeting*)

'I guess we are lucky, our shop stewards are a very reasonable bunch, and provided we stick to procedures, treat 'em with respect — which we do — and spend time explaining our actions, we have very little trouble.
(*Comment by a production manager at the same seminar*)

'Only six weeks ago, we signed a pay deal with management which was based on their agreement to limit pick-ups of grain to so many tons a week — and yesterday, what do we find? Only that the bloody transport manager has gone straight through the limit on the quiet — I don't expect the boss even knows about it, but what's the use of a bloody agreement when that kind of thing happens?'
(*Comment by a shop steward at a college course*)

'The works manager at our place isn't much good at his job at any time, but when it comes to getting round the table, he's a dead loss. He's pig-ignorant of procedures and agreements, never knows his own mind and is scared stiff of making decisions. You should hear the way his own foremen talk about him behind his back. . . .'
(*Comment by another shop steward at the same course*)

159

In taking the somewhat risky decision to paddle in what amounts to a sea of contention, my aim is to focus on certain aspects of the people who sit at either side of the negotiating table and, if nothing else, provide a little food for thought.

## The quiet revolution

Today, nearly 12 million of the 25-odd million working population of the United Kingdom are members of trade unions, with the obvious result that there exists an army of shop stewards who have been elected to represent the varied interests of this multitude — and because shop stewards, like managers, are human beings, they are all different. Some, despite ill-informed opinions to the contrary, are gifted intellectuals; most are not. Some are dyed-in-the-wool militants; the majority are not. A goodly number are skilled and interested in the art of their elected calling, but many are not — and so it goes on. I have stressed this question of individual difference for one good reason; for the first time in its history, the Trades Union Congress, to which over 10 million trade union members are affiliated, is taking massive and highly effective measures to narrow some of the differences and, in short, produce a new breed of shop steward — the 'skilled, tough professional' so accurately pictured by the personnel director in the first quotation.

Very quietly, very professionally and with supreme success, the TUC is forging ahead with a national programme of education for shop stewards. Utilising colleges and centres throughout the UK — and taking full advantage of the legal duty imposed on employers by *The Employment Protection (Consolidation) Act, 1978,* to permit shop stewards to attend courses approved by the TUC or unions — thousands of these workplace representatives are being equipped, as never before, with high levels of knowledge and skill in union matters. Bearing in mind the sobering fact that there is no equivalent, national scheme for managers, take a look at but some of the subject areas, presented by highly qualified and professional tutors, covered in the TUC *Basic* Course:

*Collective bargaining* Students develop skills in the objectives and tactics involved in collective bargaining, and the preparation and critical analysis of collective agreements.

*Job security* Students undertake a wide-ranging, in-depth study of the tactics to be employed in order to avoid redundancy, and the action to be taken in situations of unavoidable redundancy.

*Grievances and discipline* Students develop skills in the identification and representation of grievances, the action to be taken in disciplinary cases, and the preparation and critical analysis of associated procedures and agreements.

*Rights at work* Students are familiarised with individual and collective rights at work, and the tactics and sanctions involved when these rights are not recognised by the employer.

*Conduct of meetings*   Students undertake practical studies in the conduct of meetings and the tactics involved, general negotiating skills and report writing.

And so on.

The ten-day Basic Course (with specially tailored syllabuses for shop stewards from certain industries) is followed by courses which include 'Law at the Workplace', 'Bargaining Information' and 'Health and Safety'. Remember, this is no casual, come-if-you-please arrangement, but a highly geared and totally sophisticated education campaign, which can only result in the shop steward of tomorrow being an informed, capable union representative. Truly, a quiet revolution. . . .

## The other side of the table

If he is sensible, there is one fact of management training life that the thinking executive will seek to change and change quickly. Whilst most organisations will gladly send their managers scooting off on courses that have a direct bearing on their specialist functions, there is a marked reluctance on the part of companies to require managers to undertake training in 'general management techniques'. Again, most managers will happily attend the former type of training course but, almost to a man, will shy away from the latter — pronouncing it as 'textbook stuff' and strictly for the birds. There is a widespread and tragically unquestioning faith held by companies and managers alike that appointment to an executive slot generates, quite automatically and straight from heaven, the necessary level of general management expertise for the post. Hence, for example, it happens that Bill Blenkinsop, chargehand-foreman, who sparkles at his particular engineering job, tends to be promoted on these merits alone — the fact that he may have difficulty in composing a letter, conducting a meeting or coping with a wider span of man-management responsibility goes swiftly by the board. This chapter is concerned with the parties at the negotiating table, and I must pose the question — how many managers receive formal, professional training in, say, the field of collective bargaining or, for that matter, trade unions in general? *In the light of what the TUC is achieving today and the effect that its vast programme will have on tomorrow's management world, will a continuation of laissez-faire really suffice?*

## Tactics at the negotiating table

When union representatives meet with management, if they know their onions (and, most certainly, if they have been TUC trained), they will be intent on making management 'do all the work'; that is to say, instead of arguing the toss over every word and syllable that management tries to utter, they will 'plant the pearls' of their proposals or ultimatums and then sit back, letting management talk themselves to a sweaty standstill. Again, if trained and skilled in the art of negotiation, the union representatives will have fully considered all the implications of whatever it is that they wish to achieve, and will have anticipated counter-arguments and possible ploys by management. Successful performance at the negotiation table can never boil down to simply making a note of the meeting in one's desk diary and then five minutes before the event, casually remarking to one's colleague, 'Don't forget, Charlie, we've got a meeting with the union at two o'clock.' If indeed a manager takes that view, he is permanently residing in cloud-cuckoo land and will reap the whirlwind he so richly deserves. I commend the following checklist to your attention, and when it has prompted you to think objectively about this type of situation, have a go at adding further points to the list:

## Checklist for meetings with union representatives

1   *Always* hold a pre-briefing and ensure that *all* concerned attend:
   a   To learn the *full* facts of the matter.
   b   To produce and confirm *all* the documentary evidence.
   c   To anticipate all possible modes of approach by the other side.
   d   To prepare all possible counter-arguments.
   e   To anticipate all possible side issues that may be raised by the other side.
   f   To investigate and decide upon counter-proposals, not omitting to decide upon the limits to which these will extend in a bargaining situation.
   g   To allocate areas of speaking responsibility to members of the team.
   h   To hear and agree exactly what each member will say in given situations.
   i   To thrash out uncertainties and weaknesses of approach.
2   Ensure that members of the team are fully familiar with the essentials of good tactics and conduct at such meetings:
   a   No argument or interruption merely because an opponent annoys or distracts.
   b   No rising to red herrings — and the union lads are superb at this game!
   c   No disruption of the *status quo* — or you will be asking for trouble.
   d   No succumbing to the evil temptation of saying more than is actually or tactically necessary.
   e   No discolosure of all one's cards at one go — keep some aces up the sleeve, you'll likely need them.
   f   No tempers, paddies or overbearing attitudes — all of which constitute a free hand-out of ammunition for the other side.
   g   Make the other side 'do all the work'.

# Part Four
# BACK TO SCHOOL

The place of the upstart is being taken by the downstart. I know people who secretly visit evening elocution classes in order to pick up a Cockney accent.

**George Mikes**
*How to be Inimitable*

# 18
# H'articulating and uvver 'orrors

Man owes his ability to produce sound to that curious little structure, the *larynx*, sometimes called the voice box, a gristly contrivance which Mother Nature has kindly tacked to the top end of our respective windpipes. This two-inch bag of tricks — incredible though it may seem, the ladies are blessed with a smaller edition — contains the all-essential *vocal cords* which, like the reeds in a concertina, sound off when air is passed over them. However, if this were the end of the story, man's efforts at communication would be limited to a selection of distinctly unfunny grunts, moos and bellows — and although when listening to some folk, one is tempted to offer that this might have been a jolly good arrangement, the Great Designer has gone a stage further in the scheme of things. Once the vocal cords have done their noisy stuff, the sound passes to the throat, mouth and nose, where it receives the stamp of *resonance* and, by means of crafty manipulation of the tongue, teeth and lips, the well-nigh miraculous conversion into speech sounds, *articulation*.

Articulation, then, is the final and vital process by which man gallops into effective speaking life. If Mr Everyman is a proficient articulator, he will speak distinctly and he will utter his pearly words of wisdom with a minimum of muscular effort. His voice will invite attention, and because he produces the sounds of speech with accuracy and clarity, other people will enjoy listening to him.

165

## The factors that affect articulation

*Habit*  Most weaknesses in articulation are founded in acquired habits, and in this context I am reminded of the good old computer adage, GIGO (garbage in, garbage out). If, to quote an obvious example, a child has the misfortune to spend a lengthy period in the company of people who articulate badly — be it for reasons of social environment, regional dialect or accent (but please note my defence of accent in Chapter 2), or actual physical defect — such influences will play a dominant role in shaping the youngster's articulation. The big difficulty is that long established habits, like articulation or BO, tend to become unnoticed facts of life — we barely know of their existence until the proverbial best friend whispers a frank word in our ear.

*Nervous or physical defects*  Stammers, lisps, cleft palates, size 14 buck-teeth and the like are the enemies of good articulation and only specialist treatment can save the day. Having said that, there are many speakers who spray their inarticulate way through life, causing havoc and annoyance to anyone within fall-out range, simply because they have failed to do something about ill-fitting dentures. Many of these unfortunate souls, whilst well aware that their false teeth are rattling round like castanets, blissfully overlook the fact that their articulation is suffering to an often grievous degree. The moral in such cases is plain — get thee to a dentist, and quick.

## Some pointers to good articulation

*The art of listening – and learning*  Before dashing off to enrol in the nearest elocution class or, for that matter, investing a mighty sum in a load of tape cassettes labelled '1000 Easy Lessons on Good Speech', spare a thought for the much neglected art of *listening*. Switch on those ears and instead of merely listening to what you want to hear, cultivate the process of listening to everything and everyone. If necessary, become a shameless eavesdropper, and learn to spot and analyse the four characteristics of any voice that comes your way:

1 *Volume*  Ask yourself, how loud *is* the voice — is the volume suited to the occasion and the environment? What volume would *you* employ in this instance?
2 *Pitch*  Is the voice low-pitched, high-pitched or what? Does it sound *natural* — and if not, why? How does the pitch of *your* voice compare?
3 *Rate*  Examine the rate of delivery — is it too fast or too slow? Are the words tumbling out in a mish-mash of sound, or are there over-long pauses which tend to detract from the message, inviting boredom and interruption? Again compare *your* rate of delivery with that employed by the speaker.
4 *Quality*  Quality is the sum of the innate characteristics or timbre of a voice — the quality of speech that makes Mary's voice so attractive and

John's so unpleasant to the ear. How does the quality of *your* voice compare with that of the speaker?

In sum, then, the object of the listening game is *to detect, analyse and compare the vocal characteristics of other people with your own*, something we very seldom bother to do. Avid, analytical listening pays off in terms of better articulation — try it.

*Take a longer, deeper look at how sound is produced*  Speaking does not start with the tongue, it begins with breathing. Think objectively, maybe for the first time in your life, about your *lungs,* and if you need a spur to your objective thought, carry out the following experiment:

> Instead of breathing so gently in and out as you read this — the reflex action of life itself, and thank God it *is* a reflex action — take a deep breath, a lungful of air. Now breathe out, exhaling normally, to the full extent. Then, *without breathing in,* purse the lips and 'spit peas' — ten of them, as if your life depended on it. These additional, forceful expulsions will purge the neglected 'dead air' from your lungs — something that normally shallow, reflex breathing can never achieve. Replace the noisome stuff with a good, deep breath of fresh air, and I guarantee that you will now be thinking very objectively about your lungs — and they will be a little cleaner to boot.

Yes, speaking begins with breathing. When air is expelled from the lungs, it ascends the windpipe at a high rate of knots and provides the very source of energy for speech. It is therefore vital to control the usually reflex action of breathing in order to provide ample energy — not only for the manufacture of sound but also as an effective means of reducing strain and tension in the neck and throat during speech. There is a lot of common sense in the Sergeant-Major's tip to the raw recruit on giving orders, 'Sound off from the chest and stomach, laddie, not the flippin' throat.' In other words, use the abdominal wall as, if you like, a servo-motor for the control of the chest diaphragm — when exhaling and speaking, pull the abdominal wall in to help the diaphragm in its rise. So having produced an abundant and controlled airstream, what then?

Well, firstly, the airstream reaches the larynx, housed behind that knobbly part of the throat known curiously as the Adam's apple, where it is affected by the vocal cords. These two bands of elastic tissue thrum and vibrate to produce a buzzing sound, with the loudness and pitch determined purely by the force of the airstream. Then the airstream, the carrier-wave of the sound, is released either through the mouth where it is modulated to produce oral sounds or through the nasal passages to produce nasal sounds — or of course through both channels at the same time. The direction taken by the airstream is determined by the position of the soft palate at the rear roof of the mouth — a routing device of great flexibility. Further modulations of the speech sounds are effected by changes in shape and tension of the lips and the pharynx (the passage linking larynx, mouth and nose). Now, at long last, comes the turn of that ever-mobile and infinitely flexible organ, the tongue. By wiggling to and fro, by attaining a

167

wide variety of positions and thus altering the shape and volume of the mouth cavity, the tongue produces sounds of many different qualities. The tongue is responsible for the manufacture of all the vowels and about half of the consonants, for example:

An '*a*' vowel sound, as in '*mart*' — The tongue is low down in the back of the mouth.

An '*e*' vowel sound, as in '*met*' — The tongue is bunched high in the centre of the mouth.

A '*t*' sound, as in '*tip*' — The front of the tongue presses against the ridge behind the top, front teeth.

A '*k*' sound, as in '*book*' — The tongue touches the rear section of the palate.

Extend your skills in articulation and become familiar with the very wide range of distinguishable sounds which the vocal apparatus can produce by the simple expedient of mouthing words to yourself. Take careful note of the mechanics involved and constantly compare the results, your articulation, with the sounds made by other and better articulators.

## Sugaring the pronunciation pill

Broach the subject of pronunciation in almost any circle, and sooner or later someone will refer to that most beloved of intangible terms, the 'Queen's English'. When asked to expound on this intriguing topic, the person concerned will probably look slightly flummoxed and make vague references to 'English as spoken by the BBC' or 'Educated English' and so on. Many years ago I was shocked to my teenage and patriotic core by an authoritarian schoolmaster who informed me that the Queen's English emanated from, of all places, Dublin University and nowhere else. I have never discovered — that is, to my entire satisfaction — the truth behind the term. It may be of course that the Queen's English is merely another name for 'Standard English', the pasteurised, de-accented pronunciation favoured by the god-like figures who spawn BBC newsreaders — done, so we are told, in order that all lesser mortals may easily understand every word and syllable of the latest disaster or political pronouncement. Be that as it may, there is no national authority to pontificate and guide on matters of pronunciation — although in these days of enslaving bureaucracy, that could soon change. No, we are left with a simple rule of thumb — *for pronunciation to be good, it must be acceptable.* It must be topical, for pronunciations change as the years go by. It must be a native pronunciation, unsullied by a foreign accent, and it can be characteristic of any region of the British Isles.

It is wise to note that pronunciation also involves the various ways in which a sentence can be annunciated to give it a variety of meanings. The first exercise in the self-tutorial to Chapter 3 provides an example of the importance of emphasis and nuance in pronunciation. Remember also that placing the stress on one syllable of the word can change the actual meaning of that word — as in 'refuse' (the noun) and 'refuse' (the verb). A further and significant aspect of pronunciation is that it will often reveal information about a speaker's personality and social or ethnic origins. Hence a 'domineering' voice may yield a valuable clue that the owner is a right so-and-so, and an accent will denote the American from Little Rock who — despite the anguished howls of the purists — is speaking English.

## Acronyms and slang

It seems that one cannot halt the march of progress, and one symptom of the trek to super-civilisation, whatever that may turn out to be, is the mushrooming of acronyms — names which have been made up from initials. Once an acronym has been coined and put to wide usage, it does not take many years for the new name to be admitted to the hallowed columns of English dictionaries, when it becomes a fully paid-up member of the language club. I suppose it is a natural feature of acronyms that, once born, the meanings of the component initials become shrouded in obscurity — thus those who are old enough to remember the Second World War will probably be familiar with such names as Anzac, Ensa and Fido, but not perhaps aware that the acronyms spring from the Australian and New Zealand Army Corps, the Entertainments National Service Association and, wait for it, Fog Investigation and Dispersal Operation. Plainly, the use of acronyms saves a speaker much time and trouble — after all, who would be fool enough to talk about 'radio detection and ranging' when one can use the acronym (and fully accepted word), radar?

There is no reason why a speaker should not resort to the use of an occasional acronym, *provided that his audience is aware of its meaning*. Some time ago I listened to a speaker who was supposed to be giving a very basic talk on the use of computers, and it was sheer hell. I still have difficulty in remembering that Fortan and Cobol mean, would you believe, *Fo*rmula *Tran*slation and *Co*mmon *B*usiness *O*rientated *L*anguage, respectively. Only the other day I overheard a conversation between a college lecturer and a governor, during which the governor asked the lecturer about his teaching responsibilities. 'Oh, I have a pretty mixed bag on my timetable at present,' came the reply. 'For a start, there's Yops and Tops, a sprinkling of Sec and of course Tec and Bec. . . .' The governor nodded wisely, but I could not help wondering if he fully understood that the man was referring to the Youth Opportunities Scheme, the Training Opportunities Scheme, secretarial courses, Technical Education Council and Business Education Council courses.

As for slang — well again there can be nothing wrong with using slang words or expressions which have general acceptance and which will not cause offence. The trouble starts when a speaker who is used to one community addresses people outside the community. For instance, I fancy that not all of us would be entirely familiar with a typical injunction transmitted by a Citizens' Band radio

169

fan — 'Wake those brakes, man — the smokey bears are wall-to-wall, tree-top tall, with a bear in the air heedin' your speedin'. . . .' ('Drive slowly — police about in numbers, including a helicopter.') At the risk of labouring the point, let me add that there are some of us who do not respond to good music with such comments as, 'Uptight, outa' sight and in the groove — dig those heavenly vibes — they're cosmic, baby!'

An occasional use of acceptable slang — remember the moral, study your audience — can lend zest to any presentation, but an over-indulgence in slang will kill it, stone-dead.

## Self-tutorial (Part One)

For the purpose of this discovery exercise in the articulation of vowel sounds, you will require *(a)* seclusion, *(b)* a mirror and *(c)* pencil and paper. So having closeted yourself away from public gaze, have a go at the following, introductory part of the exercise:

### Production of 'a' sounds

Remembering to watch yourself in the mirror, place the tongue low down and relaxed in the back of the mouth, keep your jaw open and lips relaxed, and say — 'a'. Now say the following words:

| | | | | | |
|---|---|---|---|---|---|
| sad | lad | cad | fat | sag | pal |
| lap | tap | sap | mat | sat | tag |

### Production of 'aw' sounds

With the tongue still flattened in the back of the mouth, jaw open and lips slightly protruding, say — 'aw'. Now say the following words:

| | | | | | |
|---|---|---|---|---|---|
| cause | law | taught | pawl | haul | caudle |
| award | awl | naught | call | sawn | awning |

### Production of 'ah' sounds

With the tongue again flattened in the back of the mouth, jaw open and lips less protruding, say — 'ah'. Now say the following words:

**ᴜᴜmart**

| | | | | | |
|---|---|---|---|---|---|
| mart | dark | garter | tarn | part | laugh |
| marl | lard | marker | bark | card | epitaph |

### Production of 'e' sounds

With the tongue arched in the centre of the mouth, jaw open and lips relaxed, say the following words:

| | | | | | |
|---|---|---|---|---|---|
| led | said | lent | pen | septic | tent |
| pet | went | tell | fed | rented | when |

### Production of 'ee' sounds

With the tongue arched and raised forward in the mouth, jaw open and lips relaxed, say the following words:

| | | | | | |
|---|---|---|---|---|---|
| need | peat | seek | peel | lean | beer |
| leap | free | seem | heat | deem | seed |

Right, introduction over — from now on, you are on your own. Select and practise saying at least 12 words for each of the following vowel sounds:

*a   Production of 'oo' sounds (as in 'boot')* — say 'oo' by arching the tongue and

171

pushing the lips forward to form a small, rounded shape.

b   *Production of 'oh' sounds (as in 'lode')* — say 'oh' by slightly arching the tongue at the back of the mouth and pushing the lips forward to form a slightly larger, rounded shape than in the previous example.

c   *Production of 'i' sounds (as in 'kit')* — say 'i' by placing the tongue forward and moderately high in the mouth, with jaw open and lips relaxed.

d   *Production of 'u' sounds (as in 'cut')* — say 'u' by arching the tongue in the centre of the mouth, with jaw open and lips relaxed.

Note that in completing the above exercise, you have barely scratched the surface where articulation is concerned. If it has whetted your appetite, you should refer to the suggested reading list at the rear of this book — or of course enrol in a local elocution class.

## Self-tutorial (Part Two)

This is a discovery exercise in the use of a dictionary as a guide to correct pronunciation — so, quite plainly, you will need to acquire, by fair means or foul, a decent dictionary. Having obtained the volume, examine the *Guide to Pronunciation* which will be found somewhere within the first few pages of the work. You will see that the guide contains a list of symbols which, as the dictionary explains, indicate correct pronunciation. It is necessary that you familiarise yourself with these symbols — for if you misinterpret them, your pronunciation will be hopelessly wrong.

Having learned the symbols, *check* and *practise* the dictionary pronunciation of the following words:

| | | |
|---|---|---|
| chiaroscuro | iconography | perispomenon |
| tropaeolum | degaussing | girandole |
| kolkhoz | asyndeton | zouave |
| ratiocinate | nigrescent | scaramouch |
| trapezoid | usury | bifurcation |

## Self-tutorial (Part Three)

Just for the hell of it, what is the exact meaning of each of the following acronyms?

| | | |
|---|---|---|
| Balpa | Aslef | Cento |
| Unesco | Nalgo | Unicef |
| Seato | Gatt | Efta |

(Answers on page 191).

172

> Be not deceived: evil communications corrupt good manners.
> **The Bible**

# 19
# A postscript on burning the communication candle at both ends

The big white company chief and his acolytes can squat in their corporate boudoirs and spawn plans and policies until Doomsday, but all will come to naught unless they are communicated to the hard-working souls who have to implement them. Conversely if the ideas, views and experiences of those who earn their daily bread in an enterprise are not conveyed to the heady heights of top management, the gods of the company stratosphere will remain in ignorance of much of what is happening or likely to happen at minion level. Anyone who has worked in an organisation of any size will know that there is only one way in which the gulf between 'them and us' can be bridged, and that is by two-way, eyeball-to-eyeball communication. Huh, easily said!

## Formal communication

Formal communication — a dreadful term, smacking of an eviction order or a death sentence — is, firstly, concerned with that most powerful of administrative religions, the sacred flow of official instructions from seniors to juniors, implemented in strict accordance with prevailing commandments or, as so often is the case, on a when-it-pleases-His-Highness basis. This usually means that a deluge of written notes, memos, instructions and orders descend from a great height on those beneath, with little regard for the simple fact that *unless this mass of boomph is preceded by oral presentation, it will be largely ineffective.*

173

Those who are managed, the souls who carry the can for implementing the shower of paperwork, must have the opportunity for discussion — a chance to air variations in interpretation, resolve misunderstanding and achieve full acceptance of whatever is required.

Secondly, the pundits tell us that formal communication is concerned with the lateral exchange of information at various levels within the outfit. There is no doubt that this can best be achieved by holding a regular programme of staff meetings when, once again, views can be aired and policies dissected and discussed. The absence of such oral exchange will create a momentary vacuum — momentary because it will be swiftly filled by those agents of the devil, conjecture and rumour.

Thirdly, and this is usually where the crunch comes, we are informed by those who dictate our corporate existence that formal communication is concerned with the sacrificial offerings by we lower supplicants of ideas, views and experiences on the altar of senior management. With the exception of the multitude of operating statements, returns and what-not which are always required to be sent 'up the line', we members of the lower orders in the hierarchy never seem to achieve this third aim of formal communication, and a thinking management would do well to ensure that regular staff or command meetings fill the gap. Such meetings are the very essence of eyeball-to-eyeball communication, and they represent a major and vital component in the effective company machine. Ideally there will be a meeting 'chain' so that it will not be necessary for each manager to attend a welter of sessions. Each executive should be required to attend a meeting under his own superior and also chair a meeting of his subordinates — and so on. Let there be no mistake; a reliance on paperwork to fill this particular void is absolutely no substitute for the spoken word.

## Joint consultation

Thus far, although I have referred to the 'lowly orders' of the hierarchy, I have had managers in mind. Plainly we must now think in terms of that far more important clump of folk who *really* bear the brunt of the company burden — the foremen, supervisors and all the people they represent — in short, the workers, bless 'em. There seems to be some agreement that the concept of staff meetings cannot be carried down to the lowest levels in an enterprise. As a result and following much knitting of management brows — including such dire arguments as 'foremen and chargehands will often lack the skill and experience to conduct such meetings' and 'operatives will not be sufficiently interested to play a constructive part' — the experts have come up with an answer, namely joint consultation.

The reader who seeks a pat description of consultation need go no further in his search than the report of a leading court case [*Agricultural etc. Industry Training Board* v. *Aylesbury Mushrooms Ltd* (1972)], in which the judgement noted that *'the essence of consultation was the communication of a genuine invitation, extended*

174

*with a receptive mind, to give advice'*. The ideas and views of the people who matter, the men and women at the sharp end of an organisation, can be of substantial value, but if they are denied the opportunity for expression of these ideas and views, it does not merely follow that there will be a profound silence. Far from it, the absence of a chance to speak out will cause deep frustration, and infinitely more sinister, those who are gagged by an unthinking management will seek militant and destructive outlets for their energies. When, on the other hand, an opportunity for consultation is provided, more than a few of the workers will obtain deep satisfaction from the knowledge that they are making a valuable contribution and that management has used some, if not all, of their ideas.

Note, if you will, the emerging importance and potential vitality of a *'speaking management'* and a *'speaking workforce'* — and then send the barriers for scrap, for we are talking about a *'speaking organisation'*.

## Informal communication

Believe it or not, the process of informal communication has been defined as 'those aspects of face-to-face relationships which are not recognised by the participants as, nor preconceived for the purpose of, achieving a particular objective. . .'. Little wonder that we tend to shy away from management text-books — Lord help us, if the man is trying to say *'the grapevine'*, why the hell doesn't he? (There is a good answer to that one. In addition to appearing erudite, the wily so-and-so knows that a long definition takes up a lot of space and brings the end of the book that much closer — which is exactly why I have repeated it in full.) The grapevine brings us galloping back to those two nasties, rumour and speculation. It is impossible for any organisation to eliminate totally these parasites of the uninformed, but effective, *spoken*, formal communication can drastically lessen their evil effects. All of us engage in rumour and speculation, and we all know how satisfying it can be to arrive at explanations, however ill-conceived, of the unknown — and how emotionally relieved we feel as a result. Being human, and very animal at heart, people get extremely anxious when they are left out of the picture and angry when they are not consulted. Good, two-way formal communication has to be the answer.

## A speaking checklist for the company

This book is not a treatise on corporate endeavour, but it is about speaking; and if the company chap is to get anywhere with his individual speaking efforts within the organisation, he needs a policy that will help, not hinder. Here then is a bare-bones checklist on some general points:

1   Are regular meetings held — and are they properly organised? Does *everyone* have a say, or just the guy at the head of the table?
2   Are there any identifiable barriers or blockages in the speaking pipelines? (Of course there are — what about *doing* something towards eliminating them?)

3   Are all the managers *made* to speak and discuss with their respective charges, or is it just left to happen?
4   Is consultation practised — and if so, is it genuine-bedouin stuff? Do the people at the sharp end get a fair crack of the whip, or are they patronised?
5   Are staff appraised — and if so, is the appraisal system open and discursive?
6   Exactly how accessible are managers — *can* subordinates take advantage of *genuinely* open doors?
7   Is the importance of lateral management relationships understood — and is there a high degree of discursive association?
8   Is there any hostility between individuals or departments?
9   Is there a pursuit of individual rather than company objectives?

Go on, management — be devils, why not have a discussion about it all?

> Examinations are formidable even to the best prepared, for the greatest fool may ask more than the wisest man can answer.
>
> **Charles Colton (1780-1832)**
> *Lacon*

# 20
# Strictly for the keen type

This is the point at which I slap down the proverbial gauntlet, for the sole aim of this final chapter is to present a *pot-pourri* of exercises and questions, a do-it-yourself examination and assessment, directed at the keen reader who enjoys a bit of a challenge. Being a somewhat devious type, I have made the whole thing thoroughly unfair by salting the mixture with a generous helping of material not contained in the preceding chapters, so something other than 'parrot knowledge' will be required. However, in an effort to assuage any outraged feelings, answers (or suggestions, where direct answers are inappropriate) are provided — do not look them up beforehand, for that, me hearties, is *cheating*.

## Exercise 1

The following words or phrases often rear their ugly heads in business communication — and like it or not, you should understand them. Write down the meaning of each one.

    addendum
    *ad hoc*
    *ad infinitum*
    *ad libitum*
    *ad referendum*
    *ad valorem*

alumnus
amendment
*annus mirabilis*
*a posteriori*
*a priori*
*arrière-pensée*
*au contraire*
*au fait*
blasé
bona fide
*cause célèbre*
*caveat actor*
*caveat emptor*
*c'est-à-dire*
*certiorari*
*ceteris paribus*
closure
*comme il faut*
co-option
*cui bono*
*de facto*
*de trop*
dropped motion
*et alia*
*et sequens*
*ex cathedra*
*exempli gratia*
*ex-officio*
*ex post facto*
*fait accompli*
*force majeure*
*habeus corpus*
*idée fixe*
*idem*
*id est*
*in absentia*
in attendance
in camera
*in toto*
*intra vires*
kangaroo closure
lie on the table
*locum tenens*
*mal à propos*
*mea culpa*

modus
*mutatis mutandis*
*nemine contradicente*
*n'importe*
no confidence
*non sequitur*
*nota bene*
*obiter dictum*
*pari passu*
*per capita*
*per contra*
*per diem*
*persona non grata*
prima facie
*pro tempore*
proxy
quasi
*quid pro quo*
quorum
*raison d'être*
reference back
resolution
*savoir-faire*
*sine die*
*sine qua non*
*status quo*
*sub judice*
subpoena
*ultra vires*
verbatim
*vide infra*
*vide supra*
*viva voce*
*vox populi*

Well, now, just in case you are inclined to mutter, 'damned silly exercise — never heard of it and I'll certainly never use it. . .', bear in mind that many company chairmen and chief executives are fond of using such horrors. A spot of gamesmanship might not come amiss. . . . Check out the answer section when your bad mood has subsided.

## Exercise 2

The wild use of *clichés* in any form of presentation invites disaster, but there is always the occasion when one comes in handy. Brush up on your stock-in-hand by providing a cliché for each of the following:

*a*   To provide what a recipient cannot appreciate.

*b*   Two perils or extremes of which it is hard to avoid one without running into the other.

*c*   A person who sees objections and weaknesses only.

*d*   A comment reserved for the moment of departure.

*e*   Take the step that commits one to an undertaking.

*f*   A good thing unappreciated by the ignorant.

*g*   Something that begins on a small scale but threatens great extension or promise.

*h*   To settle a debt with borrowed money.

## Exercise 3

Please imagine that you have been invited to deliver a short talk (of approximately 15 minutes' duration) to a group of CSE-standard school-leavers on any *one* of the following topics:

Your job
A hobby
A recent do-it-yourself task
A recent crisis

Remembering that you have not met the group before, prepare a set of speaking notes for the occasion.

## Exercise 4

Think of any person you know fairly well who is approaching retirement age, and prepare a set of speaking notes for a suitable, short address at the individual's retirement dinner.

## Exercise 5

Not a word to a soul but, just for the purposes of this rather morbid exercise (a speaker must be prepared for anything), imagine that your present boss has been struck down with a fatal coronary. If you are 'top dog' and have no boss, use your 'leading subordinate' for this solemn role. Prepare speaking notes for a brief eulogy at the memorial service.

## Exercise 6

During a discussion it is necessary for the discussion leader to exert various controls — what are these?

## Exercise 7

Describe the effective steps to be taken by a speaker in order to 'weigh up the opposition' prior to a meeting on a contentious issue.

## Exercise 8

A speaker is approached by a branch of the Women's Institute and invited to speak for 45 minutes on any one of the following topics, but he rejects the list as it stands. Examine the list and determine the probable reasons for his rejection:

Marine life
Premium Bonds
Thoughts on hobbies
Corporation Tax

## Exercise 9

Imagine that you have agreed to deliver a talk on a suitable subject to the residents of an old folks' home. In preparing for the assignment, what general considerations would you bear in mind?

## Exercise 10

Place the following lists of items for inclusion on an agenda in the correct order:

Discussion of an item adjourned from the last meeting
Apologies for absence
Any other business
Reading of minutes of previous meeting
Date of next meeting
Matters arising from the previous minutes
Treasurer's report
Chairman's opening comments
Election of officers to the committee
Motion to increase monthly subscriptions
Reading of letter from club president

## Exercise 11

This exercise is intended for the reader who dictates letters during the course of his or her work. Ask the poor lass who receives your dictation to supply you with a frank list of your shortcomings and weaknesses as a dictator (using that word in its kindest sense. . .). Stress that you are anxious to improve on your standard of dictation and that only she can help in this respect. If you conduct the exercise carefully and act on the results, you will earn her lasting gratitude.

## Exercise 12

A limited number of gestures can add zest to almost any presentation. Think up and practise some appropriate gestures to suit the following:

a    '. . . and he shouted, "You are all against me!" '
b    'He had the strength of Hercules.'
c    'He had but one attribute. . . .'
d    Contrasting a microchip with a matchbox.
e    'I could just discern him at the summit. . . .'

## Exercise 13

Some of us are uncertain regarding the formalities of performing introductions — are you? What are the correct methods of introduction in the following cases?

a    Mrs Briggs and Mr Williams meet for the first time in your company.
b    Mr Harvey, a retired director, and Mr Cleveland, a newly appointed director, meet for the first time in your company.
c    Two acquaintances, Sir Robert Cunliffe and Mr Simpson, meet for the first time in your company.
d    You wish to introduce your wife (or husband) to an acquaintance, Mr Alger.

## Exercise 14

Prepare and deliver a five-minute talk on a subject of your choice to your family or a circle of good friends. Ask your audience to note down, or signify in an agreed manner, each time you resort to an 'um' or an 'er' (etc.) during your talk. Try to make them take the exercise seriously, for it is an important business — 'ums' and 'ers' can be very annoying to an audience.

## Exercise 15

Examine the following sentences and note down any weaknesses in construction:

a    'To my delight, I found that the arrangements were absolutely ideal.'
      'Thank you so much, it was all very wonderful.'
b    'I repeat, I issued definite orders to that effect. . . .'
      'I have stated the actual facts in my report. . . .'
c    'The reason why I refused to go is because I dislike flying.'
      'I am pleased to report that he displayed enthusiasm and zeal in his work.'
d    'I am relatively confident that the project will be successful.'

## Exercise 16

Who knows, the great day may come when you are required to speak on television. . . . Now, come on, resist the temptation to splutter 'Rhubarb!' and think very seriously of what is involved with such a commitment. Note down the points that, in your opinion, it would be wise to bear in mind when speaking 'live' in front of the camera.

## Exercise 17

All right, so you will never appear in front of the TV camera (fatal last words) — but what about the business of coping with a microphone at, say, a conference? Note down the 'rules' for such a contingency.

## Exercise 18

Carry out a frank search of your vocabulary-cupboard and list the 'pet words' to which you are currently addicted. If in doubt, ask someone who is a close associate to help you with the list.

*(For answers-cum-crib-bank, see pages 184-191.)*

# ANSWERS-CUM-CRIB-BANK

## Exercise 1

| | | |
|---|---|---|
| addendum | — | an amendment that adds words to a motion, an additional remark |
| *ad hoc* | — | for a special purpose |
| *ad infinitum* | — | without limit |
| *ad libitum* | — | without limit |
| *ad referendum* | — | for further consideration |
| *ad valorem* | — | according to the value |
| alumnus | — | graduate of a college (etc.) |
| amendment | — | a proposal to alter a motion by adding or deleting words, a correction or addition |
| *annus mirabilis* | — | a wonderful year |
| *a posteriori* | — | through experience |
| *a priori* | — | known beforehand, by reasoning |
| *arrière-pensée* | — | second thought, reservation |
| *au contraire* | — | on the contrary |
| *au fait* | — | familiar with |
| blasé | — | indifferent, bored |
| bona fide | — | in good faith |
| *cause célèbre* | — | a prominent case, lawsuit or cause |
| *caveat actor* | — | 'let the doer beware' |
| *caveat emptor* | — | 'let the buyer beware' |
| *c'est à dire* | — | 'that is to say' |
| *certiorari* | — | 'to be made more certain' |
| *ceteris paribus* | — | other things being equal |
| closure | — | a motion which is submitted with the object of ending an unwanted/interminable debate |
| *comme il faut* | — | correct, proper |
| co-option | — | Power given to a committee to allow others, usually with specialist knowledge, to serve on the body |
| *cui bono* | — | to whose advantage? |
| *de facto* | — | in fact, actually |
| *de trop* | — | unwanted, superfluous |
| dropped motion | — | a motion that has to be abandoned because there is no seconder or because it is the wish of the meeting that it should be dropped |
| *et alia* | — | and others |
| *et sequens* | — | and the following (*abbrev.*: et seq.) |
| *ex cathedra* | — | by virtue of one's office |
| *exempli gratia* | — | for instance (*abbrev.*: e.g.) |
| *ex-officio* | — | by virtue of office |
| *ex post facto* | — | done afterwards but retroactive |
| *fait accompli* | — | an accomplished fact |
| *force majeure* | — | compelling force |
| *habeus corpus* | — | an order to bring a person before a court |

| | | |
|---|---|---|
| *idée fixe* | — | an obsession |
| *idem* | — | the same |
| *id est* | — | that is (*abbrev.*: i.e.) |
| *in absentia* | — | in absence |
| in attendance | — | people who have no right to be present at a meeting (e.g. the secretary, if a non-member) |
| in camera | — | in private, behind closed doors |
| *in toto* | — | entirely |
| *intra vires* | — | within the powers of authority of |
| kangaroo closure | — | the chairman's right to hop from one amendment to another omitting those which, in his view, are trivial or time-wasting |
| lie on the table | — | metaphor describing the disposal of a matter or document when a meeting decides to do nothing about it |
| *locum tenens* | — | a deputy |
| *mal à propos* | — | ill-timed, out of place |
| *mea culpa* | — | through my fault |
| *modus* | — | method |
| *mutatis mutandis* | — | after making the necessary changes |
| *nemine contradicente* | — | no one contradicting (*abbrev.*: nem. con.) |
| *n'importe* | — | it does not matter |
| no confidence | — | a vote of no confidence is passed by a committee when it lacks confidence in the chairman and wishes to oust him from office |
| *non sequitur* | — | not a logical consequence |
| *nota bene* | — | pay particular attention (*abbrev.*: N.B.) |
| *obiter dictum* | — | incidental or casual comment |
| *pari passu* | — | likewise, in the same degree |
| *per capita* | — | each |
| *per contra* | — | on the other side |
| *per diem* | — | by the day |
| *persona non grata* | — | an unacceptable person |
| prima facie | — | at first view, first-hand |
| *pro tempore* | — | for the time being (*abbrev.*: pro tem.) |
| proxy | — | a member who acts for another, or the document which entitles a person to attend a meeting and vote on behalf of another |
| quasi | — | as if, as it were |
| *quid pro quo* | — | equivalent return |
| quorum | — | the number of persons required to hold a valid meeting, as set out in the rules governing the body |
| *raison d'être* | — | justification |
| reference back | — | the action of a committee in referring a matter for further investigation |
| resolution | — | a motion which has been carried |
| *savoir-faire* | — | common sense |
| *sine die* | — | without naming a day |

| | | |
|---|---|---|
| *sine qua non* | — | an essential condition |
| *status quo* | — | the state existing |
| *subjudice* | — | under consideration |
| *subpoena* | — | an order commanding appearance in court |
| *ultra vires* | — | beyond the vested powers (of) |
| verbatim | — | word for word |
| *vide infra* | — | see below |
| *vide supra* | — | see above |
| *viva voce* | — | orally |
| *vox populi* | — | popular opinion, the voice of the people |

## Exercise 2

*a*    To cast pearls before swine.
*b*    Between Scylla and Charybdis.
*c*    The devil's advocate.
*d*    A *Parthian* shot.
*e*    Cross the Rubicon.
*f*    Caviare to the general.
*g*    The thin end of the wedge.
*h*    To rob Peter to pay Paul.

## Exercise 3

The speaking notes — remember, 'triggers' — will obviously bear the stamp of your own design, but the format should have taken account of the following main features:

*Greeting* · · · · · · · · · · · · · · · · · · · · · · *Personal intro*

*Intro topic*

*Give reason for choice?*

*Structure*

*Introduction* · · · · · · · · · · · · · · · · · · · ·

*Body* · · · · · · · · · · · · · · · · · · · · · · · · · · ·

*Conclusion* · · · · · · · · · · · · · · · · · · · · · · ·

186

In composing your speaking notes, you should have borne in mind the following 'basic approaches' to your subject, and selected accordingly:

Why?
How?
Argue for?
Argue against?
Plain description?

Lastly, bearing in mind your school-leaver audience, *what visual aids did you select?*

## Exercise 4

1 *Select appropriate 'message' or 'thought',* i.e. 'Some people make a mess of retirement.'
2 *Give it a 'twist',* i.e. 'Some neglect it — others are afraid of thinking about it.'
3 *Give it a second 'twist',* i.e. 'But some people — those lucky people who enjoy life — look upon retirement as a second, big opportunity.'
4 *Add the punch-line,* i.e. 'John is one such person.'
5 *Illustrate briefly why John is so 'special'.*
6 *Contradulate him* (remember, no 'wishing good luck').
And that is that!

## Exercise 5

One effective method of approach to the obituary is to utilise an amended version of the formula in Exercise 4, above — with the obvious exception of the final, congratulatory section. An alternative approach is the 'I first knew John. . . .' gambit, with subsequent and brief allusions to the various highlights in his life — concluding with the '. . .that is why he was so special' theme.

## Exercise 6

There are two essential 'areas of control':
1 *Control of the subject:*
    *a* State, and re-state, the main objects of the discussion.
    *b* Restrict inconsequential and 'tangential' chit-chat.
    *c* Re-cap and summarise progress at regular intervals.
    *d* Clarify, where necessary, the remarks of others.
2 *Control of individuals:*
    *a* Gag the garrulous.
    *b* Encourage the shy or reluctant to speak up.
    *c* Remove tension when things get rough.

  *d* Display an interest in each speaker.

  *e* Be friendly, but firm.

A necessary piece of parrot-knowledge, this — how did you do?

## Exercise 7

The process of 'weighing up the opposition' is a vital prerequisite to effective performance when contention is in the air:

1 What, exactly, will be the objections/arguments?

2 What form is this opposition likely to take?

3 How effective is it likely to be (i.e. will you be a 'dead duck' from the word go — or is there hope for your survival?)

4 How may the opposition be countered or overcome —

  *a* By factual argument?

  *b* By outright rejection?

5 How will other members of the group react to the opposition?

6 Exactly how important is the issue — is it worth the candle?

  Having weighed up the opposition, the next step is to consider one's preliminary manoeuvres and skirmishes — did you think of this element of the tactical plan? If not, refresh your memory by re-reading the appropriate section in Chapter 10.

## Exercise 8

*Marine life* The subject is far too wide for adequate presentation during a 45-minute session. The speaker would be wise to go back to the WI and suggest that, if they really want such a topic, he 'narrows it down' to something more manageable, i.e. 'Man-Eating Sharks', 'The Great Barrier Reef', etc.

*Premium Bonds* A talk of 45 minutes on this subject to a 'general audience' sounds a pretty grim prospect. It is likely that the speaker has rejected the topic because he doubts his ability to fill the necessary period with interesting and entertaining material.

*Thoughts on hobbies* A terribly vague topic, inviting generalities and consequent boredom. Whilst a truly proficient and entertaining speaker could probably make the ladies laugh their way through the 45 minutes, the amateur speaker would do well to avoid such vague assignments.

*Corporation Tax* For the Women's Institute? All right, so they may be ravenously keen on learning about the convolutions of corporation tax, but it will take a damned sight longer than 45 minutes. The speaker would probably question the choice, and if the WI was adamant, remind them that his talk would probably be very generalised and, as a consequence, boring.

## Exercise 9

The key to this exercise is 'preliminary reconnaissance'. Salient points will include:

Type of room, seating, lighting, etc.

Potential audience — provision for the deaf and those with poor sight.

Compatability of planned duration of talk with needs of the old folk.

You would also be wise to consider the use of large and simple visual aids and, because senior citizens enjoy mulling over this kind of thing, the provision of hand-outs after your talk.

## Exercise 10

Apologies for absence.

Reading of minutes of previous meeting.

Matters arising from previous minutes.

Reading of letter from club president.

Chairman's opening comments.

Discussion of an item adjourned from the last meeting.

Treasurer's report.

Election of officers to the committee.

Motion to increase monthly subscriptions.

Date of next meeting.

Any other business.

## Exercise 11

There is, of course, but one answer to this exercise — heed the poor girl's comments and *do something about it*. It is an unfortunate fact of executive life that few managers dictate well (and doing it well means dictating at the right speed for the lass concerned, maintaining a smooth delivery without 'ums and ers', helping with difficult names and technical terms, etc.). If you are brave and keen enough to stand a good object lesson, closet yourself away from the public gaze and dictate some material on a tape recorder. Play it back and subject yourself to a critical self-analysis — and then iron out those weaknesses!

## Exercise 12

Plant yourself in front of a mirror and repeat the gestures — ask yourself, are they larger than life? Do they graphically represent that which you are trying to illustrate? *Do they help?*

## Exercise 13

a   Always introduce the man to the woman — 'Mrs Briggs, may I introduce Mr Williams?'

b   Introduce the younger person to the older person — 'Mr Harvey, may I introduce Mr Cleveland?'

c   A man or a woman is always introduced to an established dignitary — 'Sir Robert, may I introduce Mr Simpson?'

d   When introducing members of the family, the words 'Mr' or 'Mrs' should not be used — 'Mr Alger, I would like to introduce my wife/husband'.

189

## Exercise 14

The chances are that you have not attempted this exercise — 'Load of rubbish, I'm not clowning around like that. . . .' A pity — but just in case you were brave and keen enough to have a go and things didn't get too hilarious, ponder on the consequences of habitual expressions. 'Ums' and 'ers' are bad, but everlasting repetition of things like 'You know . . .' can be excruciating to an audience. Think on't.

## Exercise 15

These little beauties are known to grammarians as *redundancies*, and speakers often allow redundancies to slip out, especially when speaking off-the-cuff.

| | | |
|---|---|---|
| a | 'absolutely ideal'<br>'very wonderful' | The words 'ideal' and 'wonderful' have been 'intensified' when, in fact, this is wrong — 'absolutely' and 'very' are *redundancies*. |
| b | 'definite orders'<br>'actual facts' | The nouns 'orders' and 'facts' do not require the addition of such adjectives — 'definite' and 'actual' are *redundancies*. |
| c | 'the reason why —<br>is because . . .'<br>'he displayed<br>enthusiasm and zeal' | Once a meaning has already been conveyed, it is superfluous to repeat it — 'because' and 'zeal' are *redundancies*. |
| d | 'I am relatively<br>confident' | Relative to what? No 'yardstick' has been mentioned against which the degree of confidence can be compared — 'relatively' is a *redundancy*. |

## Exercise 16

Speaking on television can be a fairly traumatic experience for the best of us, but there are some basic rules that will help you out:
1   Forget all about the microphone — be it suspended on an arm over your head, round your neck or in the hands of an interviewer, do *not* attempt to speak into it as one used to do with the old, upright telephone. Modern microphones are extremely sensitive and will pick up your every word.
2   If you are being interviewed, you will probably not be required to face the camera — but if you wish to make a splendid emphasis at some point of the interview, then look it straight in the lens (remembering that the camera in use will be plainly indicated by, usually, a red light).
3   If, however, you are performing 'solo' and required to face a camera all the time, remember to focus *on* the lens and not past or 'through' the beast.
4   Imagine that the camera is a person, and if required to face it, do your utmost to talk naturally and sincerely.
5   At all times, try to adopt a pleasant, lively style — and speak at a moderate

pace. (What's moderate? Well, for the technical, 120-130 words per minute — get your secretary to time you.)

6    If seated, do not slouch in the chair — remember that the camera will be presenting a two-dimensional image, and this type of laxity will show up.

7    Avoid gestures and if you have to move about, do it naturally and not at the gallop.

## Exercise 17

If you are not 'first on the bill', listen carefully to the performance of the amplifying equipment when used by earlier speakers. Note the sensitivity of the microphone by comparing the positions of speakers with the associated volume, i.e. mouth-to-mike distances. It should not be necessary to speak 'into' the micriphone, but it *is* advisable to refrain from *excessive* head movements. Above all, do not attempt to lend emphasis to your words by 'spitting' them into the microphone, but it *is* advisable to refrain from *excessive* head movements. Above ever rap or knock the mike — in fact, do not touch it at all; have a spot of faith and try to start your address without tapping the damned thing and saying words like 'Can you hear me, mother?' Last but not least, be careful that you do not allow your speaking notes to caress the mike for, again, the result will be quite dreadful. Oh, yes, and enjoy yourself!

## Exercise 18

Goodness knows what pet words you will have listed, but do make a conscious effort to minimise their use when speaking — anywhere. Remember that nearly all of us possess this habit of taking pet words to our respective bosoms, and that it is a continuing process. So — having cleared them out of the way this month, conduct a further self-examination at regular intervals. Who do *you* know who bores everyone to tears with such repetitive horrors as *fabulous, fantastic, great, super* — or, for instance, that addiction of certain youngsters, *cheers*, meaning thank you?

\*   \*   \*

## Answers to Self-tutorial (Part Three) on page 172

British Air Line Pilots' Association
Associated Society of Locomotive Engineers and Firemen
Central Treaty Organisation
United Nations Educational, Scientific and Cultural Organisation
National and Local Government Officers' Association
United Nations Internal Children's Emergency Fund
South-east Asia Treaty Organisation
General Agreement on Tariffs and Trade
European Free Trade Association

# Appendix —
# Tribunal tribulations

In the halcyon days of yore, when a company's business was regarded as largely its own affair, it was possible for the manager who detested public speaking to exercise a spot of cunning and, by dint of passing a few bucks and diligently avoiding the hot-seat, so arrange his working life that he was seldom, if ever, required to put himself to the dreaded task. However, today, as any office junior will gleefully assert, 'Things is diff'rent.' No matter how assiduously a company man buries himself away in the back office, pursuing his craft out of the public eye, there is always the chilling presence of a new Sword of Damocles which, when least expected and with a deft flick of the wrist of Fate, will impale him — for all to see and hear on the dissecting slab of contemporary justice — the industrial tribunal. Whilst many of us may cling with desperate tenacity to the pious hope that 'it can never happen to me', the fact is that it can and probably will — for, to misquote an old adage, 'Hell hath no fury like the employee scorned', and, like it or not, the law provides a succulent range of opportunities for him to vent his spleen.

To make matters worse, when an inexperienced or nervous speaker finds himself saddled with a tribunal appearance, he often faces the additional and intimidating prospect that it is his first encounter of any kind with a court of law. The poor chap's imagination slides adroitly into top gear — thoughts of monumental verbal gaffes and other speaking unmentionables intermingle with nasty visions of hawk-eyed inquisitors tearing his evidence to shreds, and rendering him with consummate ease to the level of a bumbling idiot. Well — can it *really* be like that? Let us examine the tribunal scene and see if such fears are justified.

## The all-important environment

Little can be more worrying to an inexperienced speaker than his physical surroundings, and the mere thought of a court hearing conjures up a traditional picture in the mind — a sombre wood-panelled and echoing chamber, the very fabric of which exudes a sinister miasma of interrogation and penalty, a be-wigged and omnipotent judge seated on high, the unfriendly isolation of the witness stand, a bevy of detached and coolly-butchering counsel, the dock. . . . Bless me, before the reader who is a stranger to industrial tribunals collapses with apprehension, let me emphasise that the usual tribunal setting is nothing like that. The normal venue is a largish room with little or nothing in the way of judicial trappings. At the business end, so to speak, there may well be an inches-high dais — one small sop to the majesty of the law — on which the chairman and two members of the tribunal will be seated, behind a perfectly normal, run-of-the-mill table. Facing these informal seats of power will be a number of tables and chairs for the use of the two parties concerned, witnesses, the clerk to the tribunal (who, during the hearing, administers the oath, runs messages and shunts pieces of paper to and fro) and, somewhere in a dark corner, the odd newspaper reporter. Since a tribunal is a public hearing, there will also be a scattering of seats for onlookers. So, in a nutshell, there is little to worry about where the surroundings are concerned — informality has been preserved as much as is possible within a court of law.


## The proceedings

Industrial tribunals consist of a legally qualified chairman and two 'lay members', one with experience of industry from the employers' point of view and the other from the unions' side. Throughout the hearing the chairman usually bends over backwards to help whoever is giving evidence present his case. This entirely laudable approach has of course provoked an emotive scream from some ill-informed employers to the effect that tribunals are biased in favour of the applicant — which is absolute nonsense. There is a world of difference between helping an inarticulate and probably timid layman to *present* his case and helping him to *win* it, and tribunals are well aware of the difference. Be that as it may, the important thing is that inexperienced speakers have no cause for worry so far as their actual or imagined oral inabilities are concerned; help will be forthcoming. One important feature in this context is the leisurely speed at which the hearings proceed — for some inscrutable reason, the chairman is required to record all that transpires in *longhand*, and this means that the whole caboodle is punctuated by hefty pauses as the big man pushes his aching wrist through miles of manuscript composition. Thus for instance the normally terrifying business of cross-examination is perforce reduced to a sedate and halting crawl — the aspiring Perry Masons of this world stand no chance of success at industrial tribunals:

*Perry Mason-type, cross-examining a witness* 'Now, remember that you are on oath — I want you to consider my next question very carefully. . . .'

*Chairman* 'I am sure Mr Bloggs is aware that he is on oath, Mr Mason — he's only just taken it. What is your question?

*PM-type* 'Er — yes, sir — Mr Bloggs, did you or did you not say to Mr Winterson, your foreman, on the morning of 13th December at approximately 11 a.m. the following words. . . .'

*Chairman (Writing hard)* 'Just a moment, if you please, Mr Mason.'

*PM-type (Gritting his teeth as his litigational moment of drama evaporates into thin air)* 'Certainly sir. . . . Now, Mr Bloggs — did you, at that time, utter the following words. . . .'

*Chairman (His pen poised in mid-air)* 'Do please come to the point, Mr Mason. . . .'

*PM-type* *(Glaring at chairman, who regards him with a kindly, benign expression)* 'Did you say, "Get stuffed, you old bag of nails", to the foreman?'

*(Silence as the chairman writes down the question)*

*Chairman* 'Well, Mr Bloggs — did you?'

*Bloggs (Who knew all along that he would be asked the question and has now had a cosy period in which to deliberate his reply)* 'No.'

*PM-type* 'I put it to you that you did!'

*Chairman* 'The witness has just stated that he did not utter those words, Mr Mason — do you wish to pursue the subject?'

*PM-type* 'I will be producing evidence to the effect that Mr Bloggs *did* utter that statement, Mr Chairman, and. . . .'

*Chairman* '. . . and we will naturally listen very carefully to any witness you produce, Mr Mason — now, do you have anything further to ask Mr Bloggs?'

*PM-type (deflated)* 'Er — yes, sir. What *did* you say to the foreman, Mr Bloggs?,

*Bloggs* 'I didn't call him old. . . .'

## Beware of skeletons in the closet

Whilst I hope that the inexperienced speaker has rightly gained some comfort from the preceding section, it would be highly dangerous to assume that any tribunal hearing is a piece of cake — for things can and do go very wrong, particularly if the witness has failed to carry out a thorough preparation for the event.

A good maxim for the company witness to adopt, and this applies particularly to the inexperienced or nervous speaker, is simply that in many cases there is only one 'specialist' in the parties to a hearing — and that guy is the applicant, the person bringing the complaint. Lest you doubt this, consider for a moment the general background to, say, a complaint alleging unfair dismissal. When Mr Average Employee is fired from his employment, there is absolutely no doubt that the occasion will register as a very unpleasant and

195

significant day in his calendar. Not only will he remember all the aspects and events of the dismissal itself but — and this is the crucial bit — *he will recall with startling clarity every nuance and circumstance which led up to and culminated in the dismissal*. Now think of the manager primarily concerned in the case; whilst the business of dismissing the employee would doubtless be unpleasant, the episode merely represents one occurrence in his day-to-day tasks — and most managers are very busy people. He will *not* remember with such startling clarity all the many features of the case, and at the tribunal hearing may be very unpleasantly surprised at some of the evidence produced in a firm and convincing manner by the applicant — skeletons in the closet. Faced with such tactical setbacks, the inexperienced speaker can literally lose the day. The moral is simple: when preparing for a hearing, take nothing for granted and cater for every possible contingency which may arise.

## Demeanour counts

Much has been said and written about the Solomon-like task of administering justice which faces so many tribunals — deciding on the basis of probability of the evidence, tests of reasonableness and so on. To the layman, and I guess that means you and me, there is a more basic, albeit crude, approach; on many occasions one of the two parties will be lying in its teeth, and it is the tribunal's job to winkle out the rogues and pronounce accordingly. The chairman and his two sidekicks will eye everyone concerned very closely, particularly when individuals are not actively engaged in giving evidence, and will be on the lookout for anything in the way of gestures or demeanour that tends to give the proverbial game away. So in addition to dressing suitably for the occasion (I once saw the boss of a small outfit turn up at a hearing looking as if he had just crawled from underneath a lorry, which he probably had), it is vital to preserve an 'upright', convincingly genuine demeanour throughout the entire duration of the case.

## Forms of address

The chairman of the tribunal should be addressed as 'Mr Chairman' — unless of course it happens to be 'Madam Chairman' — or, more simply, 'sir' or 'madam'. A nice touch is to note the names of the two lay members (these will be displayed for your information in the tribunal waiting room) and just occasionally address these worthies in this more personal manner when they pose the odd question. However, do make certain that you ascertain which person is which, or your neat ploy will thud to the floor like a piece of wet dough.

## A drill for the intending witness

*Preparation* For the umpteenth time, there is no substitute for adequate preparation. Ensure that you are in possession of and carefully consider every scrap of documentary evidence — do not assume for instance that the 'personal file' of an ex-employee applicant is the only repository for documentary evidence; ask around and be certain that you have *everything*. Check and double check all information and do not allow opinion or hearsay to colour your judgement unduly.

Finally, write down everything that you intend to say at the hearing — go through it again and again; set *yourself* the task of detecting and dealing with weaknesses in your evidence. Ask *yourself* what questions are liable to be posed in cross-examination and how best should they be answered or countered. Do not set yourself the objective of 'parrot-learning' your evidence — the inexperienced speaker who recites his piece is easily identified as a tyro at the game and highly vulnerable — merely concentrate on getting all the facts at your fingertips. The chairman of the tribunal may allow you to refer to notes — if, in the words of the classic rejoinder, 'they were made at the time of, or shortly after, the events concerned'. Remember also that you will be required to show such notes to the other side.

*Delivery*  Give your evidence at a moderate pace — keep an eagle eye on the chairman and pause voluntarily when you see that he is busily making notes — your courtesy in so doing will be appreciated.

Do not make the fatal error of trying to emulate the police witness ('I was proceeding down. . . ' — 'acting on information received . . .' — and so on are not for you).

Use simple, telling words and *do not waste the tribunal's time with superfluous comment.*

*Questions and cross-examination*  When asked questions by the chairman or lay members and when under cross-examination, remember the golden rules:

Do not say the first thing that enters your head — *take time to think.*

If you cannot readily understand the question, ask the chairman for help.

Never volunteer more information than is required by the question — you will not help your cause by so doing.

If perchance the cross-examiner does try to trip you up, refuse to be flustered and *take your time.*

Refrain from sarcasm and other smart Alec tricks — they will do you no credit at all.

## In conclusion

I am continually surprised at the number of managers who, when conscripted to a tribunal hearing, utter plaintive cries about 'not knowing the procedure' — and there is precious little excuse for such ignorance. I know that we individually regard ourselves as the busiest men in our respective outfits and that time is always of the essence — I also know that, in nearly every case, this is absolute rubbish. There is an industrial tribunal within the reach of most managers; make it your duty to visit one and see exactly what goes on. Remember, the stakes are high in the tribunal handicap.

# Recommended reading

*Author's note*  The reader will note that the following list contains one or two 'oldies' — take my tip and do not be put off by the patina of age, for there is much sparkling wisdom in them thar' words. . . .

## Appraisal

'New context of personnel appraisal' (S. Sloan and A.C. Johnson), *Harvard Business Review* (November-December 1968).

'Re-appraising appraisal' (P. Honey), *Management in Action*, London (June 1971).

*The Interview in Staff Appraisal* (W.E. Beveridge), Allen & Unwin, London (1974).

## Conversation

*How to Win Friends and Influence People* (Dale Carnegie), Cedar Press, New York (1953).

*Plain Words* (Sir Ernest Gowers), HMSO, London (1948).

*Talking Your Way to Success* (Jacqueline Dineen), Thorsens Publishers, Wellingborough, Northants (1977).

## Meetings

*A.B.C. of Chairmanship* (Lord Citrine) NCLC Publishing Society Ltd, London (1952)

## Public speaking

*Confident Speaking* (Margaret Perkins), A. Thomas & Co, Wellingborough, Northants (1977).

*Effective Technical Writing and Speaking* (Barry T. Turner), Business Books, London (Second edition, 1978).

*How to Say a Few Words* (D.G. Powers), Dolphin, London (1953).

*Successful Public Speaking* (H.G. Garrett), Newnes, London (1964).

*The Businessman's Guide to Speech-making and to the Laws and Conduct of Meetings* (Ewan Mitchell), Business Books, London (Second edition, 1977).

## Training

*Presenting Technical Ideas: a guide to audience communication* (W.A. Mumbert), John Wiley (1968).

*Visual Presentation in Education and Training* (E.A. Taylor), Pergamon Press, London (1966).

## Television and radio

*Hello, Good Evening and Welcome: a guide to being interviewed on TV and radio* (John Brand), Shaw & Sons, London (1977).

## Voice and speech training

*Improve Your Speech* (A.M. Bullard), Anthony Blond, London (1960).

*Training the Speaking Voice* (V.A. Anderson), Oxford University Press, London (1961).

# Index

Accent, 9-10
Acoustics, 109-110
Acronyms, 169-170
Acting as company spokesman,
    120-121
Address:
  body of, 86
  checklist for subject validation, 84
  checklists for committee report or,
    95
  choice of subject, 83-84
  closing comments, 113
  committee report or, 94-96
  conclusion, 87
  dress standards, 111
  impromptu, 113-114
  introduction, 84-85
  nerves, 101-107
  opening gambits, 111-112
  preparation, 89-98
  Press, relations with, 118-122
  questions from the audience,
    112-113
  rehearsal, 96-98
  setting the stage, 110-111

  speaking gaffes, 15-16
  speaking notes, 89-94
  speaking volume, 112
Aggression, 13-14, 150
Aims of effective speaking, 8
Answering questions at interview,
    152-155
Appraisal:
  checklist for discussion, 70
  forms, 68-74
  halo effect in, 67
  leniency in, 66
  open or closed, 63-65
  self-assessment, 70-75
  varying standards in, 67
Argument, 14, 150
Articulation:
  factors affecting, 166
  improving, 166-168
Attitudes, speaking, 13-15, 32-33
Audience:
  argument with, 14
  domination of, 14
  fear of, 14
  questions from, 112-113

Body of an address, 86
Business games, 142

Case studies, 142
Central tendency, error of, 66
Charts and diagrams, 144
Checklists:
  appraisal discussions, 70
  committee reports, 95
  company communications, 175-176
  discussions, 49-50
  grievances, 40-41
  issuing orders, 28
  meetings with union representatives,
    162
  presentations, 56-57
  speaking subject, 84
Closed appraisal system, 63-65
Closed-circuit television, 143
Close, the speaking, 113
Command, 25
Committee report or address, 94-96
Communication within the company:
  checklist for, 175-176
  formal, 173-174
  informal, 175
  joint consultation, 174-175
Company spokesman, acting as,
    120-121
Component parts of an order, 24
Composing an address, 81-87
Concluding the discussion, 48-49
Conclusion of the public address, 87
Conduct of the discussion, 47-49
Contrast error in interviewing, 149
Corporate praise, 55-56

Democracy in discussion, 49
Dialect, 10
Direct questions, 152-153
Disagreement in discussion, 49
Discussions:
  concluding, 48-49
  conducting, 47-49
  democracy in, 49
  disagreement in, 49
  dishonesty in, 49-50
  expanding, 48
  introducing, 47-48
  personal sins in, 49-50
Dishonesty in discussion, 49
Dislike of audience, 14
Domination, 14, 150
Dress, 111

Education of shop stewards, 160-161
Effective speaking, aims of, 8
Elements of an order, 24
English language, 9
Epidiascope, 143
Evidence, giving, 196-197
Expanding the discussion, 48

Familiarisation with nerves, 103-107
Fear of audience, 14
Felt boards, 144
Film projectors, 142-143
Formal communication in companies,
    173-174
Formal meetings, 125-129
Forms, appraisal, 68-74

Gaffes, speaking, 15-16
Grievances, 39-42
Guest speaker, 144-145

Halo effect in appraisal, 67
Halo error in interviewing, 149
Handling grievances, 40-41
Humour, 16-17

Impromptu speaking, 113-114
Inaccuracies, speaking, 15-16
Individual praise, 55-56
Industrial tribunals, 193-198
Informal communications in
    companies, 175
Informal meetings, 129-131
Insistence on showing authority, 14,
    150
Instruction, the, 25
Interviews:
  aggression, 150
  answering questions, 152-155
  argument, 150
  contrast error, 149
  direct questions, 152-153
  domination, 150
  halo error, 149
  insistence on showing authority, 150
  logical error, 149
  losing control, 150
  mirror-image error, 149
  opening gambits, 151-152
  standard-revealing questions, 153
  tactics, 149-151
  tricks, 155-157
  unknown factors, 148
Introduction of the discussion, 47-48

Introduction of the public address, 84-85

Jargon, 12
Joint consultation, 174-175
Jokes, 16-17

Lecture, 141
Leniency in appraisal, 66
Logical error in interviewing, 149
Logicality of approach, 13
Losing control of the interview, 150

Magnetic boards, 144
Meetings:
  formal, 125-129
  informal, 129-131
  personal performance at, 131-132
  rules of order, 125-128
  sales, 130-131
  terminology, 128-129
Memory, praise and, 56
Mirror-image error, 149
Mobility, 13

Negotiating with trade unions, 159-162
Nerves, speaking, 101-107
Notes, speaking, 89-94

Objectives of effective speaking, 8
Open appraisal systems, 63-65
Opening gambits, 111-112, 151-152
Order, rules of, 125-128
Orders:
  checklist for issuing, 28
  factors dictating choice of, 24-25
  types, 25-26
  vital elements of, 24
Overhead projector, 143

Personal faults in discussion, 49-50
Personality:
  in giving orders, 26-28
  speaker's, 10
  trainer's, 139-140
Personal performance at meetings, 131-132
Phrasing, 11-12, 19-20
Plea, the, 26
Praise, 52-57
Preparation of the public address, 89-98
Presentations, 56-57, 139-140
Press conference, 131-132

Pronunciation, 168-169
Proposing a toast, 114-115
Public speaking:
  body of address, 86
  choice of subject, 83-84
  composition of address, 81-87
  conclusion of address, 87
  introduction of address, 84-85
  preparation of address, 89-98

Questions:
  answering, at interview, 152-155
  direct, 152-153
  from the audience, 112-113
  standard-revealing, 153

Recognition of speaking nerves, 103-107
Rehearsal, speaking, 96-98
Replying to a toast, 115
Report, committee, 94-96
Reprimands:
  attitude when awarding, 32-33
  examples of, 33-34
  golden rules for, 31-32
  in general, 34-35
Request, the, 25
Rhythm, 11-12
Role play exercises, 142
Rules of order, 125-128

Sales meetings, 130-131
Sarcasm in discussion, 49
Self-appraisal, 70-75
Seminar, 141-142
Setting the stage for an address, 110-111
Shop stewards:
  checklist for meetings with, 162
  dealing with, 159-162
  education of, 160-161
  negotiating tactics, 161-162
Sincerity in speech, 11
Slang, 169-170
Speaking:
  attitudes, 13-15
  checklist for the company, 175-176
  checklist for subject validation, 84
  choice of subject, 83-84
  closing comments, 113
  gaffes, 15-16
  humour, 16-17
  impromptu, 113-114
  nerves, 101-107

notes, 89-94
personality, 10
rehearsal, 96-98
with the Press, 118-122
Spokesman, acting as company,
    120-121
Standard-revealing questions, 153
Stressing words, 12
Subject knowledge, 139
Successful delivery, 109-115
Suggestion, the, 25-26

Tactics at interview, 149-151
Tape recorder, 143
Teaching:
    knowledge of students, 140-141
    lecture, 141
    presentation and personality,
        139-140
    seminar or discussion, 141-142
    subject knowledge, 139
Terminology, meeting, 128-129
Toasts, 114-115
Tone, 12, 20
Training:
    knowledge of trainees, 140-141
    lecture, 141
    presentation and personality,
        139-140
    seminar or discussion, 141-142
    subject knowledge, 139

Tribunals, industrial, 193-198
Tricks at interview, 155-157
TIC education of shop stewards,
    160-161
Types of order, 25-26

Unions, negotiating with trade,
    159-162

Validation of speaking subject, 84
    Varying standards in appraisal, 67
Visual aids:
    charts and diagrams, 144
    closed-circuit television, 143
    epidiascope, 143
    felt board, 144
    film projector, 142-143
    magnetic board, 144
    overhead projector, 143
    slide projector, 143
    tape recorder, 143
Vital elements of an order, 24
Vocabulary, 12
Volume, speaking, 12

Weaknesses of appraisal schemes, 66-
    66-70
Wedding toasts, 115
Witness, industrial tribunal, 196-197
Words of praise, 54-55